SHAKESPEARE SURVEY

ADVISORY BOARD

SHAKESPEARE SURVEY

AN ANNUAL SURVEY OF
SHAKESPEARIAN STUDY AND PRODUCTION

29

EDITED BY
KENNETH MUIR

cop. a

CAMBRIDGE UNIVERSITY PRESS

CAMBRIDGE

LONDON · NEW YORK · MELBOURNE

Published by the Syndics of the Cambridge University Press
The Pitt Building, Trumpington Street, Cambridge CB2 1RP
Bentley House, 200 Euston Road, London NW1 2DB
32 East 57th Street, New York, NY 10022, USA
296 Beaconsfield Parade, Middle Park, Melbourne 3206, Australia

ISBN: 0 521 21227 8

First published 1976

Shakespeare Survey was first published in 1948. For the first
eighteen volumes it was edited by Allardyce Nicoll under the
sponsorship of the University of Birmingham, the University
of Manchester, the Royal Shakespeare Theatre and the
Shakespeare Birthplace Trust

Printed in Great Britain
at the
University Printing House, Cambridge
(Euan Phillips, University Printer)

The Library of Congress originally catalogued Vol. I of this series as follows:

Shakespeare Survey; an annual survey of Shakespearian study & production. 1–
Cambridge [Eng.] University Press, 1948–

v.   illus., facsims.   26 cm.

Editor: v. 1–   Allardyce Nicoll.

'Issued under the sponsorship of the University of Birmingham, the Shakespeare Memorial
Theatre, the Shakespeare Birthplace Trust.'

1. Shakespeare, William – Societies, periodicals, etc.   2. Shakespeare, William – Criticism and
interpretation.   3. Shakespeare, William – Stage history.   1. Nicoll, Allardyce, 1894–   ed.

PR2888.C3   822.33   49–1639

EDITOR'S NOTE

The central theme of *Shakespeare Survey 30* will be '*Henry IV* to *Hamlet*'. The theme of Number 31 will be 'Shakespeare and the Classical World'. Contributions on that or on other topics should reach the Editor (University of Liverpool, P.O. Box 147, Liverpool L69 3BX) by 1 September 1977. Contributors are required to provide brief summaries of their articles and they should leave generous margins, use double spacing, and follow the style and lay-out of articles in the current issue. A style-sheet is available on request. Contributions should not normally exceed 5,000 words. There will be a cumulative index of Numbers 21–30 in *Shakespeare Survey 31*.

K. M.

ALLARDYCE NICOLL

As we go to press, we regret to hear of the death of the founder of this journal and the editor of the first eighteen volumes. This is not the place to pay tribute to his numerous invaluable books, which began to appear more than half a century ago, nor to the International Shakespeare Conference which he founded; but *Shakespeare Survey*, even after his retirement, owes a great deal to his wise counsel.

K. M.

CONTRIBUTORS

N. W. Bawcutt, *Senior Lecturer in English Literature, University of Liverpool*

James C. Bulman, Jr, *Teaching Fellow, Yale University*

Neil Carson, *Assistant Professor of English, University of Guelph, Ontario*

Phyllis Gorfain, *Assistant Professor of English, Oberlin College, Ohio*

F. David Hoeniger, *Professor of English, Victoria College, University of Toronto*

E. A. J. Honigmann, *Professor of English Literature, University of Newcastle upon Tyne*

Henning Krabbe, *Professor Emeritus, University of Odense, and Chairman of the Danish Shakespeare Society*

†J. W. Lever, *Professor of English, Simon Fraser University*

D. J. Palmer, *Senior Lecturer in English Literature, University of Hull*

Roger Prior, *Lecturer in English, The Queen's University, Belfast*

Richard Proudfoot, *Lecturer in English, King's College, University of London*

Willem Schrickx, *Professor of English and American Literature, University of Ghent*

Nick Shrimpton, *Lecturer in English Literature, University of Liverpool*

James Edward Siemon, *Visiting Lecturer in English, University of California at Los Angeles*

Peter Thomson, *Professor of Drama, University of Exeter*

E. F. J. Tucker, *Assistant Professor of English, Southern Methodist University, Texas*

Roger Warren, *Lecturer in English, University of Leicester*

Stanley Wells, *Reader in English Literature and Fellow of the Shakespeare Institute, University of Birmingham*

CONTENTS

PLATES

SHAKESPEARE'S ROMANCES SINCE 1958: A RETROSPECT

F. DAVID HOENIGER

In his review in 1958 of trends in the critical response to the Romances (*Shakespeare Survey 11*, 1958) Philip Edwards concluded that we had heard enough about their universality, and boldly called for more 'mundane' studies. Many though not all have followed his counsel since; so much so indeed that some may have forgotten how much we owe the current wave of enthusiasm for the Romances to T. S. Eliot and G. Wilson Knight. However perverse or 'trite' (Edwards's word) the universalisers sometimes were, they did stimulate and certainly never hurt anyone. Recent decades have likewise seen many well-received performances of several of the Romances, though *Cymbeline* remains puzzling to both critics and producers (who therefore seldom risk it), and it is curious how seldom *Henry VIII* is staged nowadays, considering how popular the play was until fifty years ago.

My survey will attempt to give recent 'mundane' studies the due they deserve but not confine itself to them. But it both should and must be selective. Too much writing on the Romances has anyhow been repetitious or supererogatory, and whoever wishes could write an article on six different recent views of how exactly we should respond, step by step, to the first half of I, ii, or to the final scene of *The Winter's Tale*. Much is omitted deliberately or hesitantly, though my readers may well wish I had omitted more. I have no room to deal with bibliographical studies or problems of authorship. I will refer seldom to *Henry VIII*

and, very reluctantly, not at all to *Cardenio*, the seventh of the Romances Shakespeare was involved with, nor to *The Two Noble Kinsmen*, where Shakespeare yet once more explored fresh directions and emphases, well pointed out in three recent essays by Philip Edwards (*Review of English Literature*, October 1964), Richard Proudfoot (in *Later Shakespeare*, Stratford-upon-Avon Studies 8, 1966), and Clifford Leech (Introduction, Signet edn., 1966). The divisions of this survey, while sometimes perhaps suggesting a wrong emphasis for certain writings, will, I hope, be found convenient.

Influence of coterie theatre, Blackfriars, masque, music

In their comments on these familiar subjects, recent critics have either concentrated on fresh data or reacted to extreme earlier views. While Shakespeare's use of masque-like devices in the Romances can hardly be debatable, and we can readily assume that his audiences welcomed them, few now would claim as great an influence of court masques even on *The Tempest* as Enid Welsford did. Nosworthy (Arden *Cymbeline*, 1955) points to the lack of gravity and paucity of content of court masques, and to their fundamental unlikeness to drama. He asks rhetorically why Skakespeare, if he was so much taken with the new form, never wrote a court masque. Such an extreme reaction is healthy though, as Fitzroy Pyle reminds us in an appendix to his *The Winter's Tale: A*

Commentary on the Structure (1969), few other plays around 1610 show as much influence of the masque as some of Shakespeare's Romances. While considering this subject, we surely need to keep in mind the whole context of experimentation with new devices and forms – in drama, sculpture, architecture, music, and so on. Opera made its beginnings then, and *The Tempest* has a kinship to *The Magic Flute*. Inigo Jones's stage devices for the court masque, however original, were in the air; and masque-like effects were used much earlier than 1610 by dramatists writing for both public and private theatres.

In spite of Sternfeld's splendid work on music in Shakespearian drama, and discoveries by Cutts and others, little of direct bearing on musical effects in the last plays has in recent years been added to our knowledge. Moreover, we remain crucially ignorant about how music contributed to the mood or effect of plays, for instance Marston's, in the coterie theatres before Shakespeare's company took over Blackfriars. But we should always welcome comments by those few scholars expert in both music and drama, like R. W. Ingram's in 'Musical Pauses and the Vision Scenes in Shakespeare's Last Plays' (*Pacific Coast Studies in Shakespeare*, Eugene, Oregon, 1966), who likens the verse in the Jupiter episode in *Cymbeline* to that of operatic libretti. Gower in *Pericles* has in recent years been staged more than once as chanting his 'song', and I mentioned in my Arden edition that both Pericles and Marina are musicians. Nosworthy has provided a useful list of musical effects in the four Romances, and comments: 'Each of the Romances is an advance upon its immediate predecessor, philosophically as well as technically, and music comes to occupy a conspicuous and effective position in the moral and metaphysical fabric' (*Shakespeare Survey 11*, p. 68). And in a sanely balanced comment Pyle suggests that 'Without the musical tradi-

tion of Blackfriars to draw on, *The Tempest* and the long fourth act of *The Winter's Tale* could hardly have been written as they were written. The point is of obvious critical value, but particular rather than general. It does not account for the distinctive tone of the last plays' (p. 180). To which one can add, for the tone of *Pericles* indeed not.

Bentley's well-known thesis that Shakespeare planned the Romances specifically for Blackfriars was answered by Edwards but the issue remains alive. Some point to *Pericles* and to the performances at the Globe Simon Forman saw. Others see no likeness between the very popular nature of Shakespeare's comedies, early and late, and almost anything that was staged at Blackfriars before Shakespeare's company took it over. One might ask how much in essence Beethoven's music was affected by the invention of new instruments, but the answer is: surely to some extent. Others have been more respectful towards Bentley's view, allowing some importance to practical considerations (different theatre and audience) in a dramatist who besides writing 'for himself' appears to have been interested in real estate and in making money, and to have treated his audiences consistently gently. But careful critics emphasise how little we know about fundamental facts, how small the evidence is for supporting Bentley's or a different thesis. That is the subject of Daniel Seltzer's thorough, however negative, chapter on 'The Staging of the Last Plays' (in *Later Shakespeare*). We theorize about acting styles, lighting in Jacobean theatres, etc: we know next to nothing. Seltzer indicates a laborious route by which we can come to know a little more. But the results would not amount to safe evidence for broad conclusions.

Related is the subject of the influence on Shakespeare's Romances of coterie drama. Here speculation has been rife but again, safe evidence is hard to come by, and counter-arguments are easily raised. All is rather quiet today on the front of Beaumont and Fletcher whose *Philaster* may after all have been produced after *Cymbeline*, and attention has concentrated on Marston. Some recent critics have sought in Marston's earlier drama the origins for the histrionics and exhibited 'artlessness' of Shakespeare's last plays, especially *Cymbeline*; the techniques of distancing characters, their Brechtian 'Verfremdungs effect'. And for *Cymbeline* at least the approach deserves a welcome, like any from a fresh direction that helps enlighten us about that particular, puzzling play. R. A. Foakes (see p. 8) was in part anticipated by Arthur Kirsch (*English Literary History* 34, 1967) who suggests that in *Cymbeline* Shakespeare's genius 'is less distractingly present' thus allowing us to see in it better than in the other Romances the influence on them of the dramaturgical movement in the private theatres. Comparing and contrasting *The Malcontent* and *Cymbeline* as experimental tragi-comedies, Kirsch suggests how Shakespeare exploits in *Cymbeline* 'the deeper paradoxes of such tragi-comedy through the imagery'. This may be pertinent however much we should recall that Marston never wrote popular drama. If Shakespeare after 1600 learned anything from a contemporary about dramatic experimentation, Marston is a worthy candidate. Only let us remember the remarkable independence of other artists of genius in their later work.

Emblematic plays complimenting Stuart royalty

It is one thing to stipulate that Shakespeare planned the Romances for Blackfriars, quite another to assert that he designed them for special occasions at court. Glynne Wickham differentiates the 'emblematic play', a term familiar in discussions of some medieval drama and Calderón, from allegory and parable. Emblematic plays often take the form of romance, but in them 'references to factual matters of a topical nature have been inserted'. What reaches the eye in them is purely pleasurable, but what reached the understanding of original audiences 'usually takes the form of moral or political instruction' (*The Elizabethan Theatre III*, Toronto, 1973, p. 85). In more than one article Wickham has suggested that all of the Romances are in this sense emblematic, but as the case made is quite unconvincing except perhaps for *Cymbeline*, I will confine myself to that play.

In several articles by others who in part anticipate Wickham's views on *Cymbeline*, not only contemporary history and royalty but also ancient British history and more are involved. Long ago Northrop Frye intimated that Christ was born during Cymbeline's reign. Then Philip Brockbank suggested (in *Shakespeare Survey 11*) that different parts of the history of ancient Britain which Shakespeare drew upon for *Cymbeline* may prove relevant to the play's interpretation. Responding to these clues, Robin Moffet proposed in '*Cymbeline* and the Nativity' (*Shakespeare Quarterly* XIII, 1962) that the play's action, moving as it does through confusion and paradox to unity and self-knowledge in humility, hints at the Christian revelation which lies just beyond. His argument is presented cautiously and with good detail. Similarly reserved about the play's merits was Emrys Jones who in 'Stuart Cymbeline' (*Essays in Criticism* 11, 1961; in Palmer, D. J. ed., *Shakespeare's Later Comedies*, Harmondsworth, 1971) linked the play's ending to the *pax Romana* under Augustus on the one hand, and to King James' motto as *Beata pacifici* on the other, also drawing attention to the rich association of Milford Haven for King James and his family. Next, Bernard Harris in 'What's past is Prologue' (*Later Shakespeare*, 1966) added further data to those of Brockbank, Moffet and Jones, emphasising contemporary references to Christ's birth in

Cymbeline's reign and how in Daniel's masque of 1610, Queen Anne herself in the part of Tethys referred to Milford Haven; the article moves on to the *Pastor Fido* and other matters. Finally, Glynne Wickham presented Jones's view all anew, but specifically claimed that *Cymbeline* was composed for the occasion of Prince Henry's investiture as Prince of Wales in June 1610 (*The Times Literary Supplement*, 1969, and elsewhere).

Lovely material and speculation all this, about which Hallett Smith is excessively unkind in an appendix to his *Shakespeare's Romances* (San Marino, Calif., 1972) where he quotes, for instance, a Spanish admiral on the suitability of Milford Haven for invading Britain, and repeats the old truth, too often forgotten, that no shred of external evidence exists for a single play of Shakespeare's time that it was devised for a special occasion or court performance. Wickham makes much of Shakespeare having been a Groom of the royal chamber, and of King James as patron of Shakespeare's company. But others have indicated that James talked more about peace-making than he acted, and that he was not a popular king. To infer anything about plays from compliments in masques is anyhow dubious. Cymbeline and his Queen hardly suit a play which wants to compliment royalty. Yet we had better keep an open mind for, as Geoffrey Bullough tells us, Shakespeare's use of the Scottish story of Hay and his two sons, who in battle against the Danes turned defeat into victory, looks like a tribute to one of the King's oldest friends, Sir James Hay. 'The King and his courtiers would recognise the Hay ancestry in the feat of Belarius and the two boys' (*Drama and Narrative Sources 8*, 1975, pp. 11–12).

Sources and romance

Twenty years ago scoffing at source studies was fashionable, now they are welcomed. In *The Winter's Tale*, writes Fitzroy Pyle, 'a single book stands out as having been the constant object of the writer's attention in the act of composition' (p. x); so one should pay it attention. Two major works which happen to fit the dates of my survey neatly, provide a model: Kenneth Muir's *Shakespeare's Sources*, 1957; and the eighth and final volume, devoted to the Romances, of Geoffrey Bullough's monumental work, 1975. While some may still wonder about the reasons for the painstaking work that went into these books, inferences for the interpretation of the plays will be clear to those who read them.

By the time Edwards wrote in 1958 scholars had become aware of the need for a better understanding both of the general nature of romance in the forms that reached Shakespeare and of how he moulded it into the unique shape and content of his last plays. Danby had looked closely at Sidney and Montemayor in relation to Beaumont and Fletcher's and Shakespeare's plays. Later Northrop Frye (see pp. 9–10) was to investigate and reflect further on conventions of romantic comedy. But quite a number of recent critics have concentrated on re-examining Greene's prose romance *Pandosto* and the very different play Shakespeare developed from it, *The Winter's Tale*; among them Pafford (Arden edn. 1963), Pyle, and others. How illuminating such an approach can be is shown especially by John Lawlor (*Philological Quarterly* 41, 1962; in Palmer) and by Stanley Wells (in *Later Shakespeare*), neither of whom limits himself to discussing significant changes Shakespeare made. By documenting as he does the great popularity of *Pandosto*, Wells may imply that Shakespeare could count on his audience's awareness of how he changed it. Parts of Greene's tale were made by him more 'wondrous', others more intense or 'realistic'. Lawlor comments on why Shakespeare brings young and old together already in Act IV, and observes:

If the writer of dramatic romance is to penetrate our deeper consciousness, he must not allow us to remain merely vigilant about man as agent, alert to connect act and consequence. Against that, he must show us the direction of counter-movement, including the scope of fortunate accident. But, much more important, we must encounter for ourselves the quality of a union between human beings which, cutting across all separate categorizations, is felt as itself an instance, and the highest instance, of 'great creating Nature'.

(In Palmer, p. 309)

Similarly, one might reflect on what the origins of Autolycus and of his tricks imply for the play, the character derived from Greek mythology, his tricks from London connycatchers, but both fitted into a story of pure romance. Thus Autolycus, as some have remarked, is a timeless figure. Does he today wear the garb of the reporter who sifted through Dr Kissinger's garbage for the sake of regaling urbanised Mopsas with tales which are true? The altered medium is the same message. With *Cymbeline* such an approach is much more difficult, but Brockbank and Bullough have indicated how informative a look at details in the chronicles Shakespeare used can be, and Homer Swander (in *Pacific Coast Studies on Shakespeare*) draws larger inferences from the way Shakespeare changed Posthumus from his prototype in Boccaccio and other versions of the wager story.

For *The Tempest* Kermode's account (Arden edn.) has been followed by a veritable avalanche of detailed study and speculation about Shakespeare's use of the Bermuda or Virginia Pamphlets. With their descriptions of tempests and providential deliverance, the golden world and the brazen, colonisation and the American Indian, the impact of these documents on Shakespeare's imagination has been the subject of much writing. Kermode cautioned that we ought not to forget that *The Tempest* can be richly appreciated without any knowledge of the Bermuda pamphlets, a warning too often forgotten. I am told that in a pleasant recent production of *The Tempest* at Williamsburg, Virginia, the effect was Mozartian, and Caliban reminded no one of North American Indians, nor Prospero of a colonising governor. And he does after all want to return to Milan. Thus one may wonder about the emphasis in the long fourth chapter of D. G. James' *The Dream of Prospero* (Oxford, 1967) which I yet found fascinating reading, troubled only by 'probabilities' which are mere surmises. But his book approaches *The Tempest* from several directions. Rewarding likewise is Leo Martz's chapter, 'Shakespeare's American Fable', in *The Machine and the Garden* (New York, 1964). Martz discusses how Shakespeare adapted many remarkable details from the Bermuda pamphlets for the play's world of conflict, strangeness and wonder, but his central interest is in major themes in American literature which *The Tempest* remarkably anticipates.

That Shakespeare also knew Richard Eden's *History of Travaile*, 1557, is discussed by Hallett Smith in *Shakespeare's Romances* (pp. 140–3). There he could read not only about Setebos but also about 'strange music' and a primitive ideal commonwealth anticipating Montaigne's. The chief relevance of voyager literature to our subject is surely that it conveyed the experience of the new world as romance and as travellers' tales true or false, inviting both faith and skepticism, a theme in the last plays. Virginia looked at first like an Arcadia; a Spaniard upon first seeing Mexico's capital stood rapt with wonder and recalled Amadis de Gaule (see Parry, *The English Reconaissance*, Cleveland, 1963). Yet for *The Tempest*, it is time to remind ourselves of the echoes from Virgil, Ovid, and St Paul. Old voyages and 'wonder', not only new, lie behind the play.

Most of the narrative romances are such poor stuff that we are prone to doubt whether we can learn from them much about Shakespeare. That we can is indicated in the

Cymbeline chapter (less elsewhere, I think) of Carol Gesner's *Shakespeare and the Greek Romance* (Lexington, Kentucky, 1970). Gesner emphasizes that Heliodorus', and Achilles Tatius', plots of fortune or providence and their wandering heroines also included pseudo-history. Irony, mockery and paradox are employed by them in ways anticipating *Cymbeline* (my article in *Studies in English Literature*, 1962). Accounts of romance have been all too general, ignoring the vast differences in plot and characterisation and tone between Alexandrian, pastoral and chivalric romance. Of these, the last is probably least relevant for Shakespeare.

Structure

Clifford Leech began his article on 'The Structure of the Last Plays' (*Shakespeare Survey 11*): 'The experience of time makes us aware of both cycle and crisis'. He observes that while the majority of plays concentrate on a crisis, the Romances do not, and goes on to discuss how the Romances vary among one another in combining the experience of cycle with that of crisis. *Pericles* and *Henry VIII* do so least, and are the most purely cyclic among the Romances. Beyond the play's ending, Marina and Lysimachus may well experience the blows of Fortune, and we know what was to happen to Anne Boleyn, Cromwell and the rest. Though in *Cymbeline* Shakespeare evidently took pains to produce a sense of finality in the last two scenes, it likewise, as Leech sees it, emphasizes flux. But in *The Winter's Tale*, by introducing, unlike *Pandosto*, Hermione's statue and revival, yet no longer youthful but 'wrinkled', Shakespeare superbly combined the experience of flux with that of finality, a sense of what has gone forever, not only of what is to come. And though in *The Tempest* Shakespeare from the outset concentrates on crisis, yet we are left at the play's end with a strong sense

of flux, for Prospero, no longer magician, will face new tasks, and Miranda is too innocent for what may lie in store for her. That of the five plays, the first and last should be the most purely cyclic calls for reflection.

Leech's stress on the effect of final scenes is shared by others. Patrick Swinden in *An Introduction to Shakespeare's Comedies* (1973) writes with telling detail of Prospero's 'grudging' reconciliation after Ariel's prompting. For his view of the play's structure, he acknowledges a debt to Anne Righter (New Penguin *Tempest*, 1968) who dwells on the 'peculiar alternation between movement and stillness', on how in conversation the eyes of the play's characters seldom seem to meet, and on how the scenes convey an 'impression of self-containment'.

But again, the majority of essays have been devoted to *The Winter's Tale*, perhaps in response to earlier writers who regarded its structure as 'split'. It is not so in the view of David Young in *The Heart's Forest* (New Haven and London, 1972) though after his chapters on pastoral in *As You Like It* and anti-pastoral in *Lear*, he naturally emphasises the play's tragic and comic parts (the book incidentally includes good pages on *Pericles* and *Cymbeline*). Pyle in his work already cited draws attention to the note of serenity and hope in the opening scenes of each of the first three acts of *The Winter's Tale*, and to how they make us look forward beyond the tragic part. Ernest Schanzer (*Review of English Literature* v, no. 2, 1964; in *The Winter's Tale: A Casebook*, ed. K. Muir, 1968) lists later echoes of the play's earlier scenes and proposes Time's hourglass as an image for the play's overall form with a hinge in the middle. Inga-Stina Ewbank's article in the same journal and issue (likewise in *The Winter's Tale* Casebook) emphasizes more how Shakespeare transformed Greene's triumph of fortune into a real triumph of Time, and turned the conventional 'into a dramatic exploration of the manifold meanings of Time', as we experience them. Good detail and good sense of theatre here. Time and structure are likewise the subject of William Blissett's article (*English Literary Renaissance*, Winter 1971) where he makes still more than Ewbank of the emblematic implications of Time, Time as *tempestas* in the play's first half, followed by Time as *temperentia*. For discussions of structure, critics have the blessing of Aristotle and the opportunity to include almost anything.

Unsolemn approaches and the plays in the theatre

Shakespeare wrote for actors and the stage, and far more Shakespearians today than earlier in the century take for granted that ignoring this fact almost inevitably results in misinterpretation. And since we know how unsolemn many episodes of Shakespeare's plays are in performance, we prefer less solemn writing about them too. Shakespeare the wise philosopher is out, Shakespeare the wit and the theatre man is in. Elucidations of Shakespeare's 'epistemological' concerns of course still occur but risk being found a bore. Their authors are invited to read John Crow's 'Deadly Sins of Criticism' (*Shakespeare Quarterly* IX, 1958), a minor Dunciad on some modern responses to the Romances. Since then we have had, note the titles, Molly Mahood's *Shakespeare's Word-Play* (1957) (of which *The Winter's Tale* chapter has been reprinted in both Palmer and Muir's *Winter's Tale* Casebook) and Anne Righter's *Shakespeare and the Idea of the Play* (1962) as well as articles on 'histrionics' and 'artlessness' in the last plays. We have indeed had a number of lists of all the references in the Romances, or in one of them, to 'play' in its various senses, to games and to acting. With puns we face of course the problem that we sometimes may see where Shakespeare hoped we would not, and with histrionics or games

the fact that Beaumont and Fletcher and Marston used them aplenty. The approach to structure has the side-result of discovering fresh echoes; e.g. Autolycus pretending that his shoulder-bone is out recalls what the bear did to Antigonus (Frye, *A Natural Perspective*, New York, 1965). This is entertaining, but did the echo result from conscious design or quirks of Shakespeare's imagination?

The past twenty years have not merely seen many productions of *The Winter's Tale* and *The Tempest* but also shown how astonishingly successful and deeply moving *Pericles* can be on the stage. The title of John Russell Brown's book, *Shakespeare's Plays in Performance* (1966, Penguin edn. 1969), is characteristic of the new emphasis in our time, as is that of his chapter on 'Playing for laughs: the Last Plays' (though Brown rightly indicates that laughter is called for only here and there in the Romances). Discussions of how exactly we ought to experience specific episodes in the plays have been particularly plentiful, especially on *The Winter's Tale*. They began with Nevill Coghill's well-known article (in *Shakespeare Survey 11*, 1958) and one of the best of them is by W. H. Matchett (in *Shakespeare Survey 22*, 1969). Another favourite has been the episode in *Cymbeline* where Imogen awakens beside Cloten's headless body and takes it for her husband's, some stressing more the serious, others more the comic in the grotesque effect.

Watching the plays on stage enlightens one of effects which critics have slighted or ignored. Recent productions of *The Winter's Tale* are surely in part the cause for the current interest in Autolycus, now the subject of entire articles; and, on the other hand, for the lessened emphasis on the art and nature debate between Polixenes and Perdita. And I think I am not alone in being struck by how well audiences accept the first two acts of *Pericles*. After Gower's first chorus, we are perhaps prepared for a verse which does not sound like Shakespeare's but is more like what we get (see P. Brockbank, in *Shakespeare Survey 24*, 1971, p. 107). These first two acts pass by very quickly in the theatre.

But the best theatre criticism is of the kind that keeps the whole play in view, and that shows awareness that Shakespeare's art is more than mere theatre art. I recommend this passage by Michael Goldman:

A producer searching for keys to a production of *The Tempest* must begin with the atmosphere.... The quality of the enchantment is central, ... The play's events are less important than the way they are felt: how they are received by the characters, how they appear to us, and how they are related to the arts of theatrical illusion in general.

> (*Shakespeare and the Energies of Drama*,
> Princeton, 1972, p. 137)

Links with Shakespeare's earlier plays

But now let us leave these practical concerns and take stock of some fresh suggestions on an old subject. Three matters are of primary interest: whether one can point to specific moments in earlier Shakespeare which, as it were, intimate the birth of the idea of the Romances in Shakespeare's mind (as early as *The Comedy of Errors*, then forgotten, later recalled?); whether one can do still more and trace a complete pattern of development in Shakespeare's work ending in the Romances, as Wilson Knight tried to do; and whether comparison with particular earlier plays can help us define better the peculiarity of one of the Romances. *Othello* and *Much Ado* obviously invite comparison with *Cymbeline* and *The Winter's Tale*, but recently Ernest Schanzer has drawn attention to striking similarities of the imagery in *Macbeth* and in the first half of *The Winter's Tale* (New Penguin edition, 1969).

In *The Heart's Forest* (Yale, 1972) David Young contrasts Shakespeare's handling of pastoral in four plays: *As You Like It*, *Lear*, *Winter's Tale*, and *The Tempest*. In *Shake-*

speare and the Comedy of Forgiveness (New York, 1965) R. G. Hunter traces the genre of the comedy of forgiveness from medieval drama through the 'dark' comedies to the last plays. Northrop Frye in *A Natural Perspective* (New York, 1965) discusses the popular and half-primitive materials which mark Shakespeare's comedies from early on, but with some emphasis on the Romances. There have been further reflections on *The Comedy of Errors* and the extent to which it anticipates the Romances, by John Arthos and others. And Hallett Smith in *Shakespeare's Romances* involves some of the tragedies as well, and makes an excellent case for Shakespeare's mind beginning to conceive the idea of writing Romances as he reflected on Sidney's *Arcadia* while at work on *King Lear*.

But most interesting, I think, have been G. K. Hunter (in *Later Shakespeare*) and Reginald Foakes (*Shakespeare: The dark comedies to the last plays*, 1971) on how aspects of the art of Shakespeare's late tragedies (Hunter concentrates on these alone) and the problem plays including *Troilus* anticipate the Romances. Hunter asks whether we have been right in assuming that among the tragedies *Lear* is of chief relevance, and his own ideas will appeal to those who have wondered about the enormous shift from *Coriolanus* to *Pericles* and *Cymbeline*. He writes:

Mutability is not an important theme in *Lear*, but the heroes of the last tragedies all live within its scope, though they try to outface it; the Last Plays accept it as basic and inevitable, and the natural result is a diminution in the scope of the individuals who initiate action.

> (p. 27)

In another passage (p. 17, note 6) Hunter asks and provides an answer to the question of how the heroines of the Romances and their caricature opposites, Dionyza and the Queen in *Cymbeline*, may be related to Lady Macbeth, Cleopatra and Volumnia.

Foakes reasons that around 1600 or 1602

Shakespeare, perhaps inspired by Marston and Jonson, became interested in new techniques of a more distant characterisation in the dark comedies and *Troilus*, that later he adapted them to tragedy, after *Macbeth*, and then to Romance of 'celebration', with *Cymbeline* indicating best how he experimented (cf. Kirsch, p. 3). But in my view, Foakes writes better on the dark comedies and on *Cymbeline* than on the two greater Romances that were to follow. His and Hunter's speculation and analysis should stimulate further thinking and work, coming as it does from critics who are aware of most counter-questions we might wish to raise, for instance about techniques of distant characterisation in *The Two Gentlemen of Verona* or Shakespeare's interest in *The Jew of Malta*.

I have no room for comment on new suggestions resulting from comparison of very late work by other dramatists and artists with the Romances – see Kenneth Muir's short book where he compares Racine and Ibsen; also Norman Rabkin's comments on Thomas Mann's *Felix Krull* and the *Holy Sinner*, in *Shakespeare and the Common Understanding*, 1967. Concentrating as they do on characteristics of very late work alone, for instance its freer forms, its 'artlessness', its characters who look back and forward, such studies can provide a corrective for some of those I have discussed. Late work by great artists is often remarkably independent.

Northrop Frye

Though probably not because of his views on them, Frye is among recent critics writing on the Romances the most famous, and therefore the most infamous. Frye still likes the term 'myth', now abandoned by many, and thus appears to fit into Edwards' negative category of 'Myth, Allegory and Symbol'. Frye concentrates in his book on the conventions of popular art forms and their origins,

which Shakespeare adapted in his comedies, rather than on the individuality and unique artistry of the plays themselves – a grave omission in the view of many. And Frye irritates because he hardly ever alludes to the critical views of others, probably because he has not read them. Hallett Smith in an appendix chapter to his *Shakespeare's Romances* compiled all the thoughts and data from other critics one might ransack for the sake of denigrating the response from Frye and his followers to Shakespearian comedy and the Romances. Moreover, for all those of us who like clear guides to detailed discussion of Shakespeare's plays, *A Natural Perspective* can be singularly frustrating. I confess to being one of those who made an attempt, not without irritation, to assemble all remarks in his book with immediate bearing on each of the Romances, though aware of how Frye might chuckle at such a response – yet Frye's criticism seldom hurts a fly, an example most of us do not follow.

Now a few corrections and observations. Frye, it is true, as an undergraduate found Wilson Knight more stimulating on Shakespeare than his other teachers, and preferred Colin Still's extravagant book on *The Tempest* to numerous 'mundane' investigations. But Frye recently has stated more succinctly than others why neither *The Winter's Tale* nor *The Tempest* can possibly be allegory (e.g. Pelican edn. of *Tempest*). Secondly, when one has read through the four chapters of *A Natural Perspective* one realises that each chapter is so constructed as to end in a discussion, several pages long, of one of the Romances. The discussions are still not detailed like those by many others, but Frye may just feel that for such detailed analysis of artistry and peculiar individuality of the plays he can count on many others being only too eager to undertake the task. His own chief concern is quite different, and clear only if one approaches *A Natural*

Perspective as part of his many-volumed work. As for 'myth', he defines the term in the book, and nowhere suggests (as some attackers have intimated) that *The Tempest* is a mere variant of a myth. His discussion of structure in Shakespeare's romantic comedies is based on the assumption that analysis of structure needs to be preceded by a clear understanding of the basic nature of their action, derived in large part from popular materials; and that their very popularity raises pertinent questions as do likewise the so remarkably persistent conventions Shakespeare inherited and adapted: without that we cannot hope to understand what Shakespeare did and how he appealed in the theatre. Frye's thesis indeed needs to be answered before we conclude finally that *The Merry Wives* is pure citizen comedy but designed for a courtly audience, or that Marston's work exercised fundamental influence on Shakespeare. And if Frye's book disappoints those who demand, and perhaps rightly, that critics concentrate on illuminating in detail the artistry and content of masterpieces, my answer is that the book includes more incidental *aperçus* than most others, thoughts or comments on obvious truths easily neglected that ought to set our minds aflying. 'Like all magicians', Frye says of Prospero, 'he observes time closely' (p. 152). He then needed not to expand by asking whether thus the play's classical structure is related to the very conception of its central character.

In 1958, Edwards concluded with a bold agenda. In 1976 I do not need to.

© F. DAVID HOENIGER 1976

PUZZLE AND ARTIFICE:
THE RIDDLE AS METAPOETRY
IN 'PERICLES'

PHYLLIS GORFAIN

Since 1958 when *Shakespeare Survey* last focused on the final plays, structuralism as an important intellectual movement has both deepened and expanded our critical perspectives. Because of an apparently corrupt text and problematic authorship for its first three acts,[1] *Pericles*, among the late plays, has attracted the least critical attention. Yet a structural approach especially suits this work, particularly since it may be applied independently of textual issues. Accordingly, in the last two decades the play has inspired a number of structural studies centering on the meaning of its rambling form. We now recognize that the implausibly ordered episodes produce an analogical coherence distinct from the causality of Aristotelian plotting. Recurrent and inverted outlines of action emerge as transformations of the same deep structure, which conveys a message about its own timeless rhythm of separation, loss, and recovery.

Because the play demands our participation and belief in that cosmic scheme, critics have characterized *Pericles* as ritualistic; they also note its folklore elements, but do not fully comprehend the connection between the folkloric forms and ritual. Furthermore, explicators of *Pericles* fail to use seriously recent folkloristic and anthropological studies to illuminate the role of ritual or the way folklore enhances the fantastic in this self-conscious romance.[2]

The odd riddle which opens the action provides a useful example of an important folkloric

device which critics have neglected. While some readers have wondered how any of the dead suitors could have missed the obvious picture of incest the riddle admits,[3] or have treated the theme of incest or the specific image of the daughter who consumes her mother,[4] or have noted that the riddle commences a series of trials,[5] significant interpretation of this key incident is lacking, and intriguing problems remain unexplored.

Why does the marriage test in Antioch take the particular form of a riddle? Is the enigma really so transparent? Does the structure of this folkloric device have any relevance to its subjects, incest and the destruction of

---

[1] F. D. Hoeniger, in the Introduction to the Arden edition of *Pericles* (1963), pp. xxiii–xlix, usefully reviews textual issues.

[2] For example, a major critic such as Hallett Smith utterly discounts anthropological approaches by eliminating Lévi-Strauss, in *Shakespeare's Romances* (San Marino, 1972), p. 204. Recently W. B. Thorne, '*Pericles* and the "Incest–Fertility Opposition"', *Shakespeare Quarterly*, 22 (1971), 43–76, finds in the play the structure of a fertility rite, but he makes no real use of recent work by anthropologists, and only loosely connects the alleged ritual themes and design to folkloric forms such as the riddle.

[3] Hoeniger thinks he explains the matter: 'We must accept the convention that the riddle was difficult, even if its verses seem translucent to us,' p. lxxii, n. 1.

[4] For example, Coppelia H. Kahn, *Structure and Meaning in Shakespeare's Pericles* (Dissertation, University of California, Berkeley, 1970), pp. 176–7.

[5] Douglas Peterson, *Time, Tide, and Tempest: A Study of Shakespeare's Romances* (San Marino, 1973), pp. 80–101, points up both parallels and inversions in the series of like events.

motherhood? Conversely, does riddling bear any relationship to familial reunion and legitimate procreation? The family romance in *Pericles* brings together a separated father, mother, and daughter only to divide the generations again for reproduction and rule. When Pericles and Thaisa inherit the rule of Pentapolis, Marina and Lysimachus assume reign over Tyre. That comedic resolution overturns the horror of the first incident in which overrating of blood relations[1] requires the deathly riddle and tyranny of Antioch. If we realize that paradoxical dialogues accompany the recovery of the family and resumption of good rule, we may see how transformations of order in the family and state remain associated with similar metamorphoses in riddling. Marina's wordplay produces riddles which restore to their proper roles the governor, Lysimachus (IV, vi, 66–115); the server, Boult (IV, vi, 151–200); and the father and king, Pericles (V, i, 100–4). Just how does that neat correspondence between riddling, kinship relations, and proper social roles match the overall narrative pattern of recurrent loss, trial, and redemption?

Critics have frequently stressed the metatheatrical functions of Gower's stilted choruses. Yet they fail to recognize that the seemingly minor riddle is a complicated folkloric form which also distills a process of disorder and order to criticize the uses of fictions. Exciting parallels between the riddling, the choruses and dumb shows, and ritual emerge when one considers their structural significance.

The riddle invites and then frustrates formal expectations, and uses ambiguity to point up the necessary but arbitrary ways we organize experience. As fictions about artificiality, all the formal devices oscillate between contraries – their own concreteness and the abstract process of their own representing. Thus they stand at and for the point of coincidence where boundaries are defined and violated. Here they embody the inexorable truth that social and cognitive order is contrived. Exploring the epistemological problem that knowledge may be no more than perception yields both doubt and celebration in *Pericles*. The mixed genre of tragicomedy fittingly encloses both. Like a hall of mirrors, *Pericles* reproduces our endless substitutions of one fiction for another. The self-reflecting art and artifice unfold a secret order of the universe, but as an admitted illusion controlled by Gower. The inescapability of such magic portrays man as an artist who creates multiplying forms as he imitates the source of creativity, a prolific power which always eludes the metaphors by which he strives to replicate it.

My study of the riddle in *Pericles* posits an imaginative and structural unity in the play; it also points to larger issues concerning the relations between folk genres and literary forms. To press this inquiry, I shall focus directly on the riddling episodes in the problematic action. I shall then explain general aspects of riddling which illuminate these incidents further; in due course I shall briefly consider selected aspects of Gower's dumb shows and choruses which bear on the discussion. Because I consider homologies between a variety of elements, whose significance can be seen only in terms of their structural relationships, the interpretations I offer require comparisons between equivalent schema. My argument may thus at times appear repetitious, but only because the play must use redundancy to communicate, in multiple and structurally analogous ways, its consideration of complex relationships.

In looking at the riddling episodes, we begin with the opening chorus. Gower confides that the jealous Antiochus has constructed a fatal ordeal as a 'law' to prevent his daughter's marriage,

[1] Following a structural analysis of the Oedipus myth by Claude Lévi-Strauss, 'The Structural Study of Myth', in *Structural Anthropology* (New York, 1963), p. 215.

So for her many a wight did die,
As yon grim looks do testify.

(I, Ch, 39–40)

The explicit motivation behind the marriage riddle suggests a latent incestuous impulse behind other such trials, both in this play and in other works of folklore and literature. Ordinarily when a deserving suitor passes a marriage test, the device frees the filial generation from both parental bonds and the social restrictions the test embodies. Traditionally, a riddle trial in folklore or literature transforms our vision as it creates new relationships through marriage. But in this perverse marriage riddle, the device breeds only the hollow skulls to which Gower points.

We may consider the riddle a false artifice, for its end is deception, not revelation. Antiochus uses it as he does oaths, to dictate a world to suit his desire rather than to disclose a hidden order in the universe.

The first scene introduces Pericles about to confront the riddle. As the princess enters, her father lavishes praise on her. Pericles rivals his hyperboles, although he does not realize he is a competing lover. His ambition matches his excessive admiration of the unnamed daughter, and his inflated figures of speech display the same defects in formality as does the false riddle. He mistakes the princess's sensuous beauty for a sign of control (I, i, 12–18). Later Pericles accurately intuits what Marina's beauty means:

Yet thou dost look
Like Patience gazing on king's graves, and smiling
Extremity out of act....

(v, i, 136–8)

Then figurative speech cures the disease of language bred by false artifice in Antioch.

While the princess stands before him as the prize for victory, Pericles shifts his attention to the apparently more interesting attempt to win her. In his eagerness, he interprets the hazard as an adventure placing him in the ranks of mythic heroes. But Antiochus turns Pericles's images of conquest into emblems of death:

Before thee stands this fair Hesperides,
With golden fruit, but dangerous to be touch'd;
For death-like dragons here affright thee hard.
Her face, like heaven, enticeth thee to view
Her countless glory, which desert must gain;
And which, without desert, because thine eye
Presumes to reach, all the whole heap must die.

(I, i, 27–33)

Unable by such metaphoric means to dissuade the persistent prince, Antiochus imposes another contrived deterrent. He demands that Pericles expound 'the conclusion' (I, i, 56):

I am no viper, yet I feed
On mother's flesh which did me breed.
I sought a husband in which labour
I found that kindness in a father.
He's father, son, and husband mild;
I mother, wife, and yet his child.
How they may be, and yet in two,
As you will live, resolve it you.

(I, i, 67–71)

A riddle question should state the premise, and the answer supply the conclusion. But Antiochus's riddle violates the grammar of riddling as his incest and manipulative oaths violate the social order.

The outright description of incest in the riddle has misled readers who miss the real question because they do not understand riddles. To solve a riddle, one must identify the hidden referent. Here the hidden term reveals to whom 'I' refers. The statement of illicit sexuality does not quibble about the relationship it details, only about who participates in it. Put another way, the solution to the riddle is not 'Incest,' but the name of Antiochus's nameless daughter.

Pericles alters its written sources in having the 'I' in this traditional puzzle refer to the daughter rather than to the father.[1] The

[1] See P. Goolden, 'Antiochus' Riddle in Gower and Shakespeare', *Review of English Studies*, NS 6 (1955), 245–51.

modification sharpens the focus on the princess, and accentuates her contrast to Thaisa and Marina later. All three princesses employ either riddling or deceptive remarks. But the latter two use indirection to sanctify, not desecrate, bonds with fathers and lovers; their reunion ultimately breaks the destructive mother–daughter link provided in the riddle, and establishes a gentle bond between the formerly divided figures. Marina's wordplay transforms the effects of the nameless daughter. That princess becomes a symbol of disorder because of her undifferentiated anonymity and the silence her riddle imposes. Correspondingly, her incest blurs kinship categories, the most fundamental distinctions in human culture.

This inchoate female resembles the monsters who pose riddles in myths.[1] Structurally, those undifferentiated riddlers parallel the confusion in their riddle questions. But where the hero of tradition solves the problem, destroys the chimera, and frees a land from sterility, Pericles can neither answer the question nor cleanse the pollution he finds. Pericles's skill in discerning the truth deprives him of the marriage or office won by heroic riddle-solvers. Instead Pericles must hide his answer, flee for his life, and mask his identity later.

As he undergoes a natural ordeal in shipwreck and devised trials in Pentapolis, Pericles gains both a wife and a position at court. But he cannot regain his royal identity or resume rule until news reaches him that the riddlers have perished. Moreover, no human agency ends their perversions of proper rules. Lightning strikes them down, as if in cosmic judgement. The riddle then challenges conventions about marriage tests and heroic tests while it also questions the values of individual heroism.

Answering such a fake riddle solves nothing. To dissolve the fraudulent riddle, one must expose it as a fabrication. Yet to do this is as dangerous as to reply or to keep silent. Antiochus's pretext for murder tolerates no distinctions between winning and losing, and therefore creates an absurd universe. The end results of the counterfeit test match those of the incest it pictures; as incest denies clear categories, the sham test reduces every alternative to the same conclusion.

The tournament and dances at Pentapolis enact brief plots of division and unity. The riddle in Antioch subverts all such clear discriminations. Staged as outright entertainments with a clear moral dimension, the formalities in Pentapolis emphasize not only individual skill and honor, but also the context of honorable rule which make those virtues effective. That complementarity of individual and social control alludes to the relationship of the artist to society and to the conventions tradition yields. With its modest wooing and evident artifice, the restorative episode in Pentapolis presents a foil to the ordeal at Antioch.

The power of curative art to reorder relationships becomes clear when Marina's riddling and her story open Pericles's portals of hearing and speech. He himself then speaks paradoxically of rebirth as he ends the silence and death caused by the false speech of Antioch and the misleading statue of Tharsus. Pericles uses imagination to invert the parent–child relationship in poetry: 'O come hither, / Thou that beget'st him that did thee beget' (v, i, 194). His reversal of roles then reconstitutes normal family ties and substitutes wonder for horror.

Marina represents the answer to all her father's queries. But she is also a question, for she presents herself as a puzzle; thereby she also teaches Pericles to riddle safely.

Pericles.

                      – What countrywoman?
Here of these shores?

[1] On monsters and the undifferentiated in literature of this period see two recent essays: Michael Beaujour, 'The unicorn in the carpet', *Yale French Studies*, 45 (1970), 52–63; René Girard, 'Lévi-Strauss, Frye, Derrida, and Shakespearean Criticism', *Diacritics* (Fall, 1973), 35–8.

Marina.

                    No, nor of any shores.
Yet I was mortally brought forth, and am
No other than I appear.   (v, i, 101–4)

Marina's reply encapsulates her autobiography in the form of an oppositional riddle.[1] Although born on no shore, she is mortal. Her name later closes the opposition; it reveals she was born at sea. At the same time Marina's enigmatic reply also suggests that her birth was fatal to her mother. Her next line does not reconcile that antithesis; she implicitly warns Pericles she is not the one he seems to recognize. The line also claims that appearances reflect reality, and reassures Pericles not only that she is real, but also that her beauty is true. Taken all ways at once, Marina's completed riddle cancels the debts of Antioch.

Pericles's reply does not yet solve Marina's riddle; but it foresees that the answer will resemble birth. Pericles responds to Marina's puzzle by depicting himself pregnant with grief; 'I am great with woe, and shall deliver weeping' (v, i, 105). The anticipated delivery will bring forth joy as it frees Pericles from the immobility of mourning. In his poetry, Pericles usurps the female role; yet in his conceit rests the tragicomic thesis that art can include actions of both suffering and recovery. In the Antioch riddle, the daughter 'feed[s] on mother's flesh'; Pericles's paradox inverts the roles of father and daughter without consuming maternity and creativity. Metaphor and paradox now support reunion and yet also retain distinctive identities to recreate rather than abort relationships.

The mutuality of father and daughter eventually restores the mother and wife, Thaisa. That resurrection occurs when heavenly harmony escorts Diana to earth and signals all unification. Diana helps join man and the gods as she allows Pericles to choose to follow her directions. As he does so, he combines fate and free will.

Recognizing Marina's admittedly incredible tale as the corollary to his own history brings Pericles back to life; realizing Pericles's story complements her own restores Thaisa as mother and wife. All their tales compose Gower's song, which he offers us as a restorative. When we leave the theatre, the play may truly restore us to life if we choose to understand its directions, to see in it a riddle which reflects our own histories.

Such recognition and understanding are critical in the conversion of sorrow to joy. The designation of father and daughter by name eliminates anonymity and confers control over a knowable universe. The play again turns its initial motifs upside down:

Pericles.
. . . This is Marina.
What was thy mother's name? Tell me but that,
For truth can never be confirm'd enough,
Though doubts did ever sleep.
Marina.

                    First, sir, I pray,
What is your title?
Pericles.
I am Pericles of Tyre; but tell me now
My drown'd queen's name, as in the rest you said
Thou hast been godlike perfect,
The heir of kingdoms and another life
To Pericles thy father.
Marina.
Is it no more to be your daughter than
To say my mother's name was Thaisa?
Thaisa was my mother. . . .

                              (v, i, 198–209)[2]

[1] Following Robert A. Georges and Alan Dundes, 'Toward a Structural Definition of the Riddle', *Journal of American Folklore*, 76 (1963), 111–18. An oppositional riddle question contains at least two comments on a hidden referent; they oppose each other by contradicting laws of logic, natural form, or causality.

[2] Following Peter Alexander's one-volume edition of *The Complete Works* (1951), this lineation seems faulty.

Until she finds her father, Marina withholds her royal name and thereby refuses betrothal to Lysimachus. Pericles's obscured identity in Pentapolis did not impede his marriage, but rather a safe return to Tyre and rule. His period of trial tests his submission; Marina's tries her resistance and creativity. She remains chaste in Mytilene until the family names are exchanged. Naming then reclaims the false parenthood and language of Antioch, Tharsus, and Mytilene. Normalized sexuality mediates prostitution, the deathly confusion in royal incest, and the deathless singularity of Diana's chastity. Marina's name, which commemorates the alternating rhythm of a revitalizing and destructive sea, subsumes all the ambiguities.

The riddling and paradox also organize a system of images which underlie the form and meaning of the play as a whole. For example, the reference to the viper in the unanswered riddle figures as a key image in the play; it forms a configuration with other related images, and makes sense of a singular moment in the final scene when Thaisa recognizes Pericles's ring. Kahn has suggested that the pictorial translation of the self-consuming viper might be the form of the mythological Uroboros.[1] Always depicted with its mouth reaching for its tail, the Uroboros describes an endless circle, like the self-consuming force of the contradictory riddle. Both swallow up all distinctions, initiating a series of unstabilized relationships. The family reunion finally achieves stability in the plot by transforming mutability into a process of reproduction.[2] The ring in Ephesus symbolizes that transformation as it reverses the initial meaning of circularity. The circularity of the ring no longer connotes endless change, but rather eternal unity.

When Marina names her mother, she confirms her identity to Pericles; Pericles's ring, from Thaisa's father, confirms his identity to his wife. She produces a matching band to validate all distinct identities and mutual bonds:

> Now I know you better.
> When we with tears parted Pentapolis,
> The King my father gave you such a ring.
> [*Shows a ring.*
> (v, iii, 38–40)

Thaisa's lines at the close of *Pericles* convey the necessity for the bonds of art to mark union and separation in marriage, the family, and all the means by which we organize existence. That process, so painful and restorative in romance, underlies the tragicomic logic of *Pericles*. The pattern of circularity introduced by the initial riddle illustrates Shakespeare's elegant manipulation of single images to develop symbols and designs with multiple, often opposed, meanings.

The special fit I am claiming between romance, riddling, sexuality, and social and natural order gains support if we now examine riddles in other contexts. Folklorists regard riddling as an expressive model of discontinuity and reintegration, and recent anthropological theories about metaphors and symbols point to strong similarities between riddling and ritual.

The riddle in *Pericles* like similar riddles reveals that the play presents an anomalous reworking of a type of enigma found only in narratives. Folklorists call this special form the 'neck riddle', for it is frequently posed by a prisoner who can save his neck from hanging if he can stump a judge or king with an insoluble problem.[3] Not all neck riddles perform such lifesaving functions in their narrative frames; but all are defined by a common feature which also distinguishes the riddle in *Pericles*. These conundrums describe a personal experience of the riddler; it consternates the

---

[1] P. 177.

[2] On Renaissance notions of mutability related to themes in *Pericles* see Peterson, pp. 16–21; or Ricardo J. Quinones, *The Renaissance Discovery of Time* (Cambridge, Mass., 1972), pp. 13–17.

[3] See F. J. Norton, 'The Prisoner Who Saved His Neck with a Riddle', *Folklore*, 53 (1942), 27–57.

riddlee because it is either self-contradictory or private. Commonly the neck riddle suggests a quasi-incestuous act, committed during imprisonment. Nearly all of them also embody a paradox that life comes out of death. When the riddler reveals the answer, he explains the questionable relationship as basically innocent, and resumes normal relations with family members. The solved neck riddle realigns words and deeds, but subverts the authority of the judge or king to execute the death sentence. Mirroring the theme of life proceeding from death, the neck riddle releases prisoners from physical confinement. Physical release in the narrative action duplicates the psychological release achieved when a riddle answer dispels the tension of a difficult question; the renewal of relations in the story replicates the way riddling refreshes perceptions of order. The variant neck riddle in *Pericles* twists the normal workings of this fascinating form to point up all infractions of order.

Folklorists also explain non-narrative uses of riddling by an appeal to riddle structure. Structural definitions of the riddle vary, but all demonstrate that riddle forms depend on logical or other disjunctions in the interrogative proposition.[1] The answer divulges the secret referent, which closes the gap between apparent and hidden. Whether answering depends on an analogy between elements in different logical domains, on metaphoric transfer, or on new syntactic or phonological organization, riddles require some structural transformation. That process can then imitate transformations of actual conflicts in the social situations which provide the model for riddles. Philosophically, as riddles seem to unveil the surprising order beneath ambiguous appearances, they enclose a desired universe, for riddles promise that an unseen design explains the appearances of disorder which threaten our sense of control and faith. More pragmatically, as the riddle unravels deliberate knots, it can, by a kind of imitative

magic, be held to resolve other problems confronting a group.

That riddles occur as marriage tests in actual situations as well as in folktales and literature then becomes understandable. A psychoanalytic interpretation of this practice argues that solving an enigma enables a suitor to demonstrate skill in putting together two unlike items. In this way riddling serves as a blueprint of the sexual act; in Freudian terms, any test connotes a sexual challenge. From a broader standpoint, we may view the union of opposites and transformations of relationships in riddling as a schema of marriage, which unites and transforms two previously unrelated individuals.[2] The accord between contraries achieved in the riddle answer may also represent the child, who is born of the male and female, and who mediates the poles of the past and future. In Shakespearian drama resolved riddles are always in some sense allied with new generations. The unanswered test in *Pericles* exactly inverts those patterns and reflects the unmediated extreme of parent–child incest, which can produce no new generation.

Another riddle practice offers more insight into the structural significance of these discourses. In several cultures funeral wakes include riddle exchanges. As the wake bridges the gap between life and death, the mourners attempt to convert sorrow into consolation through play. Riddles offer them formal buffers against the threats death poses to individuals and society. The assault on order in riddling resembles the power of death; yet as the riddle retrieves clarity from deliberate confusion, it imitates the pattern which tragi-comedy also

[1] On riddle structure see Georges and Dundes; also Elli Köngäs Maranda, 'The Logic of Riddles', in *Structural Analysis of Oral Traditions*, eds. Pierre Maranda and Elli Köngäs Maranda (Philadelphia, 1971), pp. 189–232.
[2] Following remarks by Alan Dundes in 'Summoning Deity through Ritual Fasting', *American Imago*, 20 (Fall, 1963), 213–20.

represented to Shakespeare's audience; in such reversibility they could read a concise text of God's providence.

Similar dualities occur in riddle texture and in the structure of performance. A fixed-phrase style and the use of rhyme and meter in riddle texture frequently counterbalance the licensed attack on order in riddle texts. The semantic fit achieved between question and answer then echoes the musical fit in the language of the question, which itself balances stylistic order against logical disorder. In these ways riddles sanction various forms of rebellion against given expectations; in addition the rules of performance control a licensed antagonism between co-operative opponents. The answer then equalizes temporary disequilibrium between the performers. The riddler possesses secret knowledge and controls the exchange; the riddlee plays a more passive role, and may have to admit he cannot provide an answer which will subsequently be shown as obvious. Riddling thus provides traditional means to assail not only categories, but also those who hold a position of greater power outside the riddle contest. The anomalous riddling in *Pericles* plays on these features of riddle performance.

Similar disorder in ritual supports the very system it upsets. This structuralist theory derives from anthropologists who interpret rituals and taboo as structural experiments. They submit that ritual symbols use inversion or ambiguity to explore the structures they attack. In particular, Mary Douglas argues that images of the body and control of its functions provide excellent natural symbols of social order.[1] The same theories apply to ambiguity in riddles. The themes of incest and birth in the riddling of *Pericles* utilize powerful images for an artistic inquiry into the nature of order.

Anthropologists conceive of the ritual process as consisting in three stages: separation, the first phase, in which the initiate 'dies' as he is separated from the secular world; margin, or liminality, the middle stage, in which normal time has stopped, and all statuses and norms are overturned or suspended in sacred time; and reaggregation, in which the initiate is 'reborn' to normal time, and advanced to a new status, or returned to the old position with a firmer intuition of the rules of social and cognitive order.[2] The formality of riddling sets it off from normal discourse in the same way that the separation phase of ritual makes possible the ambiguity of liminality. The answer then reintegrates understanding and realigns roles as does the reaggregation phase of ritual.

In *Pericles* the plot also repeats similar patterns of trial, loss, and restoration, which mark the intervals as normal experience. Still another device reflects this same ritual pattern and significance. It clarifies the meaning of the liminality at the center of the ritual moment. Gower stands at the interstices of the dramatic form:

> . . . I do beseech you
> To learn of me, who stand i' th' gaps to teach you
> The stages of our story. . . .
>
> (IV, iv, 7–9)

Like liminality, Gower's intervening choruses both close and create 'gaps' in time and form to disrupt and enhance the illusions of reality, and to mark the stages of the story. The theatrical pun enables multi-levelled thought. A 'stage' not only spatializes the ground on which the action is played, but also measures temporal aspects of a process. The play-ground which creates units of action then symbolizes

[1] In *Natural Symbols* (New York, 1970); Roger Abrahams, 'The Literary Study of the Riddle', *Texas Studies in Language and Literature*, 14 (1972), 177–97, also connects riddling and ritual.

[2] See Victor Turner, *The Ritual Process: Structure and Anti-Structure* (Chicago, 1969); also Edmund Leach, 'Two Essays concerning the Symbolic Representation of Time', in *Rethinking Anthropology* (1961), pp. 133–6.

order in both space and time, and shows up those fundamental categories as only artifices, crude as the chorus which personifies them. Gower's narrations serve as margins dramatically opposing enacted scenes; formally distinguishing enactment, narration, and pantomime; and imaginatively separating engrossing illusion and self-aware artificiality.

Gower explains that his song is performed at calendar rites which observe the change of seasons:

> It hath been sung at festivals,
> On ember-eves and holy-ales;
> And lords and ladies in their lives
> Have read it for restoratives.
>
> (1, Ch, 5–8)

In a later metaphor, Gower conflates his role, the play, and life in the image of the hourglass: 'Now our sands are almost run' (v, ii, 1). Here lies the hint that the play, like a clock, and like the chorus, measures the passage of expired singular and critical events. Yet it also seems to recur as a ritual in a sacred, stopped time. Such events raise vision to the perspective at which cycles recur and all loss is redeemed in the restorative time of comedy.

The hourglass can be overturned, both measuring and renewing time. Gower himself embodies a similar figure. Like a phoenix, he conveys a paradox. He promises that the play restores its audience, whose time it wastes, as his art ruins and replenishes his own creative powers:

> To sing a song that old was sung,
> From ashes ancient Gower is come,
> Assuming man's infirmities,
> To glad your ear and please your eyes.
>
> (1, Ch, 1–4)

> And that to hear an old man sing
> May to your wishes pleasure bring,
> I life would wish, and that I might
> Waste it for you, like taper-light.
>
> (1, Ch, 13–16)

A mediator who stands between his own past and our present, the audience and the play, Gower stands for all mediation. His deceptively simple lines play on the paradoxical border between reality and imagination. His metaphors contend that his artistic position is a sacrificial one, resembling the intercession of Christ, who also assumed man's infirmities to requite the Fall. So should the lame metaphors of good art, as they themselves indicate.

The given plot itself, not the achievements of a hero, reconciles all the oppositions – in the story and in its episodic format. Yet Gower stresses that both human choice and submission to an order beyond human understanding control the plot, which we accept from the authority of tradition and recreate. 'I tell you what mine authors say,' he repeats, as did his historical prototype. The patience he urges in enduring the narrative parallels the virtue with which the heroes bear temporal dangers. Reversibilities in suffering then seem plausible because of the active interventions of art, which make the miraculous imaginable. Like riddles and like myth, the play experiments with alternate arrangements of order; Gower's frame then removes them to a different plane of reality. So we learn that stages and songs can undo the 'foul show' of death.

The dramatic communication of that poetic proposition employs the dumb show and Gower in an elaborate way which illustrates the play's complex use of these obvious devices. The 'foul show' which commemorates bad art and corruptible parenthood is the statue of Marina at Tharus. It represents a poor copy of Marina, who accurately reproduces and surpasses Pericles. The analogy between biological, artistic, and fraudulent reproductions develops a paradox about art and life. Marina, as a symbol of art, surpasses the life she copies; as a representation of procreative life, she shows up the insufficiencies of art.

That the misleading statue makes a

counterfeit stay against time becomes evident in its intricate framing. The dumb show mimes Pericles at his daughter's tomb, where the statue stands. 'Whereat Pericles makes lamentation, puts on sackcloth, and in a mighty passion departs' – so the stage directions indicate the stylized action of the dumb show. Gower breaks in to exclaim: 'See how belief may suffer by foul show! / This borrowed passion stands for true old woe' (IV, iv, 23–4). Ambiguity encompasses multiple meanings which establish the variability of art. The 'foul show' may be the sham art of the statue, or the poor quality of the dumb show as an artifice, of the play as a production, of the character as an element in it, of the actor as a performer. ... Similarly, the 'true old woe' may be that of fictional Pericles whom the character Pericles imitates; or that of the character Pericles which the dumb show Pericles imitates; or the woe of man, which the play imitates in this enactment of 'real' and 'false' bereavement .... The experiences depicted in the dumb show are so varied, and work at so many removes from 'true old woe' that the layered meanings become complex, and the truth of any woe questionable. As each lamination encloses and imitates the other, no easy distinction between levels of reality is possible. Yet the baroque entanglement which flaunts the accretion of artifice also clarifies the problematic relations between art and life. Dionyza and Cleon ob-

jectify their pretended woe in the 'real' statue they build as a prop in their drama of grief. That fabricated show is enacted in a keyed action (the dumb show), itself part of a keyed presentation (the chorus), itself enclosed in a keyed action (the play).[1] Offered as a song, the play imitates a story handed down through the ages, and the keyed experiences and fabrications in day-to-day life, which the audience may now see is as contrived as the 'foul show' about which Gower complains. Yet such transparent illusion evokes not dismay about, but admiration for the crude instruments with which we navigate an otherwise unknowable universe.

If these literary devices serve as metatheatre, the riddle in *Pericles* serves as a metaphor of metaphor.[2] The folkloric form becomes a means for figuring the transformations in life and art. The self-conscious play develops a similar circularity. These self-reflecting circles break open when they seem to disclose who Gower's authoritative authors might be: the ordering forces of the universe which hold out both creative and created parts for us if we have the artistry to act.

[1] Perhaps clumsy terms here, but significant discriminations offered by Erving Goffman in *Frame Analysis: An Essay on the Organization of Experience* (New York, 1974).

[2] See Richard Klein, 'Straight lines and arabesques: metaphors of metaphor', *Yale French Studies*, 45 (1970), 64–78.

'PERICLES' IN A BOOK-LIST OF 1619 FROM THE ENGLISH JESUIT MISSION AND SOME OF THE PLAY'S SPECIAL PROBLEMS

WILLEM SCHRICKX

While looking in Belgian archives for documentary evidence connected with English cultural life in the late sixteenth and early seventeenth centuries I have come across a handwritten catalogue of books which were once in the possession of the English Jesuit mission established in Saint-Omer.[1] This catalogue, headed *Catalogus librorum Missionis Anglicanae Societatis Jesu, qui Duaci in Collegio nostro relicti sunt*, is preserved in the *Rijksarchief* in Ghent. It is written on the first two pages of a sheet folded once and the sheet itself is found in dossier 76, which forms part of a number of documents now classified as *Archives des Jésuites*. The catalogue lists the titles of 124 books, the authors of which are for the most part not mentioned. An examination of these titles shows that they are mostly concerned with attacking the considerable body of anti-Catholic legislation passed by Parliament in the wake of the Gunpowder Plot of November 1605, as well as with arguing against the defenders of the Oath of Allegiance. In the article mentioned below it was shown that the *Catalogus librorum* was compiled in December 1618 or in the course of the year 1619, at a time when difficulties had arisen between the English Jesuits and Matthew Kellison, who was president of the English College of Douay from 1613 to 1641.[2] With very few exceptions the books listed in the catalogue are of a devotional or a controversial nature. Among these exceptions there occurs a remarkable title, *The play of Pericles. 4°.*, which happens to be the hundredth book on the list. There is not the least doubt that this item refers to a copy of one of the three quarto editions of *Pericles* published before 1619. Because of the compilation date of the catalogue, the reference is either to one of the two 1609 quartos or to that of 1611. As a matter of fact, the catalogue lists no books printed in 1619 and only two books published in 1618, both of which were printed in Saint-Omer, namely Fulvio Androzzi's *Certain Devout Considerations* and Salvian of Marseille's *Quis dives salvus. How a rich man may be saved.* This latter work is an English translation made by the Jesuit priest Joseph Creswell, a man who, from 1614 until his death in Ghent in January 1623, was in charge of the administration of the various Jesuit colleges in Flanders, which is why he seems somehow to have been concerned in the compilation of the *Catalogus*.[3] As to the question of the authorship

[1] See my article 'An Early Seventeenth Century Catalogue of Books from the English Jesuit Mission in Saint-Omer. A Study in Books and Their Printers', *Archives et bibliothèques de Belgique*, XXXXVI (1975).

[2] The best general treatment of English colleges on the Continent is still Peter Guilday's book *The English Catholic Refugees on the Continent, 1558–1795* (1914).

[3] It is Creswell's connection with Ghent and also with Saint-Omer and Douay which explains how the catalogue of books from the Jesuit mission was eventually to find its way into the Ghent *Rijksarchief*. On Creswell (1556–1623) see A. J. Loomie, S.J., *The Spanish Elizabethans* (New York, 1963), pp. 182–229; for dates and printers of Catholic books on the Continent see A. F. Allison and D. M. Rogers, *A Catalogue of Catholic Books...1558–1640* (1964, repr. 1968).

of *Pericles*, let me state at the outset that I agree with the view of most critics that the last three acts are substantially Shakespeare's and that the first two were written by a collaborator. As will appear, I shall give additional evidence to support the theory that this was George Wilkins.

The appearance of *Pericles* in a list of books first owned by the English Jesuits and later by the English College in Douay is interesting for a number of reasons. To begin with, it provides an isolated addition to the few known occurrences of titles of Shakespearian plays in contemporary catalogues.[1] More importantly the fact that *Pericles* is the only work of imaginative literature in a long list of devotional and controversial works is in itself intriguing. When we bear in mind that music and acting entered largely into the Jesuit system of education, it is more than likely that the play was once on the repertory of the English Jesuit theatre in Saint-Omer in the early seventeenth century. Saint-Omer at the time was an extremely important town and its geographical location on the route to France often made it a stopping-place for many visitors from England. Indeed, it is because of its proximity to England that Saint-Omer had been chosen as the site for the Jesuit seminary by the famous Jesuit priest Robert Persons.[2] Yet Saint-Omer at this period fell within the territory of the so-called Spanish Netherlands which, from 1596 to 1621, was ruled from Brussels by the Archduke Albert, whose wife Isabella was the daughter of Philip II of Spain. Consequently the cultural ties of towns like Saint-Omer and Douay were with Louvain and Brussels rather than with France. It is too often forgotten that these English educational centres, as well as neighbouring cities such as Dunkirk and Lille, were not incorporated with France until about half a century later. Under Spanish rule from Brussels, these cities were taken up into the larger movement of the Counter-Reformation which

was so powerfully afoot in the area and they experienced its vigorous resurgence much more than the French towns across the border. This is why the inclusion of such a play as *Pericles* in a Saint-Omer book-list lends significant support to the view of F. D. Hoeniger, the editor of the New Arden *Pericles* (1963), that this drama is a saint's play in which Shakespeare emphasises the themes of patience and redemption. On the other hand, when discussing the fortunes of its early performances in England, recent editors have often failed to mention that on at least one occasion *Pericles* was performed by a number of recusants who were organised as a company of players 'with authority of Whitby and Roxby to travel about the country and to act plays', as we learn from an article by Charles J. Sisson.[3] The performance of which there is evidence took place at Candlemas 1610 (2 February). It is clear therefore that *Pericles* could confidently be included in a repertory for Catholic college boys on the Continent, once it had proved its worth for a recusant audience in England. And this brings me to a more detailed discussion of the play's early performances.

I would first like to call attention to a number of particular passages in Sisson's article which editors of *Pericles* seem to have taken into account very little, if at all. The Catholic provincial company, which performed *Pericles*, was a firmly established group of actors led by an actor called William Harrison, who was 36 at the time he appeared in Star Chamber. Commenting on the status of Harrison's

[1] See T. W. Baldwin, *Shakspere's 'Love's Labor's Won'. New Evidence from the Account Books of an Elizabethan Bookseller* (Carbondale, Southern Illinois, 1957).
[2] For the foundation of Saint-Omer seminary see Hubert Chadwick, S.J., *St Omers to Stonyhurst* (1962).
[3] See the circumstantial treatment of this by C. J. Sisson, 'Shakespeare Quartos as Prompt-copies with some Account of Cholmeley's Players and a New Shakespeare Allusion', *The Review of English Studies*, XVIII (1942), 129–43.

company, Sisson writes that 'it is unreasonable to doubt that this company took its work seriously, was well-trained and capable'. He goes on to remark that 'their travelling career was chequered by fear of arrest, by pursuits, flight and escape, because of the part they played in the religious conflicts of the time, for they were Catholics and their persuasion and that of most of their audiences was reflected in their performances'; and he further shows that the actors insisted, 'in their own defence against charges in Star Chamber, that they only acted plays which were in print and allowed, exactly as they were printed'. Sisson emphasises that the company played from printed books only, not from promptbooks, so that the players followed texts scrupulously, the document of the Star Chamber proceedings itself stating that 'they onelie acted the same [i.e. the printed book] according to the contents therein printed, and not otherwise'. The repertory chosen by Cholmeley's Players is of extraordinary interest in that most, if not all, of its titles betray that their inclusion was largely determined by the fact that those who were to act them were Catholics. Four titles have come down to us, *Saint Christopher*, *Pericles*, *The Travels of the Three English Brothers* and *King Lear*. Of the first play no text seems to have survived, but, considering that the publication in England of specifically Catholic books was suppressed by the authorities, it is conceivable that the book the actors played from may have been printed somewhere on the Continent and perhaps in the Southern Netherlands where the English college presses were very active. The second play, *Pericles*, may well have been on the repertory of the Jesuit theatre in Saint-Omer and it is interesting in this connection to observe that we have evidence of at least one play that was written in English and performed there *omnia Anglicé* by the Jesuits; it was called *The Triumph of the Cross* and was staged with full costume and elaborate scenery in 1613.[1]

It was a so-called *tragoedia sacra*, a genre with which, as we will see from a significant example, the scholars of Saint-Omer had been familiar from the foundation of their seminary. The third play on the repertory of Cholmeley's Players, *The Travels of the Three English Brothers*, of mixed authorship and printed in 1607, is usually ascribed to John Day, William Rowley and George Wilkins. Consequently there were two plays on the list with which Wilkins was somehow closely involved. About the contemporary Catholic appeal of *The Travels* there cannot be the least doubt. The famous traveller and adventurer Sir Anthony Sherley, one of the three English brothers, had in 1599 gone to Persia on a mission to the Shah and in 1601 he had an audience with the Pope, an event to which *The Travels* devotes a whole scene, in which Sir Anthony addresses the Pope as follows:

> Peace to the Father of our Mother Church,
> The stayre of mens saluations, and the Key
> That bindes or looseth our transgressions.
>
> (*The Travels*, 1607, sig. D₁v°)

It is worth observing that Fr Joseph Creswell had, some time before Sir Anthony's embassy to the Pope, been instrumental in bringing about this nobleman's conversion to Catholicism, and that the same Jesuit stayed with him at the court of Madrid in April 1607. Sir Charles Cornwallis, the English ambassador in Madrid reported to the Earl of Salisbury that 'Sir Anthony Sherley's Harvest proves not suitable to his Spring' and stated that he supposed '*Creswel* many Times wisheth, that he had not medled with the Scrutiny of such a a Conscyence'.[2] If it is remembered that *The*

---

[1] See Chadwick, *St Omers*, p. 130, and also William H. McCabe, 'The Play-List of the English College of St. Omers 1592–1762', *Revue de Littérature comparée*, XVII (1937), 355–75.

[2] See letter of 3 May 1607 of the English ambassador in Spain, Sir Charles Cornwallis, printed in R. Winwood, *Memorials of Affairs of State* (London,

Travels also includes mention of the christening ceremony of a child of Sir Anthony's brother, Robert, it is clear that the play was, as it were, marked out for inclusion in a Catholic repertory. As for *King Lear*, finally, there is no space here to deal in detail with any reasons why it was played by William Harrison's company, though it is perhaps worth mentioning in passing that Shakespeare's partial use of Samuel Harsnett's *Declaration of Egregious Popish Impostures* (1603), a long book in which Harsnett reveals how the Jesuits deal with demoniacs, provides a significant link with Jesuit activities. In addition, it is relevant to point out in this connection that the First Folio omits such passages from the First Quarto as the trial scene in act III, scene vi and the list of devils mentioned in act IV, scene i (ll. 60–6), a fact which probably reflects to some extent the political or religious position of those who had to introduce cuts at some stage of the textual history of *King Lear*.

With regard to other performances of *Pericles* authenticated by archive material, it is noteworthy that, before 1620, we have evidence of only two (this in spite of the fact that *Pericles* was so popular), both performances being in honour of visiting ambassadors. The Venetian and French ambassadors to England saw the play probably in 1607 or early in 1608, whereas the French ambassador de la Tremoile was given a farewell party on 20 May 1619, a festive occasion marked by the staging of *Pericles*, of which occasion we hear in contemporary letters. Again, the visitors were assumed to favour Catholicism.

Obviously *Pericles* appealed to audiences inclined to appreciate a drama with religious overtones, and this feature leads us to an examination of both the religious and the political background determining the play's significance for contemporary audiences. Politics and religion were indeed so strongly intertwined in contemporary thought that they were bound to impinge on each other. It is especially in the first two acts of *Pericles* that it becomes clear that the initial choice of the figure of Antiochus was probably inspired by the wide contemporary use of this tyrant as a symbol of religious and political oppression in what would now be called socially involved literature. In *Pericles*, Antiochus's position as a tyrant is so repeatedly emphasised as to render his political significance immediately obvious and in Shakespearian criticism he is therefore usually identified with Antiochus III (or the Great), also because he is thus styled in Gower's opening speech. The religious aspect of this character is indeed nowhere in evidence except in act II, scene iv, where his fate is similar to that of Antiochus IV Epiphanes as described in *2 Maccabees*, ix, where he is stricken by the God of Israel not only with lightning but also with plague and worms, so that he stank intolerably. In *Pericles*, Antiochus's death by lightning is also followed by a description of its ill-smelling after-effects.

> Even in the height and pride of all his glory,
> When he was seated in a chariot
> Of an inestimable value, and his daughter with him,
> A fire from heaven came and shrivell'd up
> Their bodies, even to loathing; for they so stunk
> That all those eyes ador'd them ere their fall
> Scorn now their hand should give them burial.
>
> (*Per.*, II, iv, 6–12)[1]

There are several historical figures bearing the name Antiochus, but the Antiochus in the mind of the author of the passage just quoted would

1725), II, 308. The position of Creswell as Sherley's tutor and educator is abundantly clear from a later passage in Cornwallis's correspondence (Winwood, II, 337): 'I have here inclosed sent unto your Lordship *Creswel's Instructions to his gostlye Childe Sir* Anthony Shirley *at his Departure.*' After July 1607 Sherley paid a visit to Rudolf II in Prague.

[1] Quotations from Shakespeare are from Peter Alexander's one-volume edition (1951). The first to point out this biblical echo was R. J. Kane, 'A Passage in *Pericles*', *Modern Language Notes*, LVIII (1953), 483–4.

seem to be the son of Antiochus III, Antiochus IV Epiphanes, who reigned from 176 to 164 and from whose tyranny the Maccabees freed Judaea. But what Elizabethan dramatists had shown interest in or could have felt their interest aroused by Antiochus? One English playwright who in his reading had come across Antiochus the Great was George Wilkins. Through his work on a translation of Pompeius Trogus, published in 1606 as *The Historie of Justine* he had familiarised himself with Syrian history and had therefore set himself to a close reading of the military fortunes of Antiochus the Great. E. A. J. Honigmann[1] has suggested that, because of Wilkins's special interest in Mediterranean histories, such as the translation just referred to, his pamphlet *Three Miseries of Barbary*, the play *The Travels of the Three English Brothers*, and *Pericles* (the novel), 'it becomes more likely that *Pericles* the play originated with Wilkins too', and I agree. But there are other reasons for suggesting that Wilkins was closely involved in the composition of the first two acts of *Pericles*, however imperfect the state of the text in which they have come down to us.

Roger Prior[2] in an important article on 'The Life of George Wilkins' has, on biographical grounds, convincingly argued that there is one speech in *The Miseries of Enforced Marriage* in which the dramatist's own state of mind 'is precisely described'.

Scarborrow.
Thus like a Feuer that doth shake a man
From strength to weaknesse, I consume my selfe:
I know this company, theyr custome vilde,
Hated, abhord of good-men, yet like a childe
By reasons rule instructed how to know
Euill from good, I to the worser go.
Why doe you suffer this, you vpper powers,
That I should surfet in the sinne I tast,
haue sence to feele my mischiefe, yet make wast
of heauen and earth:
My selfe will answer, what my selfe doth aske?
Who once doth cherish sinne, begets his shame,

For vice being fosterd once, coms Impudence,
Which makes men count sinne, Custom, not offence,
When all like mee, their reputation blot,
Pursuing euill, while the good's forgot.
                                    (ll. 1, 118–33)

The idea that 'vice being fosterd' (compare *Pericles*, I, i, 96: 'vice repeated' and I, i, 137: 'One sin I know, another doth provoke') leads men to 'count sinne, Custom, not offence' is closely paralleled by two lines in Gower's opening chorus (ll. 29–30) in *Pericles*:

But custom what they did begin
Was with long use account no sin.

Furthermore, there can be little doubt that Scarborrow's speech is somehow also related to a striking one by Pericles, who, having solved the riddle, realises the full extent of the sinfulness of Antiochus and his daughter.

Pericles.
                    But, O you powers
That give heaven countless eyes to view men's acts,
Why cloud they not their sights perpetually,
If this be true, which makes me pale to read it?
Fair glass of light, I lov'd you, and could still,
Were not this glorious casket stor'd with ill,
But I must tell you now my thoughts revolt;
For he's no man on whom perfections wait
That, knowing sin within, will touch the gate.
You are a fair viol, and your sense the strings;
Who, finger'd to make man his lawful music,
Would draw heaven down, and all the gods, to hearken;
But, being play'd upon before your time,
Hell only danceth at so harsh a chime.
                                    (*Per.*, I, i, 72–85)

Editors have sometimes been puzzled by the expression 'touch the gate' in line 80, but it is plain from what follows that Pericles means that, if he fingered a viol that had been played upon before its time, he would touch the gate of

[1] E. A. J. Honigmann, *The Stability of Shakespeare's Text* (1965), pp. 196–7. I endorse Honigmann's view that George Wilkins is the translator of *The Historie of Justine*.
[2] *Shakespeare Survey 25* (Cambridge, 1972), 137–51.

Hell. Pericles knows there is sin within the 'glass of light' and the 'glorious casket' and where he had expected to touch the gate of Heaven he finds that 'Hell only danceth at so harsh a chime'. Scarborrow, on the other hand, is not a 'man on whom perfections wait' and yet he too implores the upper powers. To use a current critical term borrowed from modern psychology and also memorably used, for example, in Yeats's doctrine of the self and anti-self, Pericles as we see him in the first two acts was for Wilkins an image of his own anti-self, the saintly figure to which the man would have aspired who 'was melancholic almost to the point of madness' (Roger Prior) and who was haunted by the spectre of his transgressions.

Obviously, the reason why Wilkins was attracted by the Antiochus theme was that this ruler was for him the embodiment of sinfulness. And yet I believe that his interest in Antiochus was primarily inspired by the fact that this historical figure had for a long time been interpreted in terms of the political and religious conflicts of his time and that Antiochus was deeply tainted with sin not only because of his sexual dissipation but also because of his sacrilegious attitude towards what his opponents believed to be the true religion. That such an accretion of the Antiochus symbol had taken place in the sixteenth century, at least for readers and audiences on the Continent, can be shown from a few striking examples.

In the second half of the sixteenth century, torn as it was by violence due to fierce religious strife, the theme of revolt was frequently treated in terms of the struggle between Antiochus IV Epiphanes and Judas Machabeus, particularly by those who wished through this symbolism to express their stubborn loyalty to either the Catholic or the Calvinist cause. The two examples of this use of historical symbolism to be discussed here are both associated with the prominent political leaders of the day, William of Orange and Henry IV of France.

The Revolt of the Netherlands which had been brewing for more than a decade reached a dramatic climax in 1577, when William of Orange was hailed throughout Flanders as the *pater patriae*. It was in these troubled times that Lucas D'Heere, a Ghent poet[1] and pictorial artist whose involvement with English cultural and political life as an exile in London lasted ten years from about April 1567 to early 1577, was in charge of a programme of festivities during the triumphal entry of William of Orange on 29 December 1577. The very first item of the scenic display, 'show' or *tableau vivant*, offered to greet William of Orange was the picture of Judas Machabeus who was meant to stand as a symbol for the Prince. Nine months later the same symbolism was to crop up again in D'Heere's work. After the death of Don John of Austria on 1 October 1578 Lucas D'Heere wrote a satiric epitaph on Don John containing a passage in which Antiochus symbolises the deceased Spanish governor-general and in which Machabeus is again used to represent the Prince of Orange. To free people from Spanish domination God Almighty has begot the Machabeus of Nassau to resist the weakling Antiochus. God

> Heeft verwect om ons bevrijden
> Den Machabeum van Nassau,
> Om desen Antiochus flou
> Te wederstaen.

For the committed writers of the day Judas Machabeus was therefore the great champion of religious revival and revolt. According to the Bible, 2 *Maccabees*, x, Judas Machabeus conquered the Temple of Jerusalem, destroyed the

[1] For the evidence from Lucas D'Heere I am indebted to the detailed study by W. Waterschoot, 'Leven en Betekenis van Lucas D'Heere', *Koninklijke Academie voor Nederlandse Taal- en Letterkunde, Verslagen en Mededelingen* (Ghent, 1974), pp. 1–126. See also F. A. Yates, whose book *The Valois Tapestries* (1959) includes a substantial account of the significance of Lucas D'Heere and his work.

altars set up by foreigners, purified the Temple and erected another altar. Not only was he remembered for his military exploits against Antiochus IV Epiphanes but he could also be interpreted as a prefiguration of Jesus, who likewise chased away the merchants from the Temple. It would be interesting to collect evidence of the nascent popularity of the Machabeus theme in the sixteenth century and we shall presently turn to a particularly significant example of its use in Saint-Omer, in the very place where the foundation of the first English Jesuit mission so near to England had ushered in a new revival of learning and Catholic spirituality. But I shall first return to Shakespeare.

Geoffrey Bullough's monumental treatment of Shakespeare's narrative and dramatic sources has recently given 'considerable weight to the possible effect of contemporary events'[1] on the drama of the time. Aspects of the contemporary historical situation are often reflected in ways not readily discernible. Contemporary leaders and particularly those who enjoyed great popularity were frequently equated with figures from biblical history, and so dramatists who worked for the Jesuit theatre often chose subjects through which they could hold 'the mirror up to nature, to show...the very age and body of the time his form and pressure'. And what could be more effective than biblical stories to illustrate the contemporary religious situation?

Of the direct association of contemporary historical events with the biblical narrative of Antiochus and Judas Machabeus one more very conspicuous example has come to my notice. It derives from a so-called *tragoedia sacra* and the circumstances of its performance show that it is significantly linked with military events in the Spanish Netherlands in the area of the English seminary of Saint-Omer. One stage of the struggle between the rulers of this area and France is remembered in Donne's fourth *Satire*, where 'the losse of Amyens', which occurred on 1/11 March 1597, is referred to in line 114, an allusion which in its brevity cannot sufficiently convey a sense of the excitement of the high-spirited young men of the day over the war in neighbouring France. The defeat of the great Armada kept rankling with Philip II and in the early nineties there were unmistakable signs that Spain was re-organising her warships and her armies in the face of English unpreparedness and complacency. Philip was evidently getting ready a new and more formidable Armada to invade England before the end of the century and so the Privy Council agreed to make preparations for a new offensive against Spain in 1596, of which the expedition against Cadiz formed one of the great adventures in the life of men like Donne. But nearer home the Spaniards were fighting in France, and in the spring of 1596 Spanish troops, led by the newly-appointed governor-general of the Netherlands, the Archduke Albert, were launching an attack against Calais. Here the Spanish forces were of course not formally engaged with English troops, but with the armies of Henry IV of France, whose recent conversion to Catholicism had failed to satisfy the religious demands of the new ruler of the Spanish Netherlands. At the beginning of April the Spaniards began besieging Calais, which fell into the Archduke's hands on 14/24 April 1596. The capture of Calais was the occasion for celebrations in the area and particularly for the Walloon Jesuits of nearby Saint-Omer, who decided to receive the Archduke and his soldiers with pomp and circumstance. The reception of visitors often entailed putting on dramatic performances and so a play was staged on the subject of the sacred history of Matathias and the Maccabees and their fight against Antiochus.

[1] See Nigel Alexander, 'Shakespeare's Life, Times, and Stage', *Shakespeare Survey 27* (Cambridge, 1973), 172.

Of this play an outline has been preserved in the College *Diarium* of Saint-Omer, extracts of which were printed in an article by L. Deschamps de Pas.[1] Though its author, apparently, is not mentioned in the *Diarium* it is highly likely that the piece performed was *Machabeus sive constantia, tragoedia sacra* written by the Bruges humanist Andreas Hoius (André van Hoye), who was born in Bruges in 1551 and who died in Douay in 1631, where from about 1593 he was professor of Greek at the university. The first edition of his play on the subject of Machabeus was printed in Douay by John Bogard in 1587, but the second impression was brought out in 1595 in the same city by Balthazar Bellère, a noted Catholic printer. The performance in Saint-Omer of the Machabeus play took place about 17/27 May 1595. When the Archduke asked the Rector of the College what kind of play was to be produced the answer was that an episode from sacred history was the subject chosen because 'it applied so well to the contemporary situation and suited his Excellency, Matathias being Maximilian, the father of the Cardinal [i.e. the Archduke Albert] who, with his brothers, was represented by Judas Machabeus, the holy commander, and his brothers, whereas Antiochus was Henry of Navarre [i.e. Henry IV of France], over whom, so the young actors in the drama prophesied, the commanding Cardinal and Archbishop of Toledo, would one day triumph according to the example of Judas Machabeus'. These lines, freely translated from the Latin, are embedded in a longer text of which a portion now follows.

Insinuaverat autem serenissimus Cardinalis sibi placere ut quamdiu apud nos domi esset, sibi semper proxime assistaret Rector collegii; aderat igitur et roganti quid drammatis exhibendum esset, explicavit historiam sacram tempori apprime convenientem, et suae Celsitudinis personae non male consonam; Matathiam nimirum, Maximilianum parentem Cardinalis ipsius quem referebat cum fratribus Judas Machaboeus sacer dux, et illius fratres: et Antiochum Navarreum de quo Cardinalem ducem sacrum, et sedis Toletanae archiepiscopum exemplo Judae Machabaei triumphaturum aliquando juventus nostra nobiscum illo drammate bene ominabatur. His arridens, contemplatus aliquot emblemata emporii Caletani, Ardeae, et vicinarum arcium expugnationem ingeniose per figuras allegorias exprimentia (quae post ad se cum reliquis omnibus et jam carminibus latinis, graecis et gallicis, ibi affixis deferri cum dilucida emblematum expositione mandavit) ad solium quatuor vel quinque gradibus a tabulato communi elevatum, undique rubra bysso clausum, excepta parte anteriori, qua in theatrum dabatur prospectus, ascendit, ibique sedit, ascito sibi ad latus P. Rectore interprete rerum quae proponerentur.[2]

The triumph of 'Machabeus' over Antiochus, we are told here, was represented by a number of emblems exemplifying the conquest of

[1] L. Deschamps de Pas, 'Siège & prise de Calais & d'Ardres en 1596 par l'archiduc Albert d'Autriche et réception de ce prince à St. Omer', *Bulletin historique trimestriel. Societé des antiquaires de la Morinie*, VIII (1887–91), 625–33.

[2] 'But the most gracious Cardinal had intimated that he wished the Rector of the college to remain in close attendance upon him throughout his stay with us; and so he was present, and when asked what play was to be performed, explained that it was a historical drama with a religious theme which was particularly appropriate for the time, and very well suited to his Eminence's character, since Matathias was Maximilian the Cardinal's own father, and the Cardinal himself with his brothers was represented by the divinely appointed leader Judas Machabeus and his brothers: and Antiochus was the man of Navarre, over whom the Cardinal Archbishop of Toledo, himself a divinely chosen leader, would some day triumph through the example of Judas Maccabeus: our boys and we ourselves gave a sure prophecy of this in the play. These words caused him some amusement, and he examined some emblems on which the capture of the town of Calais, and of Ardres and the neighbouring fortified centres was cleverly portrayed by means of allegorical figures: after commanding that these and all the others, together with the Latin, Greek and French poems attached to them should be taken down and clearly explained to him, he ascended to a throne raised four or five steps above the general level, and enclosed all round by scarlet drapery except in the front where it looked out on the stage, and sat there with the Reverend Rector placed at his side to translate the action of the play for him.' (Translated by Stephen Ryle.)

Calais and Ardres by means of allegorical figures, the pictures being accompanied by Latin, Greek and French texts.[1] Though the Machabeus play was staged at the Walloon or 'Belgian' Jesuit College, it is practically certain that the English seminarists saw it performed too, because co-operation between the two colleges was particularly close. The English seminary, recently created and under the care of a 'Belgian' Jean Foucart and George Persons, the brother of the notorious Fr Robert Persons, was in its initial stages no more than a *pensionnat* so that for all their classes the students were obliged to go to the Walloon College, a circumstance which was to remain a source of friction for many years until, finally in 1614, a separation of the two colleges was at last decided upon.[2]

Hoius's play was by no means the only one written on the Machabeus theme for the Jesuit theatre. His most interesting predecessor in this field was Jakob Pontanus, whose *Eleazarus Machabeus* was performed in Dillingen in 1587 and printed in 1594 and 1600. In this work Pontanus[3] tells the story of Antiochus and the old Eleazar following the account of the Maccabees in the Bible as well as that of the Jewish historian Josephus. In England the works of Josephus were published in a translation by Thomas Lodge in 1602, but the entry of it in the Stationers' Register (ed. E. Arber, III, 119) under the date of 26 June 1598 makes special mention of 'a booke touching the Machabees'. The interesting thing about Pontanus's drama is that the Jesuit author emphasises that his tragedy is of great value for two reasons: it both offers the young men of his day a shining example of the unwavering faith of their fathers and at the same time exposes contemporary Antiochuses.[4]

From the examples given here it is clear that the figure of Machabeus was destined to become a symbol of inspiration for all those who suffered religious oppression and, after

also being represented by pictorial artists such as Rubens, this biblical hero was consecrated as *vindex religionis* in Filippo Picinelli's *Mondo simbolico* (Milan, 1653). The introduction of features from the Judas Machabeus theme in *Pericles* II, iv, in the passage quoted earlier, where Antiochus's retributive death by lightning is followed by noisome after-effects, may well derive directly, therefore, from the author's acquaintance with some continental *Machabeus* drama, such gruesome details being relished particularly by the dramatists of the Counter-Reformation. At the end of Hoius's play, for example, there is a chorus in which a messenger reports how the vengeful God destroys Antiochus, the dramatist alluding to the loathsome stench which developed after the destruction of Antiochus by the plague and worms, this stench scattering his army (*prae tetro odore, exercitus dilaberetur*), while the soldiers utterly disregarded the disgrace of desertion.

> Hic perspicaci cuncta lumine intuens
> Regum superborum vltor & vindex Deus,
> In membra subitam regis effreni luem

[1] The fact that such languages as Greek, Latin and French were used makes it practically certain that the *Machabeus* performed at Saint-Omer was Hoius's play.

[2] Chadwick, *St Omers*, p. 62.

[3] Fr Johannes Müller's book *Das Jesuitendrama in den Ländern deutscher Zunge vom Anfang (1555) bis zum Hochbarock (1665)* (Augsburg, 1930) is as yet the only full-scale account of the Jesuit drama of this period but it bristles with inaccuracies. Further performances of an Eleazar drama are on record for Aix-la-Chapelle (1603), Mainz (1604) and Paderborn (1610, 1613). An *Antiochus Epiphanes Tragoedia* was performed in Augsburg in 1619.

[4] See J. Bielmann, *Die Dramentheorie und Dramendichtung des Jakobus Pontanus (1542–1626)* (Freiburg im Br., 1928), p. 65. Incidentally, Pontanus is also the author of a *Dialogus de connubii miseriis* (1580), which calls to mind the title of George Wilkins's play *The Miseries of Enforced Marriage* (1607). But the similarity does not extend beyond the title. The *Dialogus* argues that the really serious student prefers the bachelor life to the married condition.

Immisit, ima pasceretur quae ilia.
Indomitus ille, dum nihil de pristina
Remittit ira, & properat; e curru est humi
Delapsus, & lapsu ossa collisus gravi.
Vt vermium iam foeda sentina omnibus
Ex artubus scaturiret, & tabum vndique
Difflueret: ac, prae tetro odore, exercitus
Dilaberetur, imperatoris sui
Securus, haud veritusque transfugij notam.[1]

Pontanus, needless to say, also dwells on this feature of Antiochus's death, Eleazar wishing that his enemy may 'putrefy by the illness no physician can heal and be unable to endure his own stench, worms feeding on him while still alive'. And furthermore Hoius, already in the prologue to his own play, also stresses the parallel between the plight of Judaea and the church of his own time.

Grex scenicus salvere vos multum iubet,
Humani spectatores & vestris parat
Oculis subijcere Iudaeae adflictae statum,
Ecclesiae pro tempore adflictae typum.[2]

Both in its sources and through its later fortunes *Pericles* is linked by various threads with the learned drama on the Continent, as well as with the religious issues which divided the peoples of Western Europe. In addition, the text of the play itself contains in its tournament scene (act II, scene 2) certain features for which the Jesuit theatre may likewise have offered a precedent. It is a scene for which no equivalent has been found in John Gower or Lawrence Twine, the two principal authors who provided the dramatist with his chief source material concerning Apollonius of Tyrus. On occasion of the 'triumph' or festive pageantry celebrating the birthday of Thaisa six knights – of whom Pericles is the last – appear in succession with shields on which 'devices', that is to say emblematic figures, are wrought. Though the symbolism of emblems was widespread in the sixteenth century, it is nevertheless worth noting that the use of emblems was a regular feature of the receptions organised by the Jesuit colleges for visiting princes and we have earlier come across an example from the description of the entry of the Archduke into Saint-Omer. But there are others. Thus Fr Robert Persons wrote *A Relation of the King of Spain's Receiving in the College of Valladolid* (1592) in which we are told that the royal party passed into a dining hall which was hung 'verie decentlie with grene and red tafatie and adorned with abundance of verses of many languages, Emblemes, Hieroglyphics and other learned inventions'. A similar display of emblems and hieroglyphs occurred on a later occasion when in August 1600 Philip III called upon the Jesuits of Valladolid and Antonio Ortiz wrote *A Relation of the Solemnitie* (Antwerp, 1601, translated by Fr Francis Rivers).[3] What is more, the tournament scene itself is in certain respects related[4] to the way

[1] 'Now God, who avenges and punishes proud kings, seeing everything with his keen eye, assaulted the limbs of the immoderate king with a sudden disease which fed on his inmost vitals. He, undaunted, did not restrain his old anger in the least, but hastened; and he fell to the ground from his chariot, and his bones were gravely injured in his heavy fall: so that now the foul cess-pit of worms and pestilence spread from all his limbs, and flowed out on every side: and the soldiers slipped away in the face of the noisome odour, caring nothing for their commander, and not fearing the disgrace of desertion.' A. Hoius, *Matthaeus, et Machabaeus, sive Constantia: Tragoediae Sacrae* (Douay, 1587), p. 54 v°. The impression of 1595 is identical with that of 1587, but about thirty pages of poems have been added. One of these poems is addressed to Giles Schondonck, S.J., the famous superior of the English Jesuit college of Saint-Omer from 1601 to January 1617, the month of his death.

[2] 'Members of the audience, the troupe of players greets you heartily, and prepares to set before your eyes the condition of oppressed Judaea, a symbol of the present persecuted church.'

[3] See Loomie, *The Spanish Elizabethans*, pp. 191, 214–15.

[4] For the suggestions contained in the rest of this paragraph I am indebted to Professor E. De Strycker, S.J., Antwerp.

the messenger presents the seven assailants of the gates of Thebes in Aeschylus's *The Seven Against Thebes*, verse 375 ff. Each of the seven princes carries a shield with a 'device' or picture on it and of three of them it is expressly stated that their shield carries not only a device but also a motto (verses 434, 469 and 647–8). Many Jesuit colleges enjoyed a great reputation for Greek studies but the English college of Saint-Omer occupied a position of undisputed prominence in this field, and it is therefore not impossible that the tournament scene was indirectly inspired by Aeschylus's drama.

When we look back over the account presented in the preceding pages it is perhaps justifiable to claim that in all likelihood the Antiochus theme was one that could be treated independently of the Apollonius–Pericles story and this is precisely what we find in *Pericles* where, in the words of Kenneth Muir, 'there is no integral connexion between Apollonius' wooing of the daughter of Antiochus and the later episodes of his marriage, the loss of his wife and daughter, and his final reunion with them. Apollonius happens to meet his bride when he leaves Tyre for fear of the wrath of Antiochus'.[1] The disparity in tone and style between the first two acts and the rest of the play may therefore be due partly to the existence of an Ur-*Pericles* – a theory favoured by quite a number of critics – in which Antiochus would have played a far more important part, as we see him do in the Latin plays of the Jesuit theatre; and partly, of course, to composite authorship.

We must now turn to the most puzzling of all problems concerning *Pericles*, that of the identity of Shakespeare's collaborator. What the foregoing pages have shown is that *Pericles* and *The Travels* were plays of which the appeal for Catholics was assured. The mere fact that George Wilkins collaborated in *The Travels* and that there are many points of resemblance between this play and *Pericles* – proximity of dates, ties with English Jesuits on the Continent, impact on a Catholic audience, the similarities in the choric convention – points to Wilkins as Shakespeare's collaborator. If an author of a lost Ur-*Pericles* is to be looked for, Wilkins is the most likely candidate. The literary grounds for this minor dramatist having had a share in *Pericles*, have often been canvassed. However, in keeping with the historical or literary-historical drift of my argument thus far, I shall continue to concentrate on external evidence only. Roger Prior,[2] in his article on Wilkins's life, has drawn upon the Middlesex Sessions records and has thus been able to add an important number of new facts to what we know of Wilkins. The name Wilkins occurs in five legal cases between 1600 and 1619 as George Wilkinson and in three of these it probably does not refer to George Wilkins the victualler (i.e. the dramatist, who is known to have been a victualler). But, Roger Prior continues

The third case is more doubtful, partly because this Wilkinson is a yeoman and partly because the case is dated more than two years earlier than the first Wilkins entry, at a time when he may not have been living in Cow Cross. On 19 January 1608, 'George Wilkinson, yoman, Jane Wilkinson, widow...late of St. Andrew's in Holborn co. Midd.', together with more than a score of others were convicted of 'not going to church, chapel or any usual place of Common Prayer during three months beginning on 1 Sept., 5 James I' (1607). Such entries are frequent, and indicate that the accused were Catholic recusants. But Wilkins's writings give us no reason to think that he was a Catholic.

Obviously, sufficient reasons have been advanced here to suggest that this last statement is probably no longer acceptable. Moreover, a few lines further in the paragraph just quoted from, Prior shows some hesitation when he

---

[1] Kenneth Muir, *Shakespeare as Collaborator* (1960), pp. 79–80.
[2] *Shakespeare Survey 25* (Cambridge, 1972), 137–51, esp. p. 143.

writes that Wilkins 'may have been the recusant'. In addition, as mentioned earlier, the Catholic connections of *The Travels* through Anthony Sherley's close association with Fr Joseph Creswell have to be borne in mind. And in this context there is the further fact of Anthony Sherley's adventures in Barbary where he was from October 1605 to approximately July 1606. If it is recalled that Wilkins was ready with his pamphlet *The Three Miseries of Barbary* about a year later, there are reasons for supposing that he may well have got some of his information concerning this country through Sherley.[1] As to the recusant connections of other Wilkinsons – if this is an acceptable variant of Wilkins – in the *Calendar of State Papers, Domestic Series, James I. 1603–1610*, under the date of 13 February 1606 we hear of Valentine Wilkinson and his wife visiting Erith, a small town on the Kentish bank of the Thames near Dartford, where Fr Henry Garnet, before his execution, had temporarily rented a manor house.

A last point deserves mention. Prior, in the article referred to, suggests that 'Wilkins's wife may well have been the Katherin Fowler (or Fowles) whose marriage to a George Wilkins is recorded in the register of St Laurence Jewry'. On the supposition that she was approximately the same age as her husband she would have been born about 1576 and considering that there is so much in the present argument that directs us to the Continent, it is not beyond possibility that she was a daughter or a relative of John Fowler, the most prominent Catholic printer in Flanders, who was born about 1537 and who died in Namur on 13 February 1579. But quite apart from the fact that the name Fowler is extremely common, this connection is a mere conjecture, for my attempts to trace the birth of a Katherin Fowler in the preserved parish registers of Antwerp and Louvain for the period 1567–77 have proved fruitless, although four children were born to Fowler in the decade before his death.[2]

[1] The archives of Simancas hold a manuscript document concerning Barbary by which Anthony Sherley informed Philip III, in the first days of March 1607, of the dangers presented by this country. We are thus again led to Creswell. The document is classified as *Estado, leg.* 1171, fol. 112. It is not directly related to Wilkins's *Three Miseries of Barbary*.

[2] I wish to thank Dr L. Van den Branden, who has made extensive researches in the Antwerp archives, for informing me of the baptismal entry of what was apparently Fowler's third child. The baptismal registers of the Church of Our Lady (reg. 7, fol. 165) record the baptism in Antwerp on 25 January 1576 of a son, Francis. There is no space to elaborate here on this point, but members of the Fowler family, one of whom was a well-known dealer in Catholic books, were later closely connected with Creswell in Madrid and with the Spanish embassy in London whose secretary, Dr Robert Taylor, had married a daughter of John Fowler.

© WILLEM SCHRICKX 1976

GEORGE WILKINS AND THE YOUNG HEIR

ROGER PRIOR

In a previous article in *Shakespeare Survey* I presented some facts about a George Wilkins who kept a tavern in Cow Cross, or Turnmill Street, and was probably the minor dramatist and pamphleteer.[1] It also seemed likely that he was the man who gave evidence with Shakespeare in the Belott–Mountjoy suit. This hypothesis is completely confirmed by another deposition made by Wilkins which has recently come to light. This deposition is in a Chancery suit, and is much longer than that already known. The deponent is undoubtedly the victualler of Turnmill Street, and his two signatures match that of the friend of Belott and Mountjoy. The deposition itself, together with an account of the circumstances of the case, forms the principal material of the article which follows.[2]

First, however, it will be convenient to refer to other new information about George Wilkins. Most of it is contained in an article by Professor Mark Eccles.[3] He shows that the Wilkins of Turnmill Street was closely connected with people of the theatre. When this important evidence is added to that already known, it becomes virtually certain that the victualler was also the dramatist. He also adds to our knowledge a case of 1602, in which Wilkins was charged to keep the peace towards one Richard Story. More detailed and amusing is the account of a suit of 1614, when Wilkins's wife Katherine sued a neighbour for calling her a bawd: 'Thy husband may goe horne by horne with his neighbours.' A witness for

Katherine testified to the contrary: she 'had never byn reputed or accounted a bawd or so called before that tyme'. Another witness said that Wilkins's house was frequented by lewd women. Eccles agrees with my suggestion that Katherine Wilkins was the Katherine Fowler (or Fowles) who married a George Wilkins on 13 February 1602. He records the administration of Wilkins's estate, granted to Katherine on 14 October 1618.

A new connection between Wilkins and the theatrical world is slight, but worth mentioning. He had as a friend a reputed whore called Magdalen Samwaise (pronounced 'Sammy's'). In September 1611 she was charged with stealing fifty shillings from William Usurer. Wilkins was said to have made a 'composition' in the matter of this felony, and to have

[1] 'The Life of George Wilkins', *Shakespeare Survey* 25 (Cambridge, 1972), 137–52.

[2] I found the deposition while holding a fellowship awarded by the Leverhulme Research Trust, to the trustees of which I express my thanks. The reference is P.R.O. C/24/409 part I, no. 44, Dixon *con* Harrys.

[3] 'George Wilkins', *Notes and Queries*, 220 (1975), 250–2. Professor Eccles makes some corrections to my article in *Shakespeare Survey*, not all of which are correct. He is right, however, in saying that 'Randall Borkes' (p. 144) should be 'Randall *Berkes*'. Berkes was a stationer. I take this opportunity to correct some mistakes myself. On page 144 the date of Wilkins's marriage should be 1602, not 1601. On page 145 'Richard Daniell, of St Benedict, Shoreditch' is wrong. He is described as both 'of St Benet's London' and 'of Shoreditch', but the two should not be combined. See my reply to Eccles, *Notes and Queries*, 220 (1975), 561–2.

conveyed away Magdalen. These events gain in interest when we discover that a year before Magdalen had borrowed some money from Philip Henslowe.[1] Such a loan would not seem, on the face of it, to have been very secure or profitable, but perhaps Henslowe's motives were not purely financial. The note is dated 28 August 1610. Magdalen signed it herself, in a large and careful hand. She owed Henslowe forty shillings; very possibly he advanced her a smaller sum. She was to repay the money in quarterly instalments of ten shillings each, the last instalment being due at Michaelmas, 1611. So, if Magdalen did steal fifty shillings from William Usurer in September of that year, some of the money may have been intended for her last payment to Philip Henslowe.

One of Magdalen's sureties on this occasion was a young man called John Bonner, described as a factor, of Cow Cross. He too was troubled by a usurer. He was, as will appear, a close associate of Wilkins. A few weeks later they were both implicated in another incident. In November 1611 one Anthony Gouch came before the magistrates for 'comitting a notorious outrage in the house of George Wilkins and for abusing one Bonner at the same time'. By the end of June 1613 John Bonner was dead, and in 1614 his life became the subject of a Chancery suit and of Wilkins's testimony.

The suit was brought by his five sisters (who were probably all older than he was) and the husbands of four of them against a man called Thomas Harris. The names of the complainants are given as John and Priscilla Dixon, William and Mary Johnson, Thomas and Rebecca Shingler, Robert and Abigall Finsher, and Bathsuba Bonner.[2] Their aim was to regain John Bonner's property from Harris, whom they alleged to have cheated him of it. They called two witnesses: Richard Dancy and George Wilkins. These two depositions, with the interrogatory, are the only records of the suit at present available. Others may well exist,

but so far I have not found them. Dancy is described as a merchant, of St Michael Bassishawe, aged 34; Wilkins as a yeoman of St Sepulchre's, aged 40 or thereabouts. This description, in 1614, adds a year or two to Wilkins's age as calculated from the Belott–Mountjoy deposition. There, in 1612, he was said to be 36. It is nowhere stated that Wilkins and Dancy knew each other, but they almost certainly did so, since both knew Bonner well, and had acquaintances in common. Dancy's evidence is more detailed than that of Wilkins, and does not have his occasional confusions. The testimony supports almost all the Bonners' charges against Harris.

The story is a familiar one. It describes the ruin of what Wilkins and his contemporaries commonly called, with some contempt, a 'young heir'. This gives the suit an added literary interest, for the only play known to be solely by Wilkins, *The Miseries of Inforst Mariage*, has as its theme the ruin of just such a young heir, William Scarborrow. In the previous article I suggested that Wilkins's work draws heavily on his personal experience. Here is further evidence of that. William Scarborrow is not likely to be based on John Bonner, as *Miseries* was published in 1607, probably five or six years before most of the events described in the suit. But Wilkins, keeping a tavern, was well placed to meet other young heirs of the same kind, and Bonner and Scarborrow have much in common.

Both of them own estates in the country which they lose in London. Bonner's property was in and near the city of Worcester. At the

[1] George F. Warner, *Catalogue of the Manuscripts and Muniments of Alleyn's College of God's Gift at Dulwich* (1881), p. 134.

[2] Christopher Whitfield has identified a Bonner family of Gloucestershire which was related to the Combe family. The Combes were friends of Shakespeare. See 'The Kinship of Thomas Combe II, William Reynolds, and William Shakespeare', *Notes and Queries*, 206 (1961), 364–72.

time when he lost it to Harris he was under age, in his 'nonage'. So is Scarborrow at the beginning of *Miseries*. When he woos Clare Harcop she says to him:

Clare, O God, you are too hot in your gifts, shoulde I accept them, we should haue you plead nonage, some halfe a year hence; sue for reuersement, & say the deed was done vnder age.

(ll. 236–8)[1]

The Bonners may have hoped to make precisely this plea against Harris, and it is true that the deed *was* done under age. But, unfortunately for them, Harris was well aware of the dangers of Bonner's nonage, and guarded against them. Moreover, Bonner was probably over 21 when he died, with his property then in Harris's possession. In fact, the Bonners' case seems to have rested on the weak argument that Harris only held the property in trust. None of the testimony upheld this plea.

In pawning his land to a usurer Bonner again resembles Scarborrow. Both men spend the money in taverns and, in Bonner's case, probably on whores like Magdalen Samwaise. Wilkins described it.

A Tauerne is his Inne, where amongst Slaues,
He kils his substance, making pots the graues
To bury that which our forefathers gaue.

(ll. 1,381–3)

No doubt much of Bonner's money was spent in Wilkins's own tavern. Scarborrow's violent behaviour is paralleled in Bonner's violent speech. He often threatened to kill Harris, but if he made any attempt, it is not recorded. With his impotent threats he is like another 'boy of land' – Kastril, the 'angry boy' of *The Alchemist*. Kastril comes from the country to London in order to learn how to quarrel. He plans to impress his friends at home by his London sophistication. Bonner's return to his own country ended otherwise. He was 'slaine at a ffaire at Lemster in Wales' – presumably Leominster in Herefordshire – about mid-

summer, 1613. Leominster is twenty miles or so west of Bonner's home in Worcester.

In that or the following year his sisters sued Harris in Chancery. Although we have only their side of the story, there is every reason to believe that it is substantially true. Their witnesses confirm it; Harris himself is said to have admitted it. He might well have done so, for he had not acted illegally, and the Bonner sisters probably had little chance of regaining the property lost by their young brother John. He, more than Harris, had been the agent of his own ruin. He lost his fortune through his own impatience, extravagance and stupidity. He could dispose of his money when he came of age, but he wanted it now, and did not care about the cost. He seems to have been the archetypal spoiled youngest son. Richard Dancy's testimony draws a clear picture of the situation. John Bonner in his lief tyme being in want of money and other necessaries and comeing to the defendant to bee supplyed in his wantes he the said John Bonner did to thend he might be releeued in his necessityes seale to the defendant some writinges billes bondes or other specialtyes and did not at the tyme of the sealing of the said specialties read or peruse all of them.

Bonner owned, or would in the future own, a house in Worcester, once the residence of Thomas Bonner, now deceased. His sisters suggested it was worth £40 per annum, but Dancy valued it at £22 or £23. John, not yet of age, could not sell it. To raise ready money, he turned to Harris. Exactly what Harris gave or promised to give him for the house is uncertain. Several different 'considerations' were offered, and by splitting the payment in this way he probably intended to confuse Bonner. It seems that the bulk of the money was not to be paid at once, but in the future. On 23 April 1613, it was said, Harris bound himself on penalty of £300 to pay £150 to Bonner in eighteen months time. According to Dancy this £150 was the 'most part' of the payment for

---

[1] Quotations are from the Malone Society reprint of *Miseries*, prepared by G. H. Blayney (Oxford, 1964).

the house. It was to be paid only if Bonner was then living, 'and should then Come in person to receaue itt' 'at a place in the Cittie of Worcester comonly called the Towle shoppe'. Harris never had to pay. By the time his money was due, Bonner had long been dead. Harris thus got the house for next to nothing. One can imagine the outrage of the Bonner sisters.

The delayed payment was a sensible precaution of Harris's. Since Bonner was not of age, he was not yet entitled to sell his house. Harris therefore postponed paying the £150 until after Bonner's majority, when he would know for certain whether or not the house was his. This was not his only precaution. He got Bonner to bind himself by a 'Statute Merchant', with a penalty of £500, acknowledged before the Bailiff and Town Clerk of Worcester (also called Wigorne, from the Latin name *Wigornia*), and by a Chancery recognizance of £150. In these figures we can see what value Harris put upon the house. The purpose of these bonds was, said the Bonners, 'to hinder the saile of the said messuage to other persons, and therby to worke the said John Bonner to sell or convey the...house...to him the said Thomas Harris'. Dancy agreed, and added: 'the defendant hath of this deponentes knowledg offred to reward some persons well that would procure the said John Bonner to enter the said Recognizance and Statute'. His 'drifte' was that the 'said house might be sold to none but to the defendant himself'.

It is clear that Harris had Bonner totally in his power. In Wilkins's words, Bonner 'being in want of money to supply his necessitie withall was often forced and Compelled to doe what soever the defendant would wish him to doe'. Or, as he puts it in *Miseries*,

Young heires left in this towne where sins so ranke,
And prodigals gape to grow fat by them
Are like young whelps throwne in the Lyons den,
Who play with them awhile, at length deuoure them.
(ll. 1,271–4)

To get money, Bonner bought from Harris a 'bargaine of cloth'. The word 'bargain' has an ironic ring. Dancy was present when the bargain was made, and was a witness to the bond. The price of the cloth, to Bonner, was £29. 10s. He agreed to pay £30 to Harris at some future date, on penalty of £60 if he failed. Harris gave him the ten shillings change in cash. Bonner then sold the cloth at a far lower price, possibly £8. Dancy was 'verely persuaded that the said Cloth...was not worth aboue viii li at the most to be sould for ready money'.

Bonner may have come of age shortly before his death. At that time he obtained the lease of some lands at Crowle, about five miles east of Worcester. His sisters said the lands were worth £30 or more per annum; Dancy said £17, or a hundred marks to sell (a mark was two-thirds of a pound). Harris got hold of the property immediately, thus cheating death as well as Bonner. Bonner alleged that Harris had given him literally nothing at all for the lands. Dancy heard him 'swere and protest that the defendant had meerely Cheated and Cosened him of the same and that he w[ould] be revenged'. He 'vsed wordes to the like effect very often in this deponentes hearing'.

By such means, from being 'very poore and very little' Harris admittedly grew rich at the expense of John and Thomas Bonner. Dancy has

heard the defendant Confesse that about vii or viii yeres before the death of the said Thomas Bonner he the said defendant was very little worth in substance, and now in this deponentes estimacion the said defendant is worth 1500[li] or thereaboutes and so is generally reputed and taken to bee worth and...did ...by and from the said Thomas and John Bonner gett most of his estate & substance and was by the meanes of them...exceedingly advanced in his estate.

The depositions give us some vivid glimpses of the feelings of the four men, and their oddly close, ambiguous relationship, which was a form of mutual parasitism. Harris is the chief predator: he is feeding on Bonner, and is quite frank about it. But is he enemy or friend? Though hated, he is Bonner's familiar; he drinks with him and his friends; he laughs with them; he is the necessary provider. Some words of Dancy's reinforce the cumulative impression of the evidence, that Harris was constantly in his victim's company, doling out small sums to keep him going: 'he hath heard the said John Bonner in his lief tyme often swere and protest that he the said Bonner did never receaue at any tyme of the defendant in silver or money aboue half a Crowne or v.s. at the vttmost'. The clerk has added Dancy's afterthought: 'and was most as he said in Taverne Reckoninges and such like. . .' These were the necessities that Harris supplied. There is a curious acceptance, by all four, that Bonner is being ruined. No one, it seems, tried to stop it. Bonner is aware of his own self-destruction, but unable to change. In this he is again like William Scarborrow. All he can do is utter impotent threats. He 'hath often in his lief tyme threatned to kill the defendant for his the said defendantes hard and vnconscionable dealing towardes him'. Harris does not seem to have been much moved. He 'hath often', says Wilkins, 'in laughing sort Confessed soe much in effect as the said Bonner charged him withall'.

The rôles of Dancy and Wilkins in the case are as ambivalent as that of Harris. They give evidence for the Bonners. Yet they know Harris well, and have at the least not prevented him from ruining their friend, if he was a friend. Wilkins, it is easy to see, may have had divided motives. He owns a tavern, which is also perhaps a brothel: a John Bonner with money is a sure source of income; without it he is a no less certain liability. How far, if at all, did Wilkins collaborate with Thomas Harris? *Miseries* itself must arouse our suspicions. It seems more than coincidence that a man who

wrote a detailed study of the ruin of an heir should, some years later, be so closely involved in a parallel case. Many such heirs may have come his way. In *Miseries* the chief sponger on Scarborrow, his drinking companion Sir Francis Ilford, is told how to turn 'an Ancient Gentleman' into 'a young begger'. He replies:

What a Roge is this, to read a lecture to me, and mine owne lesson too, which he knowes I ha made perfect to 9 hundred fourscore and nineteene   (ll. 548–50)

And later he laughs:

To see that wee and Vsurers liue by the fal of yong heirs as swine by the dropping of Acorns (ll. 1,054–5)

Was this how Wilkins looked on John Bonner? Let us hope not.

The full text of Wilkins's deposition follows.

21 die Decembris 1614.

1 *George Wilkins* of the parish of St Sepulchers without Newgate London yeoman aged 40 yeres or thereaboutes sworne &c. 1 That he knoweth John Dixon named for one of the Complainantes and Thomas Harrys named for the defendant but Priscilla wife of the said John Dixon William Johnson Mary his wief Thomas Shingler and Rebecca his wife Roberte ffinsher and Abigall his wief and Bathsuba Bonner named for the rest of the Complainantes in this suite this deponent doth not knowe nor to his now remembrance did knowe Thomas Bonner of the Cittie of Worcester gentleman latelie deceased mencioned in the Interrogatory but did knowe John Bonner in the Interrogatory named in his the said Johns lief tyme who as this deponent hath heard was slaine at a ffaire at Lemster in Wales. about Midsomer was xii monthes as he now remembreth./

2 That by reason hee was never at the Cittie of Wigorne or at the house where the said Thomas Bonner in his lief tyme did dwell therefore hee Canott depose any thing Certein or materiall to this Interrogatory touching the yerely worth of the said Tho: Bonners dwelling house in the said Cittie or whether the same bee scituate in the same Cittie as by the article is supposed./

3 That all that he can say to this Interrogatory is this viz That he hath heard that the defendant in the life tyme of the aforesaid Tho: Bonner was but of

small worth in substance and now as this deponent hath also heard is become...[*here half a line is lost from fraying of the paper*]...as this deponent verely thinketh the said defendant hath raised his fortunes and gotten much substance by bargens and dealinges which haue beene betwixt the said defendant and the said John Bonner./

4 That hee hath heard that the defendant in or about the tyme in the Interrogatory mencioned [23 April 1613] did enter into bond to the said John Bonner in the some of 300^li or thereaboutes or some such like some with Condicion to pay one hundred and fiftie powndes or thereaboutes to the said John Bonner at or about the feast of St Michaell the archangell. Anno domini 1614 provided alwaies that the said John Bonner bee then living if not then the said bond [*word lost: probably* is] to bee frustrate as by the said bond and Condicion may and will appere as this deponent verelie thinketh to which bond and Condicion this deponent for more Certenty herein doth referre himself. and touching the tyme of the death of the said John Bonner this deponent saieth for answer therevnto as to the i. Interrogatory precedent he hath already deposed viz That he hath heard and beleeueth it to bee true that the said John Bonner was slaine at or about Midsomer last was xii months, at Lemster in Wales aforesaid./

5 That the bond mencioned in the next precedent article was so sealed and deliuered by the defendant to the said John Bonner vpon a bargein which as this deponent hath heard was made betwixt the defendant and the said John Bonner for the said house in Worcester [and the lease of the landes in Crowle: *crossed out*] in this Interrogatory mencioned and this deponent saieth that he hath heard the said John Bonner in his lief tyme say that he had never had any consideracion for the said lease of the landes in Crowle but was plainly cheated and Cosened by the defendant of the said lease which wordes or the like in effect this deponent hath heard the said John Bonner vse to the defendant & to that the defendant hath answered little or nothing againe but more or otherwise to this Interrogatory this deponent canott materially depose./

George Wilkins

[*Page 2.*]

6 That the lease of the landes mencioned in the next Interrogatory precedent being made by the said John Bonner in his mynoritie and during his nonage vnto the defendant he the said defendant did as this deponent hath heard, draw and procure the said John Bonner to enter into a Statute Merchant acknowledged before the Bayliffe and Towne Clerk of the Cittie of Wigorne of the penalty of fiue hundred powndes or thereaboutes and also to acknowledge another Recognizance in this honourable Cort of 150 l. or thereaboutes as this deponent verely thinketh only to draw and Compell the said John Bonner to Confirme the bargens he had made with the defendant in his nonage touching the messuages and landes before mencioned at such tyme as he the said John Bonner should Come to lawfull yeres and also to satisfye some other dettes which he had drawen the said John Bonner into by other indirect meanes./

7 That he hath heard that the said John Bonner in his lief tyme did buy a bargen of Cloth of the defendant and entered into bill for payment of the money, which said Cloth as this deponent hath Credibly heard was not worth halfe the money that he the said John Bonner agreed to pay for the same./

8 That he hath heard the said John Bonner in his lief tyme say to the said defendant that he the said defendant had sould him the said Bonner a nagge or gelding for the some of xx^tie markes or thereaboutes which said Nagge or Geldinge the said John Bonner did say was not worth half the money and that he was Cosened by the defendant in the horse or gelding, which the defendant [could *deleted*] did not denye./

9 That all that he can say materiall to this Interrogatory is this (viz) That he the said John [*the following line, up to* forced *and* lies along the tear; the reading given is fairly certain, but may be wrong in parts*] Bonner being in want of money to supply his necessitie withall was often forced and Compelled to doe what soever the defendant would wish him to doe. and so much the said John Bonner hath affirmed in this deponentes hearing to the said defendant./

10 That he can say noe more materiall to satisfy the questions of this Interrogatory then as he hath already deposed to 4 & 5th Interrogatories precedent./

11 That the said John Bonner in his lief tyme hath often tould the defendant in this deponentes hearing that he the said defendant had Cosened and ouer Reached him the said Boner [deft *deleted*] in the bargens formerly mencioned to haue passed betwixt them for horses geldings Clothe and the lease of the land in Crowle and in all reckoninges and accomptes which were made or had betwixt the said Bonner and the said defendant. whereto the said defendant hath answered little or nothing to the Contrary but hath

often in laughing sort Confessed soe much in effect as the said Bonner charged him withall./

12 That the said John Bonner in his nonage and mynority hath often Sworne and protested in this deponentes presence & hearing that he the said John Bonner during his nonage had never aboue half a Crowne or v^s at a tyme of the defendant.

13 That he hath heard that at the tyme of the said John Bonners death there was a bond [left *deleted*] remaynivng in the handes of one Wyley of the Cittie of Worcester whereby it appered that the defendant was indetted to the said John Bonner at the tyme of the said Bonners death in the some of xxli or some other some of money as by the said bond as this deponent thinketh may & will appere & whereto this deponent for more certenty herein doth referre himself./And more &c./

George Wilkins

© ROGER PRIOR 1976

THEATRICAL VIRTUOSITY AND POETIC
COMPLEXITY IN 'CYMBELINE'

ROGER WARREN

In much the most helpful criticism of *Cymbeline* that I know, James Sutherland isolates two contrasting styles, one 'impetuous, violent, straining after the maximum of intensity', the other a 'natural, easy, and unforced' style. He describes illuminatingly the 'new recklessness of expression' in Arviragus's

> the bier at door,
> And a demand who is't shall die, I'd say
> 'My father, not this youth':
>
> (IV, ii, 22–4)

Undertakers do not come round to the door like dustmen to demand a corpse – a corpse, too, that is not yet dead when they arrive. What Shakespeare has to express is an avowal of love that will go a stage further than that just made by Guiderius...Clutching at some means to express this thought powerfully, Shakespeare moves naturally enough to a choice between life and death, a choice involving the (supposed) father of Guiderius on the one hand and the boy on the other...Driven on by some compelling urge for the immediate and the emphatic – perhaps visualizing the death situation in a sudden flash – he never pauses to get it into perspective, but suddenly writes down the elliptical and startling phrase, 'the bier at door', and the rest inevitably follows.[1]

What Professor Sutherland conjectures here about the style seems to me to apply to whole scenes as well: Shakespeare visualises situations 'in a sudden flash' and does not bother about matters of more normal dramatic coherence. It is the situations which interest him. In particular, 'visualizing the death situation' is central to the action of the play as well as to the language.

The two contrasted styles which Professor Sutherland mentions are also central, in a less complex and extreme form, to Shakespeare's style in his earlier comedies. Those comedies constantly set extravagant against extremely simple language (the strikingly simple, powerful blank verse in the finale of *Love's Labour's Lost* against the extravagance earlier; the simple directness of Beatrice and Benedick in the Church against the dangerous frivolity of the Court; the contrast between Orsino's language and Viola's). In *Cymbeline*, Shakespeare applies similar contrasts, not only to the language, but to the whole play. In each of the central scenes, theatrical virtuosity on an elaborate scale is set off against language of great simplicity or emotional intensity or both: the enormously elaborate series of events leading up to Imogen's waking by Cloten's corpse against the breathtaking simplicity of the dirge and the passionate intensity of Imogen's grief, the virtuoso descent of Jupiter against the language with which Posthumus responds to it, and Iachimo's emergence from the trunk against his exquisitely expressed appreciation both of Imogen's beauty and her worth. And J. C. Maxwell points out the 'contrast in the final scene between the surface virtuosity of the dénouement...and the rich poetry of the occasional phrase'.[2]

[1] 'The Language of the Last Plays', *More Talking of Shakespeare*, ed. J. Garrett (1959), pp. 151, 153, 149.
[2] *Cymbeline*, New Shakespeare (Cambridge, 1960), p. xlii. All quotations are from this edition.

These contrasts account for the play's most impressive single quality in the theatre – the capturing of single *moments*, the highlighting and displaying on stage, in an extreme form, of central human emotions – love, rapture, despair, jealousy, desire, even death and burial, ultimately reconciliation. It seems to have been the desire to capture, to exploit fully, even the sadness of death that made Shakespeare contrive the bizarre series of events that would enable him to present, not just an awareness but an *experiencing* of death and loss, to make the audience share in it fully – so that he can then take them *beyond* even that to joy and reconciliation, to make it the more valued, the richer, for our having experienced Imogen's pain and the princes' grief so fully. This seems to me a more far-reaching version of the technique of a comedy like *Twelfth Night*, where the awareness of shadows, dying roses, and the wind and the rain, far from detracting from the ultimate happiness of the lovers, enriches our sense of their 'golden time', precisely *because* the harsher aspects of life have not been excluded.

The complexity of the verse in *Cymbeline* seems to Anne Barton to contrast with 'the simplicity of the characters who speak it... This dense and image-packed verse is neither clear nor transparent.'[1] But it could also be said that the effect of the verse is actually to *complicate* the 'simplicity' of the characters, so that Iachimo doesn't *simply* emerge as a villain, nor Posthumus simply as a wronged hero, nor Cloten simply a fool, nor Imogen simply a fairy-tale princess. The very density of the verse modifies the initial presentation of the characters in the way that, for instance, Orsino's language affects our final view of him.

I

Although critics' satirical interpretation of Orsino as being foolishly in love with love has by now been taken much too far, his elaborately beautiful verse in his first scene *is* obviously

meant to contrast with Viola's extremely simple statement of loss and hence of love ('My brother, he is in Elysium') in hers, suggesting a depth of human perception and experience greater than his. This contrast recurs, in a more complex form, with Posthumus and Imogen. Indeed, Posthumus's expansive vow in his first scene,

> I will remain
> The loyal'st husband that did e'er plight troth,
>
> (I, i, 95–6)

has something of Orsino's self-centredness as a lover about it; no one can equal him:

> There is no woman's sides
> Can bide the beating of so strong a passion
> As love doth give my heart.
>
> (*TN*, II, iv, 92–4)

Posthumus's oath –

> You gentle gods, give me but this [wife] I have,
> And cere up my embracements from a next
> With bonds of death –
>
> (I, i, 115–17)

has an extravagant rashness which events soon develop. 'It might', says R. A. Foakes, 'be thought a hollow confidence in Imogen that drives Posthumus to brag so much that she is "more fair, virtuous, wise, chaste, constant, qualified, and less attemptable" than the rarest ladies of France',[2] and his language and attitude certainly contrast with Imogen's, with its echo of the comedies and anticipation of *The Winter's Tale*:

> Would I were
> A neat-herd's daughter, and my Leonatus
> Our neighbour shepherd's son!
>
> (I, i, 148–50)

Professor Foakes is surely right to accuse Posthumus of extravagance when he casts Imogen 'off readily, without even hearing out the evidence'. And G. K. Hunter's phrase

[1] Programme for the RSC *Cymbeline*, 1974.
[2] *Shakespeare: The Dark Comedies to the Last Plays* (1971), pp. 108–9.

'overwrought heroic folly'[1] exactly describes the extravagant venom which replaces Posthumus's former extravagant protestation:

> This yellow Iachimo in an hour – was't not? –
> Or less – at first? Perchance he spoke not, but
> Like a full-acorned boar, a German one,
> Cried 'O!' and mounted.
>
> (II, v, 14–17)

Here, physical loathing at Imogen's imagined easiness and animality is mingled with an indignation, a sense of injured pride. Its overblown tone, which yet contains an undertone of physical violence soon to result in the letter to Pisanio, recalls Orsino's violent and unexpected outburst when he feels himself betrayed and humiliated:

> Him will I tear out of that cruel eye
> Where he sits crownèd in his master's spite.
> Come, boy, with me; my thoughts are ripe in mischief:
> I'll sacrifice the lamb that I do love
> To spite a raven's heart within a dove.
>
> (v, i, 121–5)

The language of both Posthumus and Orsino complicates the image of the romantic hero; and the outbursts of both indicate the potential explosiveness underlying conventional romantic utterance.

When, however, Professor Foakes finds that Imogen too speaks in conventional terms, and that her love is therefore as limited as Posthumus's, I think that he misses the important contrast between their language (and so between their personalities) which I am attempting to describe. For instance, does this speech really suggest that Imogen is merely absorbed in imagining a romantic farewell? Doesn't it rather suggest that she is totally absorbed in Posthumus?

> I would have broke mine eye-strings, cracked them but
> To look upon him, till the diminution
> Of space had pointed him sharp as my needle;
> Nay, followed him till he had melted from

> The smallness of a gnat to air; and then
> Have turned mine eye, and wept.
>
> (I, iii, 17–22)

Certainly there is extremity of style here; but I find it another example of Shakespeare 'straining after the maximum of intensity'. The 'diminution' of the images seem to me to show an Imogen striving to express the extremity of her grief. The eye-balls strain as the image of Posthumus becomes smaller and smaller, first to a needle's point, then to a gnat. When he has vanished, even these extreme comparisons to tiny things give way to an abandonment of language altogether: 'and then Have turned mine eye, and wept.' The resources of speech give out, as they do when Viola, for different but related reasons, is prevented from a full expression of her love:

> I am all the daughters of my father's house,
> And all the brothers too; and yet, I know not...
>
> (II, iv, 119–20)

Imogen's language, which combines extreme, even strained, expression with great simplicity is typical of the play's style and of its attempt to capture the completeness of an emotion or situation. It does so again in the central scene beside Cloten's corpse, and again it re-works the technique of *Twelfth Night*.

When Viola expresses, obliquely, her love for Orsino, she does so by imagining a death situation, and associating it with the decay of the natural world:

> She never told her love,
> But let concealment, like a worm i' the bud,
> Feed on her damask cheek. She pined in thought,
> And with a green and yellow melancholy,
> She sat like Patience on a monument,
> Smiling at grief.
>
> (II, iv, 109–14)

There is a still quality, a depth of sadness in this scene, which recurs, and is greatly

---

[1] *All's Well That Ends Well*, New Arden Shakespeare, revised ed. (1962), p. lvi.

developed, in the mood and technique of the burial scene in *Cymbeline*, where the pain and grief goes beyond the language to the events themselves: it is as if the imagined death, with its associations from the natural world, is taken out of the imagery and enacted on the stage. The technique is similar: after using an imagined death to make us fully aware of the sadness of a situation, the scene then changes direction; in neither case is the emphasis left solely on sadness. True to the image she presents of herself, Viola 'smiles' at grief however much she feels it, and her later 'and yet, I know not' marks a change comparable to Imogen's awakening, and then to her decision to serve Caius Lucius. However much the sheer intensity of their grief and the motives may differ, each abandons lamentation for a practical decision to get on with the business of living; and in so doing each moves from the sadness which is essentially connected with separation from the person she loves to ultimate union with that lover.

II

The big difference between the two plays is that taking the imagined death situation out of the poetic texture and putting it on the stage contributes to the much greater complexity – or at any rate complicatedness – of *Cymbeline*. In attempting to present on the stage everything about an experience, the play constantly fuses poetic complexity with stage action of a particularly startling kind, as it places love, grief, despair, death, before us. And of these death is the most important, since the mock-burial is at once the central, the most complex, and the most contrived scene in the play.

Why does Shakespeare go to such bizarre lengths to present us with an elaborate funeral for someone who isn't dead, and an elaborate recognition of a headless body – except that it's the wrong body? Any interpretation of *Cymbeline* must account for this apparent

dramatic perversity. Those critics who see *Cymbeline* in terms of self-conscious 'coterie dramaturgy' feel that this technique is to keep the characters' emotions distanced and the audience detached. My impression of the burial scene is exactly the reverse – that Shakespeare is lavishing all his resources on the scene in order to create an overwhelming sense of the sadness of death, a genuine sense of loss and deprivation, both on the princes' part and Imogen's, without the loss being in the end a real one. Then, having made the audience *experience* fully the princes' and Imogen's grief and sense of loss, the play can move beyond even that to reunion and a new life. And this seems to me a more complex version of the technique used in *Twelfth Night*, which makes us aware of darkness and disturbance in its implications and undertones, in order to make the final happiness seem all the richer and fuller.

The stylistic connection between *Cymbeline* and *Twelfth Night* also helps to explain why Shakespeare has taken so much trouble to get Cloten into Posthumus's clothes for this situation, and also why Imogen is made so positively to make her erroneous identification. The retching grief of this scene in the theatre convinces me beyond doubt that it is not (as some have suggested) a scene for laughs. We are not, even remotely, supposed to preserve a mockingly distanced detachment from Imogen. 'Why,' asks Frank Kermode, 'give Posthumus the body of a paragon, and then allow Cloten's equal to it?'[1] Because, I think, Shakespeare wants to indicate a similarity in certain respects between them. The physical similarity is insisted upon to suggest another kind of similarity. When Posthumus moves from an extreme protestation of love for Imogen to an equally extreme outburst of violence against her, he matches Cloten in extravagant rashness, even to the details of the language they use:

Cloten. when my lust hath dined – which, as I say, to

[1] *Shakespeare: The Final Plays* (1963), p. 26.

vex her I will execute in the clothes that she so praised
– to the court I'll knock her back, foot her home again.

(III, v, 142–5)

Posthumus.

> O that I had her here to tear her limb-meal!
> I will go there and do't i' th' court, before
> Her father. I'll do something.

(II, iv, 147–9)

The difference is that this mixture of half-incoherent rage and a determination to humiliate Imogen before her father as well as inflicting violent pain on her is the sort of thing which occurs naturally to Cloten, whereas it is only a part of Posthumus, a reaction to Iachimo's goading: the fact remains that similar violence lurks inside both characters, as it lurks inside the Orsino of Act v. All three react from wounded pride; all three are concerned with *themselves* as betrayed or thwarted lovers. The insistence on the similarity of Cloten's body to Posthumus's is not, then, a wanton theatrically self-conscious joke; what they have in common complicates what might have remained fairy-tale figures, romantic hero and boor. For Life is more complex than such superficial views allow.

And so it is with Imogen's apparent death and burial. Here again, Shakespeare uses language which had been one of the chief features of his style in the earlier comedies, defined by J. M. Nosworthy as a 'kind of poetry, frankly lyrical in tone, which... weaves exquisite patterns round birds, beasts and flowers' and which 'represents an extension of that energy which had...gone to the making of *Venus and Adonis*'.[1] It had also gone into the imagery of the comedies, where the beauty and *normality* of the natural world are evoked to convey the beauty and warmth of love, as in Berowne's

> Love's feeling is more soft and sensible
> Than are the tender horns of cockled snails

(*LL Lost*, IV, iii, 333–4)

or the loveliest, most delicate wild flowers, the 'sweet' musk roses, and the 'fair blessed' sunbeams which are the environment of the love-bestowing fairies. This lyrical beauty reappears in *Cymbeline* both to express human emotions and to reflect human characteristics. In the burial scene, the far-reaching, evocative imagery from the natural world not only suggests the sorrow of death, but its peace as well: Imogen is almost absorbed into that world; she is not only *like* primrose or harebell, she *is* the lily or 'the bird...That we have made so much on' (IV, ii, 197–8). The magical poignancy of that moment, as of the burial scene as a whole, stems from this unforced identification of Imogen with the natural world; we are hardly aware of it as a comparison at all, and this is an important example of a scene where the ease and simplicity of the writing offsets the complicated contrivance which has led up to the apparent death. And Arviragus's flower speech is worlds away from superficial compliment: the concrete, specific presentation of the robin bringing, not just 'fairest flowers' but the more down-to-earth 'furred moss' to protect the body gives a sense of security to contrast more sharply with human ingratitude:

>   The ruddock would
> With charitable bill – O bill sore shaming
> Those rich-left heirs that let their fathers lie
> Without a monument! – bring thee all this;
> Yea, and furred moss besides, when flowers are none,
> To winter-ground thy corse.

(IV, ii, 224–9)

The exquisite dirge develops this still quality, sadness mingled with a sense of the body returning to and being protected by the earth, as Belarius emphasises in closing the episode:

> The ground that gave them first has them again.
> Their pleasures here are past, so is their pain.

(IV, ii, 289–90)

[1] *Cymbeline*, New Arden Shakespeare, revised ed. (1960), pp. lxviii–lxix.

So the emotions associated with death and burial are fully evoked; an impression of Death is placed before the audience.

And then the play takes us beyond Death; Imogen revives. Shakespeare communicates her bewildered terror in another vividly expressive image from the natural world; it has that quality peculiar to *Cymbeline* of 'an exquisite distillation of the thought into a precise, if still surprising, image':[1] Shakespeare needs something immediate yet startling to convey Imogen's terror and her attempt to grasp reality, something 'not imagined, felt':

> if there be
> Yet left in heaven as small a drop of pity
> As a wren's eye, feared gods, a part of it!
> (IV, ii, 303–5)

Then the play reworks, in a much more intense fashion, the technique by which Viola moves from expressing her love in terms of an imagined death situation to an acceptance that life has to continue.

Viola's simple statement of heartbreak, 'A blank, my lord. She never told her love' (II, iv, 109) is matched by the utterly simple, broken expression of Imogen's misery:

> I am nothing; or if not,
> Nothing to be were better.
> (IV, ii, 367–8)

Neither Imogen nor Viola feel themselves to be anything without the love of Posthumus or Orsino; and Imogen, like Viola, uses the master/page relationship to express her sadness at her apparent loss, and so the power of her love:

> I may wander
> From east to occident; cry out for service;
> Try many, all good; serve truly; never
> Find such another master.
> (IV, ii, 371–4)

But the really crucial comparison is that, after promising, again in sweet-sad verse of great expressiveness, to cover the body with wood-leaves and weeds, echoing the language and implications of the earlier burial speeches, she realises like Viola – 'Sir, shall I to this lady?' – that life must go on: 'And leaving so his service, follow you.' Both scenes express human love in images of death, and the language realises that experience as fully as possible; then, having allowed both the sadness and the peace of death their full impact, both Viola and Imogen – characteristically of Shakespeare's comic technique – move beyond even this. This attempt at inclusiveness helps to explain why the language in *Cymbeline* should range so greatly, from the hauntingly evocative to the extremely tortuous: it seems to me the expression of a man trying to pack in a great deal, to communicate this or that emotion in all its complexity, even at the sacrifice of immediate clarity. Such clarity is never sacrificed in *Twelfth Night*; Shakespeare takes the emotion as far as it will go in that brilliantly organised play; but here, he wants something more, more than could be attained even by Viola – and there is a price to be paid for that more; the greater intensity can only be attained by greater dramatic complexity and the danger there is that the complexity of device may defeat the intensity of emotion. This danger is particularly acute in the Jupiter scene.

III

It looks as if the Jupiter scene was intended to parallel the burial scene, showing the low point of Posthumus's fortunes as well, in his plea to the Gods for death, and then taking Posthumus, like Imogen, beyond the shadow of death. But whereas Shakespeare makes Imogen's scene work superbly because he endows it with such powerful writing, and so maintains the crucial balance between stage virtuosity and poetic impact, Posthumus's scene *depends* upon theatrical machinery of a startling kind. To put it simply, however successful Jupiter's apparatus,

[1] Sutherland, *op. cit.*, p. 150.

46

the language of the apparitions cannot hope to compare with the emotional and atmospheric charge of 'Fear no more the heat o' th' sun'. Setting aside all questions of authenticity, the scene is unbalanced as it stands: unlike the burial scene, virtuoso staging and evocative language are not held in balance. Since Jupiter's

> Whom best I love I cross; to make my gift,
> The more delayed, delighted
>
> (v, iv, 101–2)

lacks poetic distinction, it is not powerful enough to command attention and so communicate significance when delivered from an eagle's back in mid-air. I think that the descent of Jupiter was meant to be a sensational 'call to attention', to place Posthumus in an *extreme* situation, as the burial scene placed Imogen, so as to focus on his reactions as that scene does on hers. Usually, though, that eagle *competes* with, rather than emphasising, Posthumus's experiences. But there is surely no doubt about the poetic quality of Posthumus's speeches.

Shakespeare does all he can to give those speeches suggestiveness and emotional power, and in a very specific way. Consciously or not, he uses phrasing from his own love poetry to express the depth of Posthumus's repentance *before* he knows that Imogen was true to him. When Posthumus begs the gods to take

> No stricter render of me than my all . . .
> For Imogen's dear life take mine; and though
> 'Tis not so dear, yet 'tis a life,
>
> (v, iv, 17–23)

he is, as J. B. Leishman comments, 'speaking metaphorically, as a bankrupt, and means "Don't trouble to work out what proportion you ought to take of what I possess – take all"',[1] and is using the legal metaphors and colouring of Sonnet 125. The earlier Posthumus, in his excessive adoration and protestation, and in judging by appearances, had resembled those from whom Shakespeare dissociates himself in the sonnet:

> Have I not seen dwellers on form and favour
> Lose all, and more, by paying too much rent.

In the sonnet, Shakespeare celebrates a mutual love which is 'not mix'd with seconds' (flour of an inferior quality); rather, it

> knows no art
> But mutual render, only me for thee.

But Posthumus is unhappily aware that the 'render' he can make cannot be 'mutual' because he is worth less than Imogen; his love is 'mix'd with seconds'. So he desperately offers a one-sided 'proportion', his life, in an attempt to pay the account ('audit') he owes Imogen:

> If you will take this audit, take this life,
> And cancel these cold bonds.
>
> (v, iv, 27–8)

Here again, a mixture of complexity and simplicity expresses Posthumus's intensity: the bankruptcy metaphor is combined with the tender simplicity of 'dear life' (v, iv, 22) and at the end he turns from prayer to direct communication with her:

> O Imogen,
> I'll speak to thee in silence.
>
> (v, iv, 28–9)

'Silence' is the only way he can communicate his grief after what he has done to her, as it was ultimately her only way at I, iii, 21–2. And this admission of his own folly helps to bring him closer to Imogen, so that when they meet he may seem worthier of her. They are brought together in other ways too. As there is an upward change of direction at the end of the burial scene, so his tone changes after the vision:

> 'Tis still a dream; or else such stuff as madmen
> Tongue, and brain not; either both, or nothing,
> Or senseless speaking, or a speaking such
> As sense cannot untie
>
> (v, iv, 145–8)

[1] *Themes and Variations in Shakespeare's Sonnets*, 2nd ed. (1963), p. 113, n. 3.

recalls Imogen's

> 'Twas but a bolt of nothing, shot at nothing,
> Which the brain makes of fumes,
>
> (IV, ii, 300–1)

thus underlining the similarity of their situations. His bewildered comment that he has

> this golden chance, and know not why.
> What fairies haunt this ground?
>
> (V, iv, 132–3)

recalls not only the magical atmosphere of *A Midsummer Night's Dream*, but also Orsino's 'when...golden time convents': both Orsino and Posthumus enjoy, without perhaps contributing substantially to it themselves, a new 'golden' time.

Just as the style of the play complicates the impression of 'simplicity' given by the characters in the burial and Jupiter scenes, so it does in the trunk and final scenes. As Posthumus is more complicated than a straightforward romantic hero, Iachimo is less than a fiend. It is not Iago-like malignity which spurs Iachimo to the wager, but irritation at Posthumus's protestations: 'I make my wager rather against your confidence than her reputation' (I, iv, 109–10). As Granville-Barker says, 'No tragically-potent scoundrel, we should be sure, will ever come out of a trunk.'[1] But on the other hand, that scene is not simply a matter of 'theatrical' ostentation; Iachimo emerges from that trunk to arouse expectations which are not fulfilled: a rape scene which is not a rape, like the death scene where Imogen is not dead. Shakespeare captures our attention with the visual surprise in order to isolate and throw all attention upon Iachimo's reaction to Imogen herself. The gorgeous language gives us the impression of desire, but it has a delicacy too, which indicates sensitivity as well, a response to Imogen herself, a valuing of her for her own sake, in a way that Posthumus never does until Act v. And as in Imogen's

needle, gnat and wren images, another vivid image from the natural world is used to present Iachimo's response as vividly as possible:

> On her left breast
> A mole cinque-spotted, like the crimson drops
> I' th' bottom of a cowslip.
>
> (II, ii, 37–9)

This technique recurs when, amid all the ingenious contrivance of the final scene, moments of emotional intensity suddenly emerge, expressed by similar images:

Imogen.
> Why did you throw your wedded lady from you?
> Think that you are upon a lock, and now
> Throw me again.

Posthumus.
> Hang there like fruit, my soul,
> Till the tree die.
>
> (V, v, 261–4)

Cymbeline is not a lucid play, as the comedies are, but I think it is the very *combination* of the 'virtuoso' elements with a reworking of techniques from the comedies which gives it its particular power, enabling Shakespeare to emphasise, isolate, highlight such powerful emotions as Imogen's grief or joy, Posthumus's extravagance and jealous rashness, Iachimo's response to Imogen. Gareth Lloyd Evans found it a matter for adverse criticism at Stratford in 1962 that, though Imogen, Iachimo, and Posthumus were 'superb in speech and in timing', the neutral, empty stage and the extreme sophistication of the production meant that 'their gaiety, gravity, pride and panache is cocooned in artificiality, and that the realities of grief, joy and venom are intermittent'.[2] But so they are in a sense in the play, and the outstanding achievement of the 1962 production was to use its off-white surround, together

---

[1] *Prefaces to Shakespeare*, II, paperback ed. (1963), p. 146.
[2] *The Guardian*, 18 July 1962.

with the necessary props and lighting, to *pinpoint* those individual 'realities of grief, joy and venom'. In doing so, it underlined Shakespeare's technique of isolating individual moments and situations and so highlighting a series of human emotions as fully as possible by examining contrasts and complexities, however tortuous:

> These flowers are like the pleasures of the world;
> This bloody man, the care on't.

© ROGER WARREN 1976

NOBLE VIRTUE IN 'CYMBELINE'

JAMES EDWARD SIEMON

Cymbeline has had small notice and less praise. It was reported 'Well likte by the kinge' when played at Court in 1633, and the Folger Library holds a copy of the Second Folio in which late in the seventeenth century someone inscribed the single word 'good' on the first pages of *The Comedy of Errors*, *The Merry Wives of Windsor*, *The Merchant of Venice*, and *Much Ado About Nothing*, and on the first page of *Cymbeline*, the word 'rare'.[1] Dr Johnson, on the other hand, thought the play characterized by 'unresisting imbecility', and his view is the more prevalent today.

The play undoubtedly poses difficulties, but it has also had needless difficulties foisted upon it. Its opening scene, for example, is usually understood as clarifying stable values:

> He that has miss'd the princess is a thing
> Too bad for bad report: and he that hath her
> (I mean, that married her, alack good man,
> And therefore banish'd) is a creature such
> As, to seek through the regions of the earth
> For one his like; there would be something failing
> In him that should compare. I do not think
> So fair an outward, and such stuff within
> Endows a man, but he.
>
> (I, i, 16–24)[2]

Thus the well-informed First Gentleman. There is, of course, growing recognition that the views advanced by expository characters may be highly colored and that in his exposition Shakespeare sometimes emphasizes not the complete view of the play's world that we should hold but rather a prejudicial view of it

held by its inhabitants.[3] The critical tradition, however, has been to take the First Gentleman in *Cymbeline* as Shakespeare's spokesman. W. W. Lawrence long ago remarked, 'Every audience knows that such a faithful expositor is not misleading them, but giving such information that they may understand the rest of the play intelligently'.[4] This is the standard view and remains to this day a working premise in criticism of the play. The assumptions of the current Arden editor are representative: 'Wilson Knight (*The Crown of Life*) remarks that Posthumus's merit is a major theme of the play. Shakespeare intends us to accept the First

[1] The King's reaction is reported by Sir Henry Herbert. The annotated folio (STC 22274e; Folger Library Fol. 2, No. 7), known as the Valladolid Folio, was censored for the English school at Valladolid sometime in the mid-seventeenth century, but the hand of the annotator is thought to be slightly later than that of the censor. See Roland M. Frye, *Shakespeare and Christian Doctrine* (Princeton, 1965), pp. 275–93.

[2] Quotations are from the New Arden Shakespeare; exceptions, and the source of the reading, are noted parenthetically.

[3] See, for example, John Danby's commentary on Philo as an unreliable expositor in *Antony and Cleopatra*, *Elizabethan and Jacobean Poets* (1972), pp. 132–6; for the more conventional view of Philo, see Virgil K. Whitaker, *Shakespeare's Use of Learning* (San Marino, 1952), p. 315. *The Winter's Tale* I, i is another such scene: it does not describe the world of the play at all accurately; it states instead a criterion of value whose meaning will be explored through the play's action.

[4] *Shakespeare's Problem Comedies* (1931; rpt. New York, 1969), p. 203.

Gentleman's estimate of his virtue'.[1] Hence, when in I, v Iachimo dismisses Posthumus's reputation as unimpressive, Nosworthy sweeps aside any possibility of reserving judgment: 'Iachimo...thinks all men as mean and cynical as himself. The First Gentleman has already in I, i presented the picture of Posthumus which Shakespeare intends us to accept, and Iachimo's disparagement in the present scene damages only himself'.[2] That is, we know that Iachimo is wrong because we know that the First Gentleman is right.

Such conceptions of dramaturgy lead inevitably to severe strictures on the play's workmanship. What, after all, do you say about a play in which an undoubted paragon of masculine virtue dispatches a lecherous and cynical Italian in an attempt to seduce his wife, giving him a letter of introduction to help him on his way? The older critics knew well enough what to say: a tentative and uncertain experiment in a new form; boredom; the sad result of hands other than Shakespeare's; unresisting imbecility. Their accounts of the play's failure are not, however, satisfactory. The disintegrators are in a well-deserved eclipse, even if the reaction against them has led to a too bland disregard for the implications of textual anomalies, and there is little to be gained from worrying the assertion that Shakespeare was uninterested in what he was doing. That the author of *Much Ado About Nothing*, *The Merchant of Venice*, or *Measure for Measure*, let alone *Romeo and Juliet* or *Othello*, was unschooled in writing plays which balanced comic and tragic potential is an odd notion,[3] and the still fashionable argument that *Cymbeline* is an experimental play is repeated in isolation from any serious examination of the degree to which Shakespeare is consistently an experimental playwright. The traditional strictures must be faced, but a central question, never plainly asked, is whether they are based on sound premises. For neither Cloten nor

Posthumus Leonatus behaves in a manner entirely in accord with the First Gentleman's appraisal; nor does the play either in its spectacle or in its action sustain the absolute distinction he so emphatically draws between them.

I

Posthumus Leonatus makes his second appearance in I, v, a scene of major expository importance whose implications seriously undercut the initial assertion of his virtue. This, the wager scene, opens with a short prelude: Philario, Iachimo, and an unnamed Frenchman discuss Posthumus's career and recent history.[4] Although Iachimo's doubts about Posthumus's reputation appear to be cynically motivated, the reservations themselves are not unreasonable; his manner is offensive, but his meaning goes little beyond the observation that seeing is believing. The Frenchman expresses like doubts, and Philario's response is pointed:

How worthy he is I will leave to appear hereafter, rather than story him in his own hearing.

(I, v, 33–5)

Posthumus is here not a cynosure; he is a man whose worth will emerge in time, whose worth lies in that to come hereafter rather than in story. Whereas the First Gentleman directs our

[1] Gloss to I, i, 17–54 (p. 4). Joan Hartwig is exceptional in dissenting from this point of view. See *Shakespeare's Tragicomic Vision* (Baton Rouge, 1972), pp. 64–5.

[2] Gloss to I, v, 4–7 (p. 19).

[3] Rosalie Colie discusses such a balance or mixture in her chapter on *Romeo and Juliet* and *Othello*, 'Othello and the Problematics of Love', *Shakespeare's Living Art* (Princeton, 1974), pp. 135–67.

[4] The direction which heads the scene mentions a Dutchman and a Spaniard. Whether they are mutes or were omitted in production is unknown. Nosworthy discusses the problem in his gloss, p. 19, remarking, 'That they were depicted as drunk past the power of speech is not beyond Jacobean possibility.' Were such the case, the ironic undercutting of chivalric pretensions in the scene would be considerably greater than I take it to be.

attention backwards and to story, Philario directs it forward and to action, inviting us to judge the past by the future rather than the reverse, to test Posthumus's reputation against his behavior, and to believe because we have seen. No one supposes that Posthumus stands the test well, but it is significant that in a play which begins with such high praise for Posthumus we are soon asked to watch Posthumus to see whether the praise be just or no.

The putative source for I, v does not represent the decision to test the virtuous wife as in any way out of the ordinary.[1] If Shakespeare intended us to take Posthumus's behavior as similarly a matter of course, we could reasonably expect a scene in which it were made to seem so – a scene which either directed our attention to the propriety of Posthumus's actions or deflected our attention from anything that might trouble us. In fact, Shakespeare does the reverse; he introduces a major and troubling departure from his source tale, inventing an earlier occasion in which Posthumus caused a fracas by making the question of Imogen's superiority to all other women a fighting matter.[2] The Frenchman thinks he behaved badly:

...it had been pity you should have been put together, with so mortal a purpose as then each bore, upon importance of so slight and trivial a nature.

(I, v, 40–3)

In calling the cause slight and trivial the Frenchman may be espousing Iachimo's cynical view of women; even so, as with Philario's invitation to watch Posthumus before judging him, this observation raises the issue of rational as opposed to conventional behavior. Iachimo picks up the question, and an increasingly heated disagreement ensues. As its outcome begins to take shape, Philario (for whose cynicism there is no evidence) tries to stop it, making unmistakably clear that he thinks both Iachimo and Posthumus mad:

Let us leave here, gentlemen...Gentlemen, enough of this, it came in too suddenly, let it die as it was born, and I pray you be better acquainted.

(I, v, 103, 124–6)

When Posthumus proposes the wager, Philario protests, 'I will have it no lay' (152). The scene ends with the Frenchman's disbelieving question, 'Will this hold, think you?' and Philario's unhappy reply, 'Signior Iachimo will not from it. Pray let us follow 'em'. Thus, although none of the minor characters in this scene condemns Posthumus's code of honor as such, neither do they treat it as fine and proper; they tell us that Posthumus was a hot head when he was younger and observe with alarm that he is so still.[3] Lawrence is right in pointing to a conventional code of honor underlying Posthumus's behavior, but the shape of the scene implies reservations about that code.[4] Shakespeare reworks his source material, and what had there been morally clear cut is here morally ambivalent.

When they part, Imogen gives Posthumus a ring, begging him to 'keep it till you woo another wife, / When Imogen is dead' (I, ii, 44–5). Posthumus replies that he will never part with it:

How, how? Another?
You gentle gods, give me but this I have,
And sear up my embracements from a next
With bonds of death! Remain, remain thou here,
While sense can keep it on...

(45–9)

[1] There seems little doubt that the immediate source is *Frederyke of Jennen*. Nosworthy discusses the evidence, pp. xxi–xxv, and reprints *Frederyke of Jennen*, pp. 198–211.

[2] Homer D. Swander, '*Cymbeline* and the "Blameless Hero"', *ELH* (1964), pp. 259–70, presents an important and detailed comparison of Shakespeare's scene with its sources and analogues.

[3] Douglas Peterson discusses this scene as evidence that Posthumus suffers from Cymbeline's 'crippling inability to discern between truth and seeming', *Time, Tide, and Tempest* (San Marino, 1973), pp. 117–19; but, as I shall argue, there is an even closer analogue with Cloten's bad temper.

[4] *Shakespeare's Problem Comedies*, pp. 174–205.

It is enlightening to compare Posthumus's subsequent behavior with that of another romance hero who, like Posthumus, takes a ring saying,

> when this ring
> Parts from this finger, then parts life from hence, –
> O then be bold to say Bassanio's dead!
> (*Mer. Ven.* III, ii, 183–5)

In each play a worthy but impoverished suitor wins an heiress sought by other, objectionable suitors; the lovers exchange love tokens; and the exchange is punctuated by extensive verbal play upon buying and selling. The usury of love is, of course, a motif widespread throughout the plays and sonnets, but the similarity here of reiterated details suggests that Shakespeare is consciously modifying a stock romance pattern. Portia, to choose but a single example, would be multiplied many times herself to be worthy of Bassanio, but concludes that she is in the bargain a 'Sum of nothing' (III, ii, 158, F reading); Imogen protests that Posthumous 'overbuys me / Almost the sum he pays' (I, ii, 77–8).

Each of the lovers subsequently gives up his ring. Posthumus is at first unwilling:

> I will wage against your gold, gold to it: my ring I hold dear as my finger, 'tis part of it.
> (I, v, 137–8)

Within nine lines, however, he is prepared to strip it off:

> I shall but lend my diamond till your return...I dare you to this match: here's my ring.
> (I, v, 147–51)

It requires, by contrast, twenty-three lines, the effective pleading of Portia in disguise, and a good cause to boot before Bassanio reluctantly gives up his. Posthumus, it is true, believes he will soon have his ring back; he shows, nonetheless, none of Bassanio's scruples about keeping to his vow. As with Posthumus's initial boast, Shakespeare here too seems to have altered conventional romance details in such a way as to make us feel uneasy about his hero's behavior.

The effect is neither to point up Posthumus's commitment to a noble code, nor, as is sometimes argued, to one that is corrupt, but rather to emphasize that he is rash and short tempered. He is rash throughout the play, still losing his temper in Act v (as his reaction to the British Lord in v, iii or his striking out at the still-disguised Imogen at v, v, 228–9 makes clear), and it seems to be this aspect of Posthumus's character rather than his sublime nobility (or corrupted vanity) that Shakespeare wishes to emphasize in the wager scene.

That only Iachimo takes Posthumus's behavior as a matter of course suggests less than unqualified support for the conventions which lie behind it. On the other hand, there is no doubt that the sympathetic characters of *Cymbeline* admire him and that his nobility is directly called into question only by those whose right to make moral judgments is compromised by their own morally debased attitudes. In judging Posthumus, we must give due weight both to what we are shown of him and to what is said about him in his own world, and by whom. Meanwhile we must guard against confusing the simplistic conventions of romance with the sophisticated craft of a veteran playwright. If Iachimo is cynical, the First Gentleman is naive. His portrait of Posthumus is clearly labelled cardboard, and the opening scenes of the play invite us to compare the portrait with the man. What we first learn of Posthumus's worth lies only in his reputation:

> To his mistress,
> (For whom he now is banish'd) her own price
> Proclaims how she esteem'd him; and his virtue
> By her election may be truly read
> What kind of man he is.
> (I, i, 50–4)

The reliability of such a conception is made clear enough when Iachimo uses not only the

First Gentleman's point of view but his very language to play successfully and disastrously upon Imogen's vanity:

> He hath a kind of honour sets him off,
> More than a mortal seeming. Be not angry,
> Most mighty princess, that I have adventur'd
> To try your taking of a false report, which hath
> Honour'd with confirmation your great judgement
> In the election of a sir so rare,
> Which you know cannot err.
>
> (I, vii, 170–6)

II

The First Gentleman's account of Cloten appears to be more reliable. The Second Lord, Imogen, and Guiderius agree that he is a fool, and even the Queen seems occasionally to find him exasperating. But if we simply take their word and look no more closely at the play, we shall overlook the complexity of Cloten's role. He is more than just a fool. He makes sense in the council scene (III, i) even if, as is possible, he represents there a deeply corrupted understanding of Britain's proper relation to Rome; he has the brains to see that he needs help in wooing Imogen, 'for / I yet not understand the case myself' (II, iii, 75–6); and although he is sometimes chided for valuing Imogen only for her dowry ('If I could get this foolish Imogen, I should have gold enough' – II, iii, 7–9), in fact he knows better:

> she's fair and royal,
> And...she hath all courtly parts more exquisite
> Than lady, ladies, woman, from every one
> The best she hath, and she of all compounded
> Outsells them all.
>
> (III, v, 71–5)

As Granville-Barker perceptively remarks, 'Cloten is by no means pure ass; a diseased vanity is his trouble...'[1]

Since we are repeatedly told that Cloten is a poor thing, it is tempting to take his vain comparison of himself to Posthumus as the broadest comedy:

I dare speak it to myself, for it is not vain-glory for a man and his glass to confer in his own chamber; I mean, the lines of my body are as well drawn as his; no less young, more strong, not beneath him in fortunes, beyond him in the advantage of the time, above him in birth, alike conversant in general services, and more remarkable in single oppositions; yet this imperseverant thing loves him in my despite. What mortality is!

> (IV, i, 7–16)

Indeed, Cloten before his mirror complacently cataloguing his good points while exclaiming at the vanity of men is a comic figure. If we take the comedy too broadly, however, we can only be bewildered when Imogen wakes beside the headless Cloten and mistakes him for Posthumus:

> I know the shape of's leg: this is his hand:
> His foot Mercurial: his Martial thigh:
> The brawns of Hercules...
> ...O, my Lord! my lord!
>
> (IV, ii, 309–32)

If Imogen cannot tell the difference between them headless, why shouldn't Cloten protest that the lines of his body are as well drawn as those of Posthumus's? More to the point, Imogen's mistake would be incomprehensible had not grounds for it been fully established. Of course, Cloten's headless body in Posthumus's clothes is in a disguise, and disguises have Protean vitality on the Renaissance stage. Nonetheless, there is warrant both from the text and from the great thematic importance in the play of the deceptive nature of appearance to conclude that Cloten and Posthumus must look much alike. They cannot be identical, lest the audience anticipate Imogen in her confusion, and the interesting suggestion that a single actor play both parts oversimplifies the play's treatment of deceptive appearances.[2] To make

[1] *Prefaces to Shakespeare* (Princeton, 1946), I, 499, n. 3.

[2] Homer D. Swander, '*Cymbeline*: Religious Idea and Dramatic Design', *Pacific Coast Studies in Shakespeare*, edd. Waldo F. McNeir and Thelma N.

the two mirror images of one another is simply to invert the literalist view that they are as obviously different as any two men could be. The distinction between them turns upon Cloten's moral and psychological grotesquerie; but his person is part of the deceptive appearance of the world. The Queen has evidently passed her beauty on to her son, if not her brains, and Cymbeline's inability to grasp Imogen's preference for Posthumus living is the counterpart of her inability to recognize Cloten dead. Each is in its own way a grotesque mistake; but each is plausible.

We must, in fact, take Cloten and his behavior into account in our understanding of Posthumus Leonatus, for a parallel between them is woven carefully into the fabric of the play. Almost its first words present them as inversions of one another, Posthumus more worthy than words can easily say, Cloten bad beyond words, 'a thing / Too bad for bad report'. At a crucial point the plot turns upon their physical resemblance. They are paired in their relation to Cymbeline (the one his ward, the other his step-son); as rivals who seek first Imogen's hand and later vengeance upon her; as gamblers whom Iachimo easily outwits.[1]

Moreover, the varied ways in which they are obviously paired either for comparison or contrast are underpinned by one less immediately obvious: they have remarkably like responses to a wide range of situations and events. It is, for example, often considered a difficulty of the play that the fool absolute can speak so eloquently in rejecting the Roman demand for tribute:

Come, there's no more tribute to be paid: our kingdom is stronger than it was at that time: and (as I said) there is no moe such Caesars, other of them may have crook'd noses, but to owe such straight arms, none... Why tribute? Why should we pay tribute? If Caesar can hide the sun from us with a blanket, or put the moon in his pocket, we will pay him tribute for light: else, sir, no more tribute, pray you now.

(III, i, 35–47)

This sounds pretty good, and critics have been hard pressed to explain such words from Cloten's mouth. Most of the difficulty evaporates if we recognize Cloten as a fool relative rather than a fool absolute. He clearly can, whatever the Second Lord thinks, take two from twenty and come up with eighteen, and it doesn't require hard thought to mouth commonplaces.

More interesting than the problem of how Cloten figured out that a stronger army can defeat a weaker is the degree to which his attitude is Posthumus's:

you shall hear
The legion now in Gallia sooner landed
In our not-fearing Britain than have tidings
Of any penny tribute paid. Our countrymen
Are men more order'd than when Julius Caesar
Smil'd at their lack of skill, but found their courage
Worthy his frowning at. Their discipline,
(Now wing-led with their courages) will make known
To their approvers they are people such
That mend upon the world.

(II, iv, 17–26)

So Posthumus to Philario. Cloten is more pungent, but they do not differ greatly.

Nor do they differ greatly in other regards. Posthumus's behavior in II, iv, the scene in which his trust in Imogen is destroyed, is central to an understanding of his character and of the meaning of worth in *Cymbeline*. In its over-all shape it presents a dialectical encounter between a man who means well but does not think clearly and a skilled rhetorician.[2] Posthumus is outmatched so far that he has no sense that his self-confidence is frivolous:

Greenfield (Eugene, Oregon, 1966), p. 251. Swander's suggestion that one actor play both parts is intriguing even though it oversimplifies; but in any case it ignores such difficulties as the openings of II, iv or III, i where the entrance of one of the two follows immediately upon the exit of the other.

[1] Swander remarks some of the details contributing to this parallel in '*Cymbeline*: Religious Idea and Dramatic Design,' pp. 251–3.

[2] Granville-Barker's account of Iachimo's skill in manipulating Posthumus is classic. *Prefaces to Shakespeare*, 1. 520–3.

Sparkles this stone as it was wont, or is't not
Too dull for your good wearing?...Make not, sir,
Your loss your sport...

(II, iv, 40-8)

It is difficult not to agree that so complacent a man deserves to trip. The scene is well handled, Posthumus's complacency giving gradual way first to nervous uncertainty, and then, as Iachimo's evidence mounts, to an increasingly wide oscillation between fear that Imogen has betrayed him and relief at each piece of evidence that can be discounted:

This is her honour!
Let it be granted you have seen all this (and praise
Be given to your remembrance) the description
Of what is in her chamber nothing saves
The wager you have laid.

(91-5)

Posthumus's arrogance in praising Iachimo's memory is worthy of Iachimo himself; it reflects the early stages of his gradual assumption of Iachimo's view of things. Meanwhile, the evidence becomes increasingly difficult to discount:

Iachimo.   Then, if you can
Be pale, I beg but leave to air this jewel: see!
. . . .
Posthumus.   May be she pluck'd it off
To send it me.
Iachimo.   She writes so to you? Doth she?
Posthumus.   O, no, no, no, 'tis true.

(95-106)

As Posthumus's fear grows, so does his anger, directed first toward Iachimo:

There, take thy hire, and all the fiends of hell
Divide themselves between you!

(129-30)

. . . .
If you will swear you have not done't you lie,
And I will kill thee if thou dost deny
Thou'st made me cuckold.

(144-6)

By now all attempt at manners is lost, as the shift in pronouns makes clear in both of these

speeches. But then his anger turns against Imogen:

O, that I had her here, to tear her limb-meal!
I will go there and do't, i' th' court, before
Her father. I'll do something –

(147-9)

Again, as in the wager scene, Philario's interjections point up the rash nature of Posthumus's behavior:

Have patience, sir.
           Sir, be patient: (113)
This is not strong enough to be believed
Of one persuaded well of.

(130-2)

           Quite besides
The government of patience! You have won:
Let's follow him, and pervert the present wrath
He hath against himself.

(149-52)

Moving from complacency through fear to wrath, the scene exposes more and more fully the portrait begun earlier of a man of uneven temper, unschooled in emotional restraint. But many of the details of the scene have been anticipated, and while it develops more fully a psychological process briefly sketched in Posthumus's first encounter with Iachimo, it recapitulates one fully stated in the immediately preceding scene, II, iii.

The laying of the wager between Posthumus and Iachimo is separated from Iachimo's claim to success by five scenes. Two of these, II, i in its entirety and II, iii in its opening dialogue, are devoted to Cloten as a gambler who consistently loses and whose losses make him foul tempered and violent – a dramaturgical detail of some significance in a play where so much turns upon the winning and losing of wagers. Moreover, lest we miss the point, Shakespeare brings it home by having Cloten, like Posthumus, gamble with Iachimo:

Come, I'll go see this Italian: what I have lost to-day at bowls I'll win to-night of him.

(II, i, 50-1)

and lose:

Your lordship is the most patient man in loss, the most
coldest that ever turn'd up ace.   (II, iii, 1–2)

If one inquires too closely into what characters
are doing when they are offstage – an inquiry
that fortuitously cannot be made in the theater
– it will emerge that Iachimo is simultaneously
gambling with Cloten and secreted in a trunk
in Imogen's bedroom. Clearly Shakespeare
considered logical consistency of less importance than dramatic emphasis upon the parallel
between Posthumus and Cloten.

The parallel is carried further in the encounter between Imogen and Cloten which
follows almost immediately. Cloten begins his
address to her with considerable assurance. He is
soon discomfited by her unmistakable suggestion that he is a fool, and within twenty lines of
asserting that he loves Imogen he hears her
reply that she hates him. Piqued, he retaliates
with a diatribe against Posthumus, which
brings down upon his head the full force of
Imogen's contempt:

> His mean'st garment,
> That ever hath but clipp'd his body, is dearer
> In my respect, than all the hairs above thee,
> Were they all made such men...
>
>   (II, iii, 134–7)

Now nearly speechless with rage, Cloten does
little more than punctuate Imogen's exchange
with Pisanio – significantly an inquiry into the
whereabouts of the fatal bracelet which will
soon send Posthumus into a rage comparable
to Cloten's – with the repeated exclamation,
'His garment!...His garment!...His meanest
garment!' And like Posthumus in the scene
which follows, Cloten has here the last word.
It is Posthumus's word, revenge:

> I'll be reveng'd:
> 'His mean'st garment!' Well.
>
>   (II, iii, 156–7)

The two sequences are drawn together by
many details, some small, some large. An

allusion to the tribute demanded by Rome falls
early in each; as each reaches its climax there
occurs what in a musical analysis might be
called a counterpoint between the bracelet
motif and the offended-male-vanity motif.
Each begins with an assertion of love for
Imogen and ends with a vow of vengeance
upon her. In putting two such scenes back to
back, Shakespeare invites comparison between
the two men; in putting Cloten's scene first,
he invites us to watch Posthumus's behavior
with Cloten's freshly in mind. What we see is
that as Posthumus yields gradually to fear and
anger, his behavior becomes increasingly like
Cloten's.

It is useful, too, to consider the ways in
which the construction of the play draws our
attention to the workings of Posthumus's
imagination. *Cymbeline* is widely recognized as
a recapitulatory play – recalling in particular
Much Ado About Nothing and *Othello*. The
process by which Iachimo convinces Posthumus that Imogen is a whore involves the
corruption of Posthumus's imagination, the
substitution in his mind of Iachimo's way of
seeing women, and the analogy with *Othello*,
often cited, is apt.

Within the world of romance, where chaste
marriage represents so high a value, it is not
surprising that the corrupt are often sexually
corrupt. Iachimo, with his cynical attitude
toward chastity, fits neatly into the pattern,
but the more obviously obscene imagination is
Cloten's. We are treated to a particularly
nice example of his lubricious imagination
when he addresses the musicians preparing for
the aubade to Imogen:

Come on, tune: if you can penetrate her with your
fingering, so: we'll try with tongue too...

                    (II, iii, 14–15)

Hence, too, the details of his revenge:

She said upon a time (the bitterness of it I now belch
from my heart) that she held the very garment of
Posthumus in more respect than my noble and natural

person... With that suit upon my back, will I ravish her: first kill him, and in her eyes; there shall she see my valour, which will then be a torment to her contempt. He on the ground, my speech of insultment ended on his dead body, and when my lust hath dined (which, as I say, to vex her I will execute in the clothes that she so prais'd) to the court I'll knock her back, foot her home again. She hath despis'd me rejoicingly, and I'll be merry in my revenge.   (III, v, 136–50)

Sex and violence have already appeared together in Posthumus's imagination:

> Perchance he spoke not, but
> Like a full-acorn'd boar, a German one,
> Cried 'O!' and mounted...   (II, iv, 167–9)

He has not yet come to the point of taking sexual pleasure in violence, however, and if one agrees with Derek Traversi that Iachimo's imagination is marked by disgust for the body, then it would appear that Posthumus is here entirely of Iachimo's mind.[1] The revenge he envisions at the end of II, iv is to be literary – he is going to write anti-feminist tracts – and is akin in all but intensity to Iachimo's pleasure in making cynical remarks.

As we learn in III, ii, Posthumus subsequently devises a revenge that satisfies him better. But the full details of his plan are withheld until III, iv, the scene immediately preceding the revelation of Cloten's plan:

> Thy mistress, Pisanio, hath played the strumpet in my bed: the testimonies whereof lie bleeding in me... let thine own hands take away her life: I shall give thee opportunity at Milford-Haven: she hath my letter for the purpose: where, if thou fear to strike, and to make me certain it is done, thou art the pandar to her dishonour, and equally to me disloyal.
>
>   (III, iv, 21–31)

There is much of Iachimo still in this – plausible lies and secret scheming – but something of Cloten too. In its particular details Posthumus's plan differs from Cloten's, although the degree of distinction one allows depends upon one's readiness to take as a phallic symbol

the sword which is to be the instrument of Posthumus's revenge. At the least, both respond with violence to sexual humiliation, and just as Shakespeare places the scenes of humiliation back to back, so he puts together the scenes in which the plans for violent revenge are most fully stated. The invitation to compare is patent, and the comparison shows the disintegration of Posthumus's character as a process by which he adopts Cloten's manners and some, at least, of his morals.

Through his factor Pisanio, Posthumus leads Imogen to Milford Haven in order to murder her; Cloten follows her there to rape her. That he goes dressed as Posthumus is his own depraved whim, but his whim has a propriety about which he cannot know. Cloten adopts Posthumus's dress at more or less that point in the play when Posthumus has come to adopt Cloten's manners – manners arising from 'a diseased vanity'. That Imogen awakes to mistake the headless body of Cloten for Posthumus makes good thematic sense: it is not easy to choose between them when they are so much alike.[2] A long developing series of analogies drawn explicitly and implicitly, stated usually as contrasts by characters within the play but often set forth as likenesses by the structure of the play itself, reaches its climax here as Posthumus and Cloten unwittingly exchange fair outwards and the stuff within.

But as so often in *Cymbeline* things are not that simple. In the earlier scenes in which Posthumus and Cloten behave alike, II, iii and iv for example, we actually see them. At the moment when they are most demonstrably alike, however, we are shown one but only told about the other. Posthumus is absent from the stage from II, iv until V, i, so the parallel in

[1] *An Approach to Shakespeare*, 3rd ed. (1969), II, 267.

[2] Robert Grams Hunter makes a comparable point: *Shakespeare and the Comedy of Forgiveness* (New York, 1965), p. 158.

Acts III and IV is between Cloten's hatred as we see it acted out and Posthumus's as we learn about it from his letter. Abstractly the difference is slight, but in dramatic feeling it is considerable. Whereas we watch Cloten formulating his plans for rape and murder and gloating over them, we never see the intensity of hatred which gives rise to Posthumus's damning letter. Cloten serves thus as a surrogate for Posthumus and as a scapegoat, drawing most of our hostility down upon himself, and in his violent and well-earned death satisfying our need to see vice receive its just reward and so appeasing our hostile feelings.[1] By keeping Posthumus offstage, and directing our attention instead to Cloten, Shakespeare shelters him from the blunt of obloquy.

Meanwhile, even as it sets it forth, the play begins to palliate Posthumus's cruelty. For within those scenes in which plot and spectacle most emphatically insist upon a moral kinship between Posthumus and Cloten, other characters behave in such a way as to undercut the full emotional impact of what we are being shown and told. We see the final stage of Posthumus's moral decay only at second hand, briefly in his letter, more fully as it is reflected in Pisanio's grief and in Imogen's mingled anger and pain. That these two respond in sorrow rather than contempt asserts their conviction that vice is aberrant in Posthumus, quintessential in Cloten; and her sympathy for Posthumus even at his worst is reiterated in a scene of wonderful and multifold irony when Imogen, roused to fury at the sight of what she takes to be Posthumus's mutilated body, blames Pisanio – and Cloten (IV, ii, 312–39).

Posthumus's absence from the stage, the deflection of our anger and, separately, Imogen's toward Cloten, and the violence of Cloten's death serve as elements in a modulation of tone which prepares for the reintroduction of Posthumus to the stage. That he is unable to relate his role in the fifth act to any stable costume indicates his deep moral confusion: in a world where distinctions of dress are closely bound up with questions of role and rank, confusion over one's proper dress is an apposite expression for confusion over one's true nature. His most significant actions in the war are his defeat of Iachimo and his assistance to Belarius and the princes in turning the rout. Both are pointed in their significance: the wily Italian who has defeated Posthumus in a contrived wager is now defeated by him in a straightforward encounter; and Posthumus goes on from his triumph over Iachimo to ally his valor with that of the princes. His meeting with Guiderius and Arviragus is the last of his Cloten-like encounters, and the first in which his behavior is in fact as far removed from Cloten's as it could possibly be.

That he succeeds dressed as a poor British soldier suggests that he is no longer acting under the pressure of his own ego; he has abandoned sophistic notions of honor-in-reputation in favor of a sense of propriety in which actions are of value for their intrinsic merit rather than for the glory they may reflect. That Posthumus is unable to settle on a costume for the fifth act points to his confusion, but his rejection of 'Italian weeds' points to the terms in which his confusion will be resolved:

> Let me make men know
> More valour in me than my habits show.
> Gods, put the strength o' th' Leonati in me!
> To shame the guise o' th' world, I will begin,
> The fashion less without, and more within.
>
> (V, i, 29–33)

The recollection here of the First Gentleman's words,

> I do not think
> So fair an outward, and such stuff within
> Endows a man, but he.
>
> (I, i, 22–4)

[1] Cf. Swander, 'Cymbeline: Religious Idea and Dramatic Design', p. 253 and Peterson, Time, Tide, and Tempest, p. 111.

draws together the beginning of the play and its ending; their altered balance expresses a new understanding of what constitutes worth.

III

Posthumus Leonatus and Cloten are never wholly indistinguishable, but the neat distinction the First Gentleman draws between them disregards fact quite as insistently as the opposing distinction drawn by Cymbeline or by Cloten himself. Externals such as beauty, rank, and reputation are no guarantee of worth, however much they may be its fit accompaniments. In making his distinction so emphatically, however, the First Gentleman unwittingly offers a measure of worth which becomes a feature both of *Cymbeline*'s spectacle and of its structure. The evident physical likeness between two such ostensibly different men seems at first ironic; as the play sets forth progressively more serious and dangerous likenesses than feet Mercurial and Martial thighs, it becomes ominous.

Many difficulties over the play's workmanship have arisen from mistaking hypothesis for fact. The judgment of Posthumus's worth in I, i is at odds with much of the play's action, in part because that action is designed to explore and test the bases for such judgments. They are found wanting, and in the process *Cymbeline* comes to a new and more satisfactory understanding of what it means to be nobly virtuous. So long as Posthumus's thoughts and actions are variations upon Cloten's – even when they are superior variations – it matters very little what anyone thinks of him. Only when he comes on his own to recognize and reject his excessive concern with form is the worth attributed to him made manifest. He discards the Italian weeds which, like Cloten's court dress, proclaim his rank. More important, while still believing Imogen an adulteress, he sees the folly of identifying honor with reputation and the hasty arrogance of his assumption that Imogen must die to assuage his wounded vanity. By the time the play's action affirms an apprehension of virtue in Posthumus Leonatus, he has justified his own nobility by coming on his own to embrace its new definition of virtue:

> Heaven doth with us as we with torches do,
> Not light them for themselves; for if our virtues
> Did not go forth of us, 'twere all alike
> As if we had them not.
>
> (*M. for M.* I, i, 32–5)

DIRECTING THE ROMANCES

1. DIRECTING 'THE TEMPEST'

NICK SHRIMPTON

Productions of Shakespeare's plays at universities occupy a stretch of theatrical territory which might baffle the most skilled of surveyors. Longer, at least in theory, in ideas and understanding of the text than most professional productions, they are at the same time even shorter in terms of resources than the average amateur company. For all this, it is hard to resist the feeling that struggling with the play in production, even in these circumstances, is a critical exercise more illuminating than almost any other. Formal problems, the problems of staging, do not necessarily obscure the problems of theme or interpretation. An active sense of the relationship between the two indeed can be immensely suggestive. In the case of *The Tempest*, which I had the somewhat strenuous pleasure of directing for the English Department of the University of Liverpool in the Spring of 1974, there seem to me to be two major problems of dramatic form which are of the most immediate relevance to our sense of the play's meaning.

The Tempest was a play which I approached with considerable misgiving, knowing it on the page, and through the eyes of critics, as something fascinating but rather abstract, a diagram of redemption rather than a drama. Seeing it on the stage, in other productions, had allayed some of those fears but had left instead a feeling that it was a very atomised work, full of things that were good but unusually various. The dramatic modes employed, each severally excellent, managed somehow to range from virtually direct narration and slapstick comedy to romance demanding the most complete suspension of disbelief. Many details of action and characterisation, similarly, gave a sense of the refinement of previous experiment into unprecedentedly potent forms but with an effect of rich variety rather than coherence. There is no shortage of critical commentary on this quality of the play, and very little of it is adverse. Diverse elements of plot or character, we are told, support or elaborately parody each other. But there are some startling and central contrasts which are not capable of this kind of explanation. Repeated rehearsal makes more and more obvious, for example, the oddity of sandwiching the delicate love scene of Act III, Scene i between two episodes of unusually low drunken comedy. An interval at the end of Act II would produce a most unbalanced evening. The foolery in no way comments upon the romance sentiment as it might upon the love scenes of a more conventional comedy. So the only possible purpose of the sequence would seem to be to emphasise, by contrast, the elevated nature of chastity or art. In fact, I think, not even that point emerges. This is not calculated contrast but sheer disparity. We are left with a sense of abrupt and awkward juxtaposition. Though *The Tempest* may be organised in other ways, by imagery for instance, accounts of such design are strangely unhelpful in the theatre. This stubborn impression of diversity is the first of the two problems of form with which I found myself presented.

How then was the play to be mastered and made to speak? I realised very rapidly that my first job was simply to tell the story. Even if their responses were to be perpetually jolted by incongruous moods and manners, at least the audience should have a clear line of narrative to cling to. Yet the dynastic relationships upon which the story depends are by no means easy to understand and remember. As a first answer the costumes were designed above all to make clear who belonged to which court. The Milanese wore red, Neapolitans the same clothes in black. Such clarity, incidentally, is actually important to the moral action of the play. When Prospero invites the courtiers to:

> Mark but the badges of these men, my lords,
> Then say if they be true   (v, i, 267–8)

he is making the essential link between two plots. The badges which identify Stephano and Trinculo with the court of Naples can afford to be obvious.

The most considerable decision to be taken about the visual conception of this play, however, is that involving Caliban. He is not a spirit (whom I dressed in a blanched version of the basic costume) nor is he a member of a court. Was he then to introduce an entirely new shape and colour to my code? The only picture of such a monster with a properly Elizabethan provenance which I could find was the absurd fish creature reproduced in R. M. Frye's *Shakespeare's Life and Times: A Pictorial Record* (1968). But if Caliban is to be made by his appearance a creature so entirely unrelated to everything else on stage as a fish (or, at another extreme of eccentric interpretation, a Red Indian noble savage) then how will the comic scenes work? The answer is scarcely at all. Comedy is created by human beings, animals being incapable of it unless they are anthropomorphised. My problem was solved by John Russell Brown's remarks in *Shakespeare's Plays in Performance* on the constant

importance of clowns in Elizabethan theatre companies. If I have derived only one conviction from directing *The Tempest* it is that its low life scenes are comic three-handers. Caliban, played by a clown, remains, though exotic and grotesque, broadly human. I dressed him in Prospero's cast-offs, clothes in the red of Milan (from Gonzalo's gift of 'Rich garments'), worn to tatters by Caliban's savagery, the base nature on which art will not stick. This decision produced the important incidental benefit that the 'badges' in Act v, Scene i displayed the red of Milan for Antonio, as well as the black of Naples. But the links between different problems do not stop there. Playing the comic scenes for all they are worth involved a decision about what I have talked of as my first major formal problem. It meant that the startling juxtapositions were not to be disguised or smoothed over. Low comedy and high romance would each be played to the hilt, even when they abutted on each other. The production would somehow have to incorporate a sense of incongruity and contrast.

My concern with telling the story of *The Tempest* did not, however, consist merely of a worry about clarity, nor could it be entirely solved in the wardrobe department. There is a major problem of action and suspense. Sam Goldwyn is supposed to have asked his writers for a story which 'Begins with an earthquake and then builds up towards a climax'. *The Tempest* begins with a shipwreck and then (in terms of external narrative excitement at least) sags into a flatness from which it scarcely ever recovers. This is not the irrelevant objection that the stories of the Late Plays are not realistic ones. It is a question of how well a self-confessed fairy story is told.

The problem is presented most acutely by Act I, Scene ii (though it is also raised by the lack of action, apart from the magic table and the masque, in the second half and by the intensely static Act v). Obviously Shakespeare had good reasons for substituting a preliminary narration for the lapses of time in the middle of the other Late Plays. But the change had to be paid for. The price was an explanatory scene which takes a full half hour to perform. This was my second major formal problem in *The Tempest*.

While rehearsing the play I read of a production in which the shipwreck scene was distributed throughout Act I, Scene ii. Though I sympathised with the intention, such a solution seemed to me evasive. If the scene cannot be made interesting on its own terms then no tampering will make the play as a whole work. For, once again, decisions form a chain, each affecting another. Briefly my understanding of Act I, Scene ii, my attempt at a solution from within, was to see Prospero not as the serenely detached figure now so fashionable, but rather as a fierce and embittered old man. Simultaneously Miranda was played as a girl wild and awkward enough to sustain a quarrel with such a father. They are people not unmarked by long isolation, brooding and headstrong. The scene contains, in fact, not merely recollected drama but the present drama of a family quarrel. The storm of anger with which Prospero is at times overwhelmed needs no intrusive material. It can be presented in Shakespeare's essential medium – acted words.

It might, of course, be objected at this point that such worry about *The Tempest* on the grounds of its lack of dramatic action ignores the fact that Shakespeare can deploy a potent substitute for action in the splendour of his language, which we should admire in the same way as Prospero or Ferdinand admires the static verbal beauty of the masque. But such objections do not go quite deep enough. The point about the great speeches is not that they are a substitute for action but that they are the action, an action which has become internalised. But even an internal action must involve change and development. If Prospero delivers these speeches from a serene and omniscient moral repose, then the play loses its narrative force and direction.

The solution of practical problems is, I think, by this point fairly obviously urging me towards interpretation. Discussions of *The Tempest* in terms of colonialism, or slavery, or autobiography, or even art and nature had never seemed to me to be anything but peripheral, at least to production in the theatre. Two accounts of the play did, however, make some real claim to a grasp of the ideas around which it takes shape. The first is the argument that *The Tempest* is a play about penitence and reconciliation, the second that it is a play about revenge and forgiveness. Before undertaking a production I had been accustomed to think of it as the former. In other Late Plays, after all, penitence is obviously central. In *Cymbeline* and *The Winter's Tale* we observe a process of transition. A man sins, then repents, and the climax of the action is an exquisite movement from self-reproach to joy. Applying this model to *The Tempest* is what prompts those productions in which Prospero is played as a serene stage-manager, provoking but standing back from the supposedly central events of Alonso's redemption. I do not think that *The Tempest* performed in that way comes alive on stage. The problem is that the sin and repentance which we actually see are here distributed between different characters. It is interesting to see Leontes the sinner and Leontes the penitent. It is much less interesting to see Antonio the sinner and Alonso the penitent. After such distribution the crucial transitions are impossible. Even such changes as Alonso does make on stage are rushed and overwhelmed by other events. There is also the simple fact that attention is concentrated on the injured party, as if Hermione had been given numerous scenes in the latter part of *The Winter's Tale*. With the focus so firmly on the forgiver, could it not perhaps be that *The Tempest* is not centrally a play about penitence at all? And could not those processes of transition, so crucial to the Late Plays, in fact be demonstrated by Prospero even though his experience, like that of Pericles, is of something quite different from repentance?

Forgiveness, the alternative centre, is scarcely an original discovery as the theme of *The Tempest*. But it is, I think, worthwhile to consider the full implications of the topic. It is not a single or automatic act of forgiveness which we are witnessing. Prospero has first to pass through a period of anger, of not forgiving, of revenge. For *The Tempest* is in a real sense a Revenge Play, and as such is a work of remarkable sophistication. In *Hamlet* the moral problems of revenge are complicated by psychological and practical difficulties. In the later play all these peripheral dilemmas are removed. Prospero knows all he needs to know about the offenders, his means are irresistible, and his revenge, consisting of humiliation rather than death, involves no problems of guilt. The perfect revenge is possible. In these circumstances should a man take it? The focus is of unrivalled clarity. What is the process of moral decision which it reveals?

In Act III, Scene iii, the Prospero who had been so moved by his wrongs in the first act clearly is embarked on a programme of vengeance:

> My high charms work,
> And these mine enemies are all knit up
> In their distractions. They now are in my pow'r.
>   (III, iii, 88–90)

The climax of *The Tempest* comes one act later, in that astonishing scene in which Ariel shames Prospero into forgiveness. The air, itself touched, touches Prospero, in an image of the action of moral intuition, invisible and immaterial yet hugely powerful. Prospero's speech is one of active thought, conducted, it is important to realise, in the present tense:

> Yet with my nobler reason 'gainst my fury
> Do I take part.   (v, i, 26–7)

This is a visible, acted transition of the kind undergone by, say, Pericles from grief to joy. We witness the struggle by which Prospero wins through from fury to the assertion that:

> the rarer action is
> In virtue than in vengeance.   (v, i, 27–8)

It is, of course, at precisely this point that Prospero abjures the magic that made the perfect vengeance possible. But Prospero's mental progress from anger to 'virtue', the interest that solved my second formal problem, is not concluded yet. For at this point, of course, his forgiveness is conditional, dependent upon such things as penitence in others:

> they being penitent,
> The sole drift of my purpose doth extend
> Not a frown further.   (v, i, 28–30)

On discovering that Antonio (and possibly Sebastian) are not thus penitent, Prospero does not retreat into revenge but instead advances further into the moral heroism of forgiveness. He forgives even though his enemy does not repent or reform:

> I do forgive thee,
> Unnatural though thou art.   (v, i, 78–9)

Not 'wert' but 'art', again the tense is crucial, and is re-emphasised, to the now conscious Antonio, fifty lines later:

> For you, most wicked sir, whom to call brother
> Would even infect my mouth, I do forgive
> Thy rankest fault – all of them.   (v, i, 130–3)

Antonio is still 'wicked', his fault is not single or necessarily in the past (that interesting grammatical contradiction suggesting that there are, and will be, more faults than Prospero can at this moment know). The world does not become perfect, forgiveness is no longer connected to a restoration of perfect order. Yet the gesture, Senecan rather than

Christian in its sense of virtue for its own sake, remains valuable, even imperative.

And it is here that my first problem of theatrical form returns to the service of interpretation, taking its place beside this moral and emotional progress which supplies the seemingly absent narrative interest. For that awkward disunity is a quality profoundly appropriate to Prospero's most developed moral position. The sense of diversity given by the play's form, Stephano rudely juxtaposed with Miranda, reflects life as something neither serene nor controlled, a world unorganised by providence or grace. Instead it gives a sense of the unmasterable contradictions amidst which moral action must take place, and in spite of which moral gestures of the kind which Prospero ultimately chooses must be made. Far from needing to be played down, this, like the other chief practical difficulty which faces a director, in fact provides the most cogent of pointers to the understanding of the play.

© NICK SHRIMPTON 1976

2. VERBAL REMINISCENCE AND THE TWO-PART STRUCTURE OF 'THE WINTER'S TALE'

RICHARD PROUDFOOT

The Winter's Tale is alone among those plays of Shakespeare which can be described as tragi-comic in reflecting its mixed genre in the sharp division of its action into two halves, the first predominantly tragic, the second predominantly comic in tone and technique, divided by a 'wide gap of Time' (v, iii, 154). By contrast, the time-gap in *Pericles* (whose structure may not be wholly of Shakespeare's devising) is preceded by an important action pointing to an eventual happy outcome in the resuscitation of Thaisa by Cerimon, while the action of the later acts continues the sequence of painful adventures characteristic of Pericles into the life of his daughter Marina. The shift of mood engineered in the third act of *Measure for Measure* and confirmed in the following act by the introduction of Mariana suggests a closer parallel, not least in the proliferating comic action of the central acts, but no such sharp division of the action is felt as the time-gap imposes in *The Winter's Tale*. In structure, *The Winter's Tale* conforms to the two-part pattern discerned in other plays by Emrys Jones in *Scenic Form in Shakespeare*.[1] This feature of the play has received extensive attention in recent criticism, especially from Ernest Schanzer,[2] Fitzroy Pyle,[3] W. H. Matchett,[4] J. E. Siemon[5] and L. S. Cox,[6] whose commentaries have outlined and elaborated

[1] Oxford, 1971.
[2] Ernest Schanzer, 'The Structural Pattern of *The Winter's Tale*', *Review of English Literature*, 5 (1964), 72–82; Introduction to New Penguin edition of *The Winter's Tale* (Harmondsworth, 1969).
[3] Fitzroy Pyle, '*The Winter's Tale*': *A Commentary on the Structure* (1969).
[4] William H. Matchett, 'Some Dramatic Techniques in *The Winter's Tale*', *Shakespeare Survey* 22 (Cambridge, 1969), 93–107.
[5] J. E. Siemon, '"But It Appears She Lives": Iteration in *The Winter's Tale*', *PMLA*, 89 (1974), 10–16.
[6] Lee S. Cox, 'The Role of Autolycus in *The Winter's Tale*', *Studies in English Literature*, 9 (1969), 283–301.

the nature and extent of the parallels and contrasts of action, word and theme which create the peculiar balance between the play's two halves and also between its comic subplot and its main action.

In the course of producing the play with students of the English Department of King's College, University of London, for performance in January, 1975, I became aware of ever more correspondences of detail between the first three acts and the last two, whose accumulation confirmed the view that the tragi-comic mixture in *The Winter's Tale* is achieved by the sustaining of a balance between the two halves of its action which extends to a quite remarkable minuteness of detail as well as embracing the broadest effects of repetition and contrast. The parallel movement discernible in the two halves of the play has many effects, but above all it imparts to Acts IV and V the simultaneous qualities of development and recapitulation of material already expounded in Acts I to III. The relation resembles that between the two Parts of *King Henry IV*, where the explicitness and vigour of Part 1 yield, in Part 2, to a more sombre and searching exploration of character and theme, supported by an action whose outline, until its final reversal, constantly recalls the principal events of Part 1.

In *The Winter's Tale*, the links between the two halves of the play are of many kinds. A small but typical example is the thrice-repeated use of the word 'long' in relation to the cravings of pregnant women: two uses are in main-plot scenes in Acts I and IV, the third in a speech of Autolycus. In I, ii, the single speech which alludes directly to Hermione's pregnancy is her reply to Leontes's claim that she has twice spoken well, 'But once before I spoke to th' purpose? when? / Nay, let me have't; I long' (100–1). The echo comes in IV, iv, as Camillo conceives his plan to effect his return to Sicilia by first helping Florizel to escape

thither with Perdita and then urging Polixenes to pursuit, 'in whose company / I shall re-view *Sicilia*; for whose sight, / I haue a Womans Longing' (655–7). The contrast is sharp, in retrospect, between a longing whose issue is Leontes's jealousy and a birth 'before her time' (II, ii, 25) and one whose outcome exceeds expectation in joy and wonder. The third statement of the motif is in a different key, as Autolycus, turned pedlar, offers the first of his ballads 'for man, or woman, of all sizes', 'how a Vsurers wife was brought to bed of twenty money baggs at a burthen, and how she long'd to eate Adders heads, and Toads carbonado'd' (IV, iv, 257–9). Autolycus fits the Clown's rival girl-friends all too well with ballads of a prodigious birth (Mopsa has just alleged that Dorcas is pregnant, and her horror at the thought of marrying a usurer tends to support the allegation) and of the sad metamorphosis of a maid that 'wold not exchange flesh with one that lou'd her' into a cold fish.

The technique is Shakespeare's familiar one of using infrequently repeated words, phrases or metaphors to unify the verbal texture of a play and to hint at interrelation between moments far apart in time and not causally connected by the mechanics of his plot. The technique can be used with powerful ironic effect, as in the two references to figs in *Antony and Cleopatra* (I, ii, 3 and v, ii, 234) or the three to butterflies in *Coriolanus* (I, iii, 61–5; IV, vi, 95 and V, iv, 11–13). No such pointed irony can be detected in *The Winter's Tale*: although the general contrast between the outcomes of Hermione's longing and Camillo's is clear, the predicament of Dorcas seems more local in its effect, serving as it does to highlight the purity of Perdita. But the child of Hermione is a central figure in the multiple births of Camillo's plan and the third Gentleman is given the play's last reference to pregnancy as his narrative of the finding of Perdita prepares the way for the rebirth of Hermione herself: 'Most true, if euer Truth were pregnant by Circumstance' (v, ii, 30–1). Not much ingenuity would be needed to deduce an intention to identify the pregnant truth with both Hermione, truth in love, and Camillo, truth in service. What the verbal links seem to invite is rather a toying with such associations than any attempt to use them as the basis for a systematic exegesis. That the force of such links may be ironic or thematic is always possible, but their pervasive effect is to suggest the unity of the play at a rather deeper level of unconscious association.

To demonstrate the range and variety of these echoes it will be necessary to present them at length. Most of the passages cited from the first half of the play occur in I, ii, their echoes are mainly in IV, ii and iv. I deliberately omit the many such correspondences already noted by, in particular, Schanzer, Siemon and Cox, such as the horror of bastardy expressed by Leontes in II, iii, and echoed by Perdita in IV, iv. A few internal echoes within the two parts of the play are noted, also some similarities of detail which are not verbal. As it is hardly possible to classify these details into meaningful groups, it has seemed best to present them in approximately the sequence in which the earliest passages in each set occur in the first half of the play.

Situations early in Act IV are presented so as to recall those of Act I. In I, ii, Polixenes is urged to stay longer in Bohemia; in IV, ii, it is his turn to overrule Camillo's desire to leave Bohemia for Sicilia. The 'kind Hostesse' (I, ii, 60) who wins Polixenes's consent to stay is Hermione; the 'Hostesse of the meeting' (IV, iv, 64) who welcomes him to the shearers' feast is her daughter, whose shyness recalls Hermione's initial silence, until urged on by Leontes – as Perdita is by her 'father', the Old Shepherd. In I, ii, Leontes confides in Camillo his plans against Polixenes; in IV, ii, Camillo's aid is enlisted by Polixenes in spying on Florizel. The nostalgic vision of Leontes

and Polixenes as 'twyn'd Lambs, that did frisk i' th' Sun' (I, ii, 67) is answered, as the play changes direction in III, iii, by the Shepherd's loss of 'two of my best Sheepe' (67). The first metaphor used by Leontes to describe the onset of jealousy is 'my heart daunces, / But not for ioy; not ioy' (I, ii, 110–11); the matching of Florizel and Perdita is expressed in dance as well as in dialogue and Florizel's eulogy of Perdita culminates in 'When you do dance, I wish you / A waue o'th Sea' (IV, iv, 140–1). The devotion of Polixenes to his son, 'If at home (Sir) / He's all my Exercise' (I, ii, 165–6), is echoed in Florizel's devotion to Perdita, which has made him 'lesse frequent to his Princely exercises then formerly he hath appeared' (IV, ii, 31–2). A third use of the word associates the penitence of Leontes with these other devotions, as he dedicates himself to a life of mourning with the words, 'So long as Nature / Will beare vp with this exercise, so long / I dayly vow to vse it' (III, ii, 237–9).

The heavy irony with which Leontes commends his queen and Polixenes to 'your grauer steps' (I, ii, 173) has its gentler counterpart in Camillo's tactful offer of advice to the confused and improvising Florizel, 'If your more ponderous and setled proiect / May suffer alteration' (IV, iv, 516–17). The image of fishing links the jealous speculations of Leontes's 'I am angling now, / (Though you perceiue me not how I giue Lyne)' (I, ii, 180–1) with the attractions of Perdita, 'the Angle that pluckes' Florizel to a shepherd's cottage (IV, ii, 44). This image undergoes a third, and precious, transformation in the narrative of Paulina's steward, 'One of the prettyest touches of all, and that which angl'd for mine Eyes (caught the Water, though not the Fish)...' (v, ii, 80–2). The metaphor of angling may also be present in Leontes's vindictive soliloquy at the opening of II, iii, 'shee, / I can hooke to me:' (6–7), although the next phrases, 'say that she were gone, / Giuen to the fire', conjure up the equally apt picture of a devil armed with a flesh-hook.

The word 'play' so pervades the language of both I, ii and IV, iv, that instances need not be itemised, but the parallel between Hermione's theatrical image of her plight 'which is more / Then Historie can patterne, though deuis'd, / And play'd, to take Spectators' (III, ii, 33–5) and Perdita's acceptance of a role in Camillo's comedy of disguises, 'I see the Play so lyes, / That I must bear a part' (IV, iv, 651–2), pinpoints the contrast between their roles and the actions they are engaged in. Camillo too, who has conceded that he may at some time 'industriously' have 'play'd the Foole' (I, ii, 256–7), turns playwright-manager for Florizel and Perdita with as much care 'To haue you royally appointed, as if / The Scene you play, were mine' (IV, iv, 584–5). The anticipation, in his phrasing, of Paulina's '(for the Stone is mine)' (V, iii, 58) is a tiny link in the growing association of these two virtuous plotters which culminates in their marriage.

An important image of Leontes's jealousy is that of the opening of gates, 'there's comfort in't, / Whiles other men haue Gates, and those Gates open'd / (As mine) against their will' (I, ii, 196–8). A pastoral metamorphosis of the metaphor provides Polixenes with his least just allegation against the shepherd's daughter he regards as his son's mistress: 'If euer henceforth, thou / These rurall Latches, to his entrance open, . . .' (IV, iv, 429–30). Camillo's complicity in the supposed guilt of Polixenes and Hermione is impressed on the imagination of Leontes largely by Camillo's address in opening posterns for escape. The image of opening doors loses its sexual reference here, becoming one of the escape of the truth. It is translated into visual terms in the actions of Paulina, whose three main entrances in Acts II and III all involve irruption, into the prison in II, ii, into the seclusion of Leontes in II, iii, and into the midst of Leontes and his lords in III,

ii, to announce the death of Hermione. The image of sexual incontinence, unjustly applied in any case, is ambivalent and comes to signify the escape of the innocent and the intrusion of truth on false imaginings.

Leontes's fears of table-talk about his supposed cuckoldry, 'Lower Messes / Perchance are to this Businesse purblind' (I, ii, 227–8), are echoed as Perdita finds a sanction for dressing-up in the reflection that 'our Feasts / in euery Messe, haue folly' (IV, iv, 10–11). The trust of Leontes in Camillo's counsel (I, ii, 235–9) has its counterpart in IV, ii, where Polixenes makes his reliance on Camillo the reason for preventing his return to Sicilia. Leontes urges Camillo, as cup-bearer to Polixenes, to poison his cup, 'Which Draught to me, were cordiall' (I, ii, 318), but his response to the 'affliction' caused by the sight of his wife's statue recalls and reverses his earlier use of the word 'cordial', 'this Affliction ha's a taste as sweet / As any Cordiall comfort' (V, iii, 76–7). A related echo is the Shepherd's response on learning the true identity of Florizel, 'Oh my heart' (IV, iv, 415), which repeats the first symptom of Leontes's jealousy, 'I haue *Tremor Cordis* on me:' (I, ii, 110). The 'Goades, Thornes, Nettles, Tayles of Waspes' (I, ii, 329) of Leontes's anguish have their precise echoes in Polixenes's threat to have Perdita's beauty 'scratcht with briers' (IV, iv, 416) and in the 'head of a Waspes Nest' (IV, iv, 775) which Autolycus imagines as one of the places of torment for the hapless Clown. Camillo's promise to 'fetch off *Bohemia*' (I, ii, 334) – his only deliberate use of an evasive ambiguity, 'kill' or 'help to escape', in a scene pervaded with Leontes's hunger and thirst for *double entendres* – is the first evidence of his decision to deceive Leontes. Later, he will again deceive, not one master this time but two, Polixenes, in enabling Florizel to escape, and Florizel, in revealing the escape to his father. The conviction that Camillo is a traitor, voiced by

Leontes in Acts II and III, is echoed by Florizel in V, i, '*Camillo* ha's betray'd me' (191). The arbitrary provision of a ship for Florizel, 'most opportune to her neede, I haue / A Vessel rides fast by, but not prepar'd / For this designe' (IV, iv, 492–4), contrasts with the plausible readiness of Polixenes's ships at the end of I, ii. Camillo's dilemma when faced with the unjust command to murder Polixenes leaves him momentarily at a loss for words: 'I dare not know (My Lord)' (I, ii, 376) is his response to direct questioning by Polixenes. In II, iv, Camillo turns to comfort the distraught Shepherd and hears his earlier words echoed: 'I cannot speake, nor thinke, / Nor dare to know, that which I know' (443–4). Camillo's vindication of his good faith to Polixenes is expressed in these words (which contain an irrelevant reminiscence of Iachimo's trick on Imogen)

> If therefore you dare trust my honestie,
> That lyes enclosed in this Trunke, which you
> Shall beare along impawnd, away to Night.
>
> (I, ii, 434–6)

The first echo is from Antigonus, whose faith in Hermione leads him to offer to 'pawne the little blood which I haue left' (II, iii, 165) to save her daughter, but a more exact parallel is the Shepherd's offer to 'leaue this young man [the Clown] in pawne' (IV, iv, 796–7) till he completes payment of the bribe required by Autolycus to intercede with the king.

Four instances from later scenes may indicate how the parallels continue. Both Paulina and Leontes use printing imagery to express the likeness of children to their parents: Paulina in II, iii, pointing at the infant Perdita, 'Behold (my Lords) / Although the Print be little, the whole Matter / And Coppy of the Father' (97–9); Leontes in V, i, as he sees the first of a succession of wonders, the arrival in Sicilia of Florizel and Perdita,

> Your Mother was most true to Wedlock, Prince,
> For she did print your Royall Father off,
> Conceiuing you.   (ll. 124–6)

Though 'true' and 'truth' are words frequently heard in the play, two passages are linked by a combination of the motif of truth with an implied piece of stage business, the taking of a paper from a character who has just read, or sung, its contents. In III, ii, Leontes takes the oracle from the officer who has read it and looks at it himself before dismissing it with 'There is no truth at all i' th' Oracle' (137). Autolycus, as ballad-vendor, vouches for the truth of his ballads in response to the anxious incredulity of Mopsa and Dorcas. His third and 'passing merry' ballad, to the tune of 'two maids wooing a man', is sung by them with him. When they finish, the Clown, having just seen the girls act out something like their relationship with him, responds with the words 'Wee'l haue this song out anon by our selues' (IV, iv, 303–4). This response is usually taken to be one of delight, on the evidence of a later speech by Autolycus (599 ff), but it is followed by an interruption of the singing and the offer to buy fairings for both Dorcas and Mopsa, a diversion of the direction of the scene which may suggest that the force of his initial response is rather one of embarrassed puzzlement at the unexpected accuracy with which he has seen himself portrayed in the mirror of art. The implied gesture is for the Clown to take the ballad sheet from Autolycus and scrutinize it for a clue to the mystery, repeating, in the process, the gesture of Leontes and thus setting up a ripple of that association between art and divine providence which culminates in the statue scene.

Two characters offer divine honours as a reward for the performance of seemingly impossible tasks. When Paulina has announced the death of Hermione, she urges the lords to go and see for themselves:

> if you can bring
> Tincture, or lustre in her lip, her eye,
> Heate outwardly, or breath within, Ile serue you
> As I would do the Gods.   (III, ii, 201–4)

In the final scene of the play she will earn god-like honours herself by performing the task to the letter of lip, eye, heat and breath. Florizel's equivalent offer to Camillo,

> How *Camillo*
> May this (almost a miracle) be done?
> That I may call thee something more then man,
> And after that trust to thee   (IV, iv, 525–8)

must strike us as characteristic hyperbole: although Camillo's performance is attended with as much theatrical contrivance (forged letters, disguise and concealed identity) as is the statue scene, it nowhere suggests the collaboration of higher powers and its fortuitous instrument is Autolycus.

The appearance of Hermione's ghost to Antigonus is a critical crux. Its simplest effect is to reinforce our sense that she is dead (though our scepticism may be aroused by the ghost's lies). But Antigonus's description of his vision has a distancing effect, especially in the phrase 'her eyes / Became two spouts' (III, iii, 25–6), which at least prevents the stirring of strong feelings. The parallel phrase is used with self-conscious artistry when the third Gentleman describes the Shepherd as standing weeping 'like a Weather-bitten Conduit, of many Kings Reignes' (v, ii, 52–3). The last such verbal parallel sprang out in a rehearsal of III, iii at which the Clown (whose lines were not yet perfect) gave the name of Autolycus to Antigonus as he related his death. The associative link was once apparent between 'to see how the Beare tore out his shoulder-bone, how he cride to mee for helpe, and said his name was *Antigonus*, a Nobleman:' (III, iii, 94–7) and this speech from the Clown's first encounter with Autolycus, 'Oh good sir, softly, good sir: I feare (sir) my shoulder-blade is out' (IV, iii, 69–70). Although this selection of details concentrates on the less perceptible points of contact between the two halves of *The Winter's Tale*, one general pattern that emerges is the frequency with which the actions or words of Camillo in one half are related to the other and especially to the similar operations of Paulina.

The association of Antigonus with Autolycus raises the broader practical question of the possibilities offered for the doubling of roles by the play's two-part structure. The principal characters who disappear from the scene by the end of Act III are Mamillius and Antigonus; others are Archidamus, the court ladies, the jailor, the seaman and the officers. Archidamus is available for any of the small parts after Act I, but his function in I, i suggests a natural link with Time in IV, i and the third Gentleman in v, ii. This third Gentleman, whose narrative recalls and recapitulates the final stages of Act III, especially the oracle, Antigonus's dream and the Clown's narration of the deaths of Antigonus and his crew, is described as 'the Lady *Paulina*'s Steward'. The purpose of the identification is two-fold; to explain his presence at a scene from which the other Gentlemen have been dismissed and to sanction the heavy emphasis he lays on Paulina's own emotions. As Paulina must be attended on her first entry, in II, ii, it seems reasonable to introduce the third Gentleman as her attendant then and to let him age in Act v in the company of Cleomenes and Dion and of the poetical servant of v, i, whose earlier presence, as the servant attending Mamillius who appears in II, iii and III, ii, is recommended by his loyal concern for Hermione. The players of other small parts in part one will be needed in IV, iv as Mopsa, Dorcas, shepherds and shepherdesses, and two of the men later as the first and second Gentlemen in v, ii. The total disappearance of the attendant ladies from the Sicilian court in Act v is the result of the death of Hermione, but it serves the useful function of intensifying the isolation of Paulina.

That the players of Mamillius and Antigonus went home after Act III is perfectly possible: if they didn't, then the only roles available for them after the interval were Perdita, Florizel and Autolycus. That either could have played Florizel, a young man in his mid twenties, is improbable, but the other available doublings, though at first glance unexpected, deserve further consideration. The ages of Mamillius and Autolycus are nowhere specified, both could be older than they are sometimes played. To play Mamillius as from nine to eleven years old seems congruous with his lines (and may find some sentimental justification in the fact that Shakespeare evidently wrote *The Winter's Tale* some fifteen years after the death, aged eleven, of his own only son – a detail which emerges more clearly in *The Two Noble Kinsmen*, I, iii, where Emilia describes her childhood friendship with Flavina, who died when they were both eleven). That the roles of an eleven-year-old boy and a fifteen-year-old girl were within the range of a single boy player can hardly be demonstrated, but for all its oft-stated centrality in the second half of the play the role of Perdita is a comparatively small one and leads the action only in the early stages of IV, iv. Such a doubling would appropriately stress the youth and innocence of Perdita and would reinforce an association of her with the values attributed to Mamillius from I, i on-wards. The doubling of Perdita with Hermione (though beautifully executed by Judi Dench in Trevor Nunn's Royal Shakespeare Company production) remains an aberration, if only because it must distract the attention of the audience from the emotions of Leontes at the climax of V, iii to the mechanics of having the same actress speak the lines of both Perdita and Hermione within a single scene. The doubling of Antigonus and Autolycus seems less promising, though there is shoulder-bones in both. Antigonus does, however, come as close as any character in the early acts to introducing a comic note into the action. Also, just as Autolycus is a city rogue rusticated, Antigonus brings into the court of Leontes the language of the

countryside, or at least the stable and the hunting-field. Whether or not the doubling could be carried off, a further oblique link (beyond assonance) exists between the two characters. Antigonus calls on 'Wolues and Beares' as well as 'Kytes and Rauens' to nurse Perdita (II, iii, 185–6): he, in due course, meets *his* bear and his fate is instrumental in saving the infant. No wolf enters the play, however, before Autolycus, whose name is too appropriate for the faint-hearted kite in wolf's clothing of Shakespeare's imagining for it to be imaginable that he was unaware of its meaning. The 'snapper-vp of vnconsidered trifles' (IV, iii, 26–7) is no nurse to Perdita, with whom he never exchanges a line of dialogue, but he does become an instrument to aid his late master, Prince Florizel, in a 'peece of Iniquitie', the snapping-up of unconsidered Perdita, whom Polixenes 'counts but a Trifle' (V, i, 224). (The third term in this link of passages is Perdita's own lack of regard for 'such trifles' as the pedlar's wares (IV, iv, 349)).

These doublings, if adequately executed, could hardly fail to affect our response to Act V. The return of the performer of Mamillius as Perdita would reinforce the sense of restoration to Leontes of what his folly had lost and would also assert the identity of husband and wife when the same face whose resemblance to his own struck Leontes in I, ii triggers the memory of Hermione in V, i. The doubling of Antigonus and Autolycus could have no such simple effect on the emotions of the ending, if only because Paulina never encounters Autolycus. What it would do would be to add another layer to the already lacquered artifice of V, ii, in which Autolycus serves as a slightly unexpected auditor of the third Gentleman's narration of the death of Antigonus. 'Like an old Tale still' (59) has been read as a formula inviting either credulity or incredulity: what is unquestionable is Shakespeare's repeated reference to the artifice of his story. That the

6

doubling of two pairs of roles should point in one case to similarity and in the other to contrast would at least be in keeping with the play's total pattern of symmetry and contrast. Doubling may have been a technique which Shakespeare wished to restrict or even discourage in his latest plays: although *Pericles* invites extensive doubling, *Cymbeline* makes it virtually and *The Tempest* absolutely impossible, except for the smallest of parts.

Shakespeare's perennial motif of the deceptiveness of appearances pervades *The Winter's Tale*, but here, as elsewhere, the techniques of the two halves of the play differ widely. The emphasis in Acts I to III is on the words, actions and features of characters, that in Acts IV and V (except in the scenes involving Leontes) on costume. These emphases are among the qualities which associate the early acts with the world of Shakespearian tragedy and the later ones with that of Shakespearian comedy. In the opening action, it is Leontes who scrutinizes his wife and finds his version of truth in the negative image of their words and acts, and who is driven by his nostalgia for childhood innocence to find himself in the image of Mamillius, whose 'greatest Promise' (I, i, 33) is still unbroken. His reading of the characters of Camillo, Antigonus and Paulina depends less on visual scrutiny: the rage of his infected imagination simply reverses the appearance of each into its opposite, traitor, fool and pandar. In II, iii, where Paulina subjects him to the test of confrontation with 'The silence...of pure innocence' (II, ii, 41), it is questionable whether Leontes should ever look at the baby: if he does, it can only be at the one moment at which he almost relents, 'But be it: let it liue' (II, iii, 156). Hermione recognises the futility of a plea of not guilty before a judge who is also her accuser, 'mine Integritie / Being counted Falsehood, shall (as I expresse it) / Be so receiu'd' (III, ii, 25–7). Shakespeare sums up the infatuation of Leontes, and clinches the audience's conviction that he is infatuated, in his totally ambiguous line 'All's true that is mistrusted' (II, i, 48). Leontes's insistence on the evidence of the senses becomes strident as he tries to bully Antigonus into line:

> You smell this businesse with a sence as cold
> As is a dead-mans nose: but I do see't, and feel't,
> As you feele doing thus: and see withall
> The Instruments that feele.   (II, i, 151–4)

The implied action, Leontes's striking his hand, presumably against his throne, suggests not so much conviction as the desperate search for evidence palpable enough to be unambiguous. This gesture is among the earlier wounds healed when Leontes accepts the warm touch of Hermione's hand as evidence that she is alive.

In Act V, the motif of seeing is revived in a series of sights, imagined or real, which present themselves to the eyes and fancy of Leontes. The first is his theatrical vision of Hermione's spirit re-entering 'on this Stage / (Where we Offendors now appeare)' (V, i, 58–9). It is followed by the arrival of Florizel and Perdita, reincarnating Polixenes and Hermione as well as recalling Mamillius and his lost sister, and finally by the statue, whose sight transports Leontes into an ecstasy of gazing which he would have continue twenty years. That this thirst of seeing is unassuageable and that words cannot convey the quality of feeling in the scene of reunion, 'a Sight which was to bee seene, cannot bee spoken of' (V, ii, 41–2), are two points made by the Gentlemen who relate it. That gazing may not nourish is a joke exorcised from the final action by Perdita's reply, 'You'ld be so leane, that blasts of Ianuary / Would blow you through and through' (IV, iv, 111–12), to Camillo's bantering compliment, 'I should leaue grasing, were I of your flocke, / And onely liue by gazing' (109–10).

Trust in the evidence of sight, well or ill founded, is not confined to Leontes. The flight of Polixenes is urged not only by Camillo's words but by what he has read in the expression of Leontes, 'I saw his heart in's face' (I, ii, 447). Antigonus, with a *reductio ad absurdum* of Leontes's insistence on Hermione's guilt, prepares to mistrust his wife too, 'Then when I feele, and see her, no farther trust her:' (II, i, 136). Even Leontes, however, concedes that his case against Hermione and Polixenes lacks visual evidence. Though Camillo can thus describe Leontes's passion to Polixenes, 'with all confidence he sweares, / As he had seen't' (I, ii, 414–5), yet Leontes later admits that his proofs of undue intimacy between Polixenes and Hermione 'lack'd sight onely, nought for approbation / But onely seeing, all other circumstances / Made vp to'th deed' (II, i, 177–9). His lack of such evidence may even be tacitly admitted in an earlier speech if, as is possible, 'farre' is read as the comparative rather than the positive form. 'To mingle friendship farre, is mingling bloods' (I, ii, 109), that is to say, the behaviour he has seen goes just to the verge of what is definable as friendship rather than love, sexually expressed.

In part one, disguise and deception exist only in the imagination of Leontes: in Acts IV and V, little is what it seems to be and disguise is everywhere. Frequent reference to clothes begins with the first spoken line of Autolycus, 'I haue seru'd Prince *Florizell*, and in my time wore three pile' (IV, iii, 13–14). His own fortunes are reflected by two changes of costume, from rags to his pedlar's gear and then to the shed garment of Florizel in which he passes (with the vulgar) for a great courtier, 'Seest thou not the ayre of the Court, in these enfoldings?' (IV, iv, 726). The Clown is impressed, but the Shepherd sees that though 'His Garments are rich, ... he weares them not handsomely' (745–6). The Shepherd and Clown undergo a similar transformation in three stages, from the 'very nothing' of Act III to the 'vnspeakable estate' of Act IV (IV, ii,

38–40), which makes the Clown and Perdita the most eligible young people of their countryside, and finally to the hot-house blossoming of their fortune in V, ii, and the robes which are 'Gentlemen borne' (130). The comic reversal which leaves Autolycus as the servant of his principal dupe, after his attempt at aiding the operations of Fortune has been foiled by the untimely sea-sickness of Perdita and Florizel, is expressed clearly by changes of costume.

Other disguises proliferate. That of Florizel as a shepherd may denote him truly in his love but conceals the rank which is its main obstacle (and still unknown to the old Shepherd). That of Perdita, which she finds inappropriate, reveals her true nature and is Shakespeare's means of introducing her as simultaneously shepherdess and princess, a foreshortening demanded by the brief time available for exposition in the second half of the play. Her final disguise, as the princess Florizel claims she is while believing he knows her not to be, is even more accurate in revealing her. The first disguise of Perdita easily permits Florizel's association of her with Flora: his lighter allusion to the love which transformed 'the Fire-roab'd-God / Golden Apollo' to 'a poore humble Swaine, / As I seeme now' (IV, iv, 29–31) strikes a more strained posture, but gives particularity to Perdita's later image of love as 'Bright Phoebus in his strength' (124), as well as adumbrating the role of Florizel in the working out of Apollo's purpose.

Florizel's disguise poses another, more practical, problem in production: before the long scene, IV, iv, is over, he exchanges costumes with Autolycus, receiving the pedlar's clothes. In the costume he has received from Florizel, Autolycus then proceeds to pass himself off as a courtier before the Shepherd and Clown. If this costume is the shepherd's disguise worn by Florizel at the opening of the scene, it will have the double disadvantage of failing to look courtly and of being recognizable by the Shepherd and Clown. Their failure to see through such a disguise, especially when their attention is drawn to Autolycus's clothes, seems to require a degree of impercipience beyond what is elsewhere suggested.[1] A practical solution, which gains some support from the lines, is to have Florizel remove his shepherd's disguise before his exchange of costumes, so that what Autolycus receives is the more courtly garment he was wearing beneath it. Time, and a motive, for the removal of Florizel's disguise are provided after Polixenes has left the stage in anger, ordering his son to follow (IV, iv, 433). Florizel is silent for twenty lines while Perdita accepts her disappointment and counsels him to go and the Shepherd expresses his dismay and reproves Perdita. During this time he must stand away from Perdita, having perhaps moved after his father as he left the stage as if hoping to stop him. When he speaks, it is to address Perdita: 'Why looke you so vpon me? / I am but sorry, not affear'd: delaid, / But nothing altred: What I was, I am' (IV, iv, 454–6). The removal of his disguise, which has lost its purpose with his discovery, reveals him as the prince who will now claim Perdita in his own person and without deception. Before he speaks, however, she has time to look at him in doubt of the meaning of his action in removing the disguise, which could signify an intention of obedience to his father. The discarded shepherd's smock then becomes available for Perdita to take as temporary cover before leaving the stage in flight from the wrath of Polixenes. The 'truth' of Florizel's love for Perdita is strongly and passionately stated, and is sustained, both before his discovery by Polixenes and later, at the court of Leontes in v, i, by a great fluency in falsehood.

The most conventional disguises are those adopted by Polixenes and Camillo to allow them to attend the sheep-shearing feast. That of Polixenes evidently includes a white beard and seems to suggest to him the vision of an aged and bedrid father with which he attempts to goad Florizel into some display of filial loyalty. Florizel turns the suggestion to good use in v, i, alleging the infirmity of his father '(Which waits vpon worne times)' (141), as his excuse for arriving in Sicilia as his deputy. More important is the effect of the disguise in associating Polixenes, who 'has his health, and ampler strength indeede / Then most haue of his age' (IV, iv, 400–1), with old age in a scene in which the contrast between generations is everywhere stressed. The removal of his disguise reveals Polixenes as no 'ancient Sir' but in the full vigour of his 'middle age'. By contrast, the 'penitent...and reconciled King' (IV, ii, 22–3), Leontes, must seem much older, as the result of his privations, when he reappears in v, i.

The most notorious stage tricks in *The Winter's Tale* are the culminating events of the play's two halves, the departure from the stage of Antigonus *pursued by a Beare* (III, iii, 58) and the re-entry to it of Hermione from the pedestal of her 'statue'. Apart from their placing, in the final scenes of Acts III and v, they have in common their unexpectedness (though Shakespeare scatters frequent premonitory and preparatory hints), their implausibility and their effect of at least reversing the emotional tone and direction of the scene, if not of effecting a larger shift of perspective. What each contributes to the action is by way of epilogue to a completed passage: the apparently gratuitous deaths of Antigonus and his crew remove a loose end of plotting and prevent any but a providential resolution of the plot, while the restoration of Hermione

[1] J. H. P. Pafford, in his note on IV, iv, 1 (p. 89), in the New Arden edition of *The Winter's Tale* (1963), argues persuasively for the view that these difficulties count for nothing in the theatre, where 'the flimsiest disguise is always a complete success'.

adds a deeper sense of emotional healing beyond the expected terms of the oracle's fulfilment. It is in keeping with the play's preoccupations, and with the increasing reliance on visual spectacle, especially of an emblematic kind, which can be discerned in Shakespeare's plays from *Macbeth* to *The Tempest* and *The Two Noble Kinsmen*, that on each occasion much is made of the evidence of the eyes. Both bear and statue are presented to the eyes of the audience: the Clown's narrative is reinforced by at least one glance off-stage, 'he's at it now' (III, iii, 102) and Paulina stresses to Leontes the importance of visual proof as she prepares him to accept the return of the statue to life as his wife. The bear is on stage very briefly, just long enough to effect the required modulation from the sombre mood of Antigonus's abandonment of Perdita to the jubilation of the Shepherd's finding of her. (No line in the play so invariably provokes happy laughter as the Shepherd's 'what haue we heere?' (III, iii, 64)). The statue is exposed to both audiences, on stage and off,[1] for nearly eighty lines of slow dialogue, all drawing ttention to it and enforcing speculation about what we are 'truly' seeing. Every likely speculation is answered in the lines, while the lapse of time is sufficient for second and third thoughts about the spectacle before us. Paulina's offers to draw the curtain again allow for the possibility that it is 'truly' a statue, while the responses of Leontes and Polixenes encourage the hope that this 'so much wrinckled' figure (v, iii, 28) is indeed Hermione.

In v, iii, as in the scene of her trial, Hermione may be, as Schanzer says, the visual focus, but in each case the progression of the scene is marked by the responses of Leontes to what is presented to him. In III, ii, he will neither see nor hear her truth to him. The spectacle of her weakness and public humiliation, which provoke a response from the silent attendant company, move him as little as her

eloquent defence. His conception of truth is distorted from 'All's true that is mistrusted' to the arrogant presumption of 'There is no truth at all i' th' Oracle' (III, ii, 137) and even his response to the first blow, the death of Mamillius, is selfish fear of Apollo's anger not compassion for Hermione. The news of her death, the third of the scene's mounting climaxes, is alone sufficient to turn him from futile self-reproof and helpless placatory gestures to a dawning sense of the results of his mad fever of jealousy and to the prospect of a hard repentance, imaged forth in Paulina's words,

> A thousand knees,
> Ten thousand yeares together, naked, fasting,
> Vpon a barren Mountaine, and still Winter
> In storme perpetuall,
>
> (207–10)

or of rapid decline and death. As the blindness and egocentricity of Leontes in III, ii obliterate Hermione, so his attentiveness to the statue becomes the sanction for its movement, and his first words of greeting, 'Oh she's warme' (v, iii, 109), signal not only the unfreezing of the cold stone but the successful end of a penitence for which a mere sixteen years have sufficed. One other resolution is effected in these words, which temper the heat of passion and the winter of penitence to a human warmth. In I, ii, the first hint of a difference, from which Leontes's jealousy will soon spring into being, is marked by Hermione's willing response to her husband's challenge to woo Polixenes to stay longer,

---

[1] The Folio stage direction at the start of viii reads '*Enter Leontes, Polixenes, Florizell, Perdita, Camillo, Paulina: Hermione (like a Statue:) Lords, &c.*' The final '*&c*' may mean no more than the '*attendants*' to which editors generally expand it, but could plausibly be extended to include all six characters from v, ii, who leave the stage with the evident intention of being present at the unveiling of 'the Queenes Picture' (168). The presence, in the background, of the Shepherd and Clown might even add force to Paulina's 'Least they desire (vpon this push) to trouble / Your ioyes, with like Relation' (v, iii, 129–30).

'you (Sir) / Charge him too coldly' (29–30): the jealousy itself explodes, in Leontes's first extended aside, with 'Too hot, too hot' (108).

Producers of *The Winter's Tale* may be well advised to take their hint from the text and arrange the action of parallel scenes in such a way that the audience is helped, by grouping, gesture or the placing of entrances and exits, to perceive, however unconsciously, the inter-relation of different parts of the play. On an unlocalized stage, the use of the same stage areas could reinforce the verbal and thematic associations between, say, I, i and IV, ii or III, i and v, ii. Visual hints should also be given, early in IV, iv, of that scene's constant allusion back to I, ii. Other pairs of associated scenes include II, iii and v, i. The narration in v, ii involves a complex of echoes of Act III, especially of scene iii, with its own narratives of Antigonus's dream and of his death. The allusions in the Autolycus scenes to parallel events in the main plot are more often in terms of contrast than of similarity and invite a less imitative use of the stage. The parallel between III, ii and v, iii requires visual expression, but the statue in v, iii also stands in an important relation to the bear in III, iii. A brief description of my staging of these crucial moments may illustrate one way of using visual means to reinforce a sense of the play's structure.

In III, iii, the entrance of the bear was in silhouette from up-stage centre and it moved slowly in on Autolycus, on its hind legs, down a stage-space narrowed by the partial closing, in funnel shape, of three sets of curtains. The same setting of the curtains to create a confined stage-space was used only for two other scenes: IV, i, for the choric speech of Time; and v, iii, where the statue, standing on a rostrum with steps in front of it, was at first concealed at centre stage behind the second set of curtains, then revealed in the distinctive perspective of the partly-drawn curtains. The revival of Hermione was accompanied by a very slow drawing-back of all three sets of curtains to leave the stage clear, a setting only previously used for the sheep-shearing feast at the opening of IV, iv. The return from the play's deepest emotions to the conventions of the comic stage, which is heralded by Hermione's questioning of Perdita about the means of her survival and confirmed by the offer of Camillo in marriage to Paulina, was visually realized by the final isolation of a small group of actors at the centre of the bare stage.

The clue of verbal parallel and echo in *The Winter's Tale* leads to the heart of no mystery but that of the imaginative focus and complexity of detail of Shakespeare's mature art. I have tried to suggest where the correspondences provoke thought about broader issues (of which the most interesting is, perhaps, the extent of the parallel hinted at between the two benign plotters, Camillo and Paulina), but I believe that the verbal net is woven as it is for other purposes than that of indicating thematic patterns. Shakespeare's means of unifying the two halves of this play, of persuading his audience that, for all their overt contrasts of mood, style, even genre, they are the symmetrical halves of a single whole, include the repetition in the second half of a substantial number of words and phrases already used in Act I to III, not always in significantly associated passages, so as to impart to the later acts, in almost musical manner, an underlying sense of familiarity, almost of recapitulation. That the process was in some degree a conscious one seems likely in the light of the whole play's emphasis on artifice as the means to the end of art, and of its final creation, in the statue scene, of a living emblem of the renaissance view of poetry as a 'speaking picture'.

© RICHARD PROUDFOOT 1976

SHAKESPEARE AND THE IDEAS OF HIS TIME[1]

J. W. LEVER

There is scarcely a work on Shakespeare which does not touch on what he thought, what his age thought, or on the relationship between the two. In the following pages only the more influential comments of the last fifty years on Elizabethan ideas of nature and supernature, politics and society, psychology and ethics, can be referred to; only in their broader aspects; and only so far as they bear directly on Shakespeare's mind and art.

A common fallacy would have it that Shakespeare studies in the late nineteenth and early twentieth century consisted mainly of sentimental biography, character-analysis and patriotic effusions on the history plays. In fact much of the groundwork for an understanding of Elizabethan thought was laid in this time. T. A. Spalding had distinguished in *Elizabethan Demonology*[2] the conflicting attitudes of the time to ghosts and supernatural manifestations. Edward Dowden's seminal essay 'Elizabethan Psychology'[3] clearly anatomised the 'little world of man'. In the political–historical field C. L. Kingsford traced the line of Tudor histories and their influence on Shakespeare.[4] Others had considered Shakespeare's possible debt to the advanced thinkers of the age. Edward Meyer's *Machiavelli and Elizabethan Drama*[5] concluded that the Shakespearian villain was based on popular travesties of a Machiavelli known only through Gentillet's distortions. (Much later, Mario Praz in his 1928 British Academy Lecture 'Machiavelli and the Elizabethans'[6] would establish that the

true Machiavelli was far from unknown in English intellectual circles; but he still questioned any influence upon Shakespeare.) Sensitive comparisons with Florio's Montaigne were drawn by Elizabeth R. Hooker,[7] claiming literary links but not an identity of attitudes. G. C. Taylor's better known *Shakspere's Debt to Montaigne*[8] with its parallel texts presented a more detailed but not more convincing case.

These studies took for granted a 'transcendent genius' in Shakespeare which eluded attempts to formulate his opinions. His treatment of the spirit world was said to draw its strength not from contemporary theories but from a dramatic evocation of mystery. It was denied that the history plays served any political or moralistic ends; W. D. Briggs indeed claimed in *Marlowe's 'Edward II'*[9] that they shadowed forth only 'a series of inexplicable catastrophic processes'. Perhaps he had in

---

[1] Circumstances over which we had no control have made it necessary to hold this article over from *Survey 28* where it properly belongs. – Editor.

[2] 1880.

[3] In *Essays Modern and Elizabethan* (1910).

[4] *English Historical Literature in the Sixteenth Century* (Oxford, 1913); *English Literature in the Fifteenth Century and the Historical Plays of Shakespeare* (Oxford, 1914).

[5] Weimar, 1897.

[6] Reprinted in *The Flaming Heart* (New York, 1958).

[7] 'The Relation of Shakespeare to Montaigne', *PMLA*, XVII (1902).

[8] Cambridge, Mass., 1925.

[9] 1914.

mind a touch of Senecan agnosticism; J. W. Cunliffe's *The Influence of Seneca on Elizabethan Tragedy*[1] had furnished a body of parallel texts. The repugnance to 'didactic' interpretations, inherited from the Romantics, continued well into the twenties, though there was now a growing readiness to admit Shakespeare's serious concern with the 'properties of government'. Yet J. A. R. Marriott in 'Shakespeare and Politics'[2] still held that the plays' essential interest lay in the fate of individuals, and though H. B. Charlton in 'Politics and Politicians'[3] viewed the histories as dramatisations of national issues, he saw them too as carrying the sceptical hint that 'unscrupulousness is an invaluable asset in the art of government'. In general Shakespeare emerged less as a spokesman for his own or other men's theories than as the conscious dramatist drawing attitudes and opinions into the magnetic field of characters in action. Even Sir Mark Hunter's 1929 essay 'Politics and Character in Shakespeare's Julius Caesar'[4] was no clear exception. Hunter made Shakespeare into a kind of Elizabethan Tory, equating Caesar with the monarchy, the tribunes with trade unionists, and the conspirators with Liberals or worse. Yet he too acknowledged Shakespeare's marvellous empathy and 'divine humanity'. Guy Boas in 'Shakespeare and Christianity'[5] found a similar benignity governing Shakespeare's religious outlook. None of his major characters was committed to a distinctive doctrine. Instead there was a broad 'Christian emphasis' on the virtues of innocence and suffering, charity and compassion. Eschatology was left a mystery beyond the range of secular drama; so too were fine points of dogma. Need this mean that Shakespeare had no religion? Only if religion were made into 'a very narrow thing...a very different thing from what Christ intended it to be'.

Such affirmations and denials had long received general support; but a harsher climate of opinion was setting in. Talk of a 'divine humanity' or a 'Christian emphasis' was giving way to a demand for doctrinal rigour. T. S. Eliot's 'Shakespeare and the Stoicism of Seneca' (1927)[6] sounded the attack on what he saw as the confusion of Renaissance values and Shakespearian standards. Eliot himself was deeply divided between the newfound appeal of Thomist theology, with its structure of formal logic, and his own poetic sensibility. His solution was to reject the validity of the imagination as an instrument of knowledge and to view poetry as the outcome of a kind of higher 'emotion'. Against it was set 'thought ...orderly and strong and beautiful', as manifested in the system of Aquinas and informing the epic of Dante. Shakespeare, alas, could only work through 'the mixed and muddled scepticism of the Renaissance', whose models were Seneca, Machiavelli and Montaigne. Hence the lamentable 'aesthetic' stance of his heroes, notably Othello, whose self-assertion in the face of damnation amounted to an absurd attempt at 'cheering himself up'.

In this recoil from secular humanism Eliot reflected a widespread attitude amongst intellectuals of his generation. Alienated from the debased values of bourgeois society, fearful of radical change, many took refuge in scholasticism and visions of an ideal hierarchical order. Eliot's strictures against Renaissance scepticism, however, were based on impressions formed from nineteenth-century historians. The newer trend of his time was to minimise the significance of the Renaissance as a distinctive culture, to stress its continuity with the middle ages, and to explain any strains of

[1] New York, 1893.

[2] *Cornhill Magazine* 1927.

[3] *Essays of the English Association*, 1929.

[4] *Essays by Divers Hands*, Royal Society of Literature, London, 1931.

[5] *The Shakespeare Review*, Stratford-upon-Avon, 1928.

[6] In *Selected Essays* (1932).

scepticism as a kind of incipient 'modernism' or even 'Counter-Renaissance'. Hence it became possible to reconsider Shakespeare and his fellow-Elizabethans as authentic voices of the old tradition. Willard Farnham in *The Medieval Heritage of Elizabethan Tragedy*[1] invented a genre of 'Gothic tragedy' sprung from the *de casibus* monologues of the *Mirror for Magistrates*, where originally Senecan concepts of 'a world of inherent disorder' were replaced by the 'divine order' of retributive justice. Shakespeare, though aware of 'deeper ethical difficulties', was thought to have followed this formula. Howard Baker's *Induction to Tragedy*[2] sought explicitly to deny Seneca's influence, mainly by showing that verbal parallels might be derived from medieval or classical adages. Alice Harmon likewise explained away G. C. Taylor's comparisons by pointing to common traditional sources for both writers.[3] Scholarship of this kind had a limited validity: earlier critics had too often ignored the universal practice of imitation. But it was equally at fault in disregarding the special qualities of vision in the outstanding minds of the age. Whether Shakespeare borrowed this or that phrase from Montaigne mattered less than that he shared Montaigne's readiness to question received ideas and human pretensions. Seneca's Roman awareness of man's predicament in the face of cosmic and political terror voiced the apprehensions of sixteenth-century Europe in an era of church and state despotism; to deny to Shakespeare any response to such awareness was to insulate him from his time. Hardin Craig did indeed point out the profoundly Senecan spirit in Shakespeare's tragedies.[4] But such recognition was rare amongst scholars out to recast his drama in a 'Gothic' mould.

Meanwhile the work of refurbishment went on. C. J. Sisson in 'The Mythical Sorrows of Shakespeare'[5] scoffed at the Romantic view – shared by Eliot – of a Shakespeare who pro-

jected his 'emotional' problems as tragedy, and took the opportunity to suggest a writer well content with his career and his times. In '*Measure for Measure* and the Jacobean Shakespeare'[6] R. W. Chambers with a persuasive rhetoric presented this play not as a product of Jacobean disillusion, but a wholesome parable of spiritual dedication and royal sagacity set in the mainstream of high Anglicanism. In more general terms Douglas Bush's *The Renaissance and English Humanism*[7] ridiculed the outmoded concept of a liberal-minded Renaissance and placed Shakespeare securely in an Elizabethan milieu that revered 'constituted authority', scorned the mob, and served the established political and religious order.

A more rigorous kind of historicism, cultivated mainly in the United States, had proceeded from similar assumptions since the nineteen-twenties. Shakespeare, it was held, could only be truly understood in terms of the accepted ideas of his age, only appreciated through the responses of the average Elizabethan play-goer. Since character-creation was still seen as Shakespeare's greatest accomplishment, intensive research was devoted to contemporary psychological beliefs. Murray W. Bundy's 'Shakespeare and Elizabethan Psychology'[8] examined persistent 'ethical ideas' as stated by Charron, Huarte and others. Their insistence on the need for reason to rule the passions was taken as the key to Shakespearian tragedy. Not the modern idea of self-realisation, but the traditional aim of self-knowledge, was

[1] Berkeley, Cal., 1936.
[2] Louisiana, 1939.
[3] 'How Great Was Shakespeare's Debt to Montaigne?', *PMLA*, LVII (1942).
[4] 'The Shackling of Accidents', *Philological Quarterly*, XIX (1940).
[5] *Proceedings of the British Academy*, 1935.
[6] *Proceedings of the British Academy*, 1938; reprinted in *Man's Unconquerable Mind* (1939).
[7] Toronto, 1939.
[8] *Journal of English and Germanic Philology*, XXIII (1924).

said to underlie the treatment of character, especially of the typical tragic hero. Hardin Craig reached similar conclusions in 'The Ethics of *King Lear*' and 'Shakespeare's Depiction of the Passions'.[1] For Shakespeare, Craig declared, 'passion was the general name for the enemy in the human heart'. His pupil Ruth L. Anderson developed the argument in her erudite monograph *Elizabethan Psychology and Shakespeare's Plays*,[2] a conspectus of the main writings of the age on the working of the passions, the co-ordination of reason and the senses, the detailed symptoms of jealousy and villainous intent. Like Bundy, Anderson made no claim that Shakespeare's drama was didactic or that he merely repeated set descriptions. Her object, she concluded, had been solely 'to point out the extent to which his characters embody contemporary thought, and their greater reality when we know them as did the Elizabethans'. The claim was modest, yet not altogether beyond challenge. Did Shakespeare's characters indeed 'embody contemporary thought' rather than a universal vision expressed in Elizabethan idiom? Did his villains or jealous men assume greater 'reality' when their passions were diagnosed according to the treatises? Did the traditional standards of reason and 'measure' govern audience responses to Antony and Hamlet? Was self-knowledge indeed the end-product of tragic experience in Shakespeare, 'self-realisation' only an Ibsenist heresy?

Such questions seem hardly to have occurred to Lily B. Campbell. *Shakespeare's Tragic Heroes: Slaves of Passion*[3] concentrated on Bradley's Big Four, whose ruling passions were carefully analysed 'in accordance with the medical and philosophical teaching of the period'. More than half the book was taken up with accounts of 'fundamental ideas held by Shakespeare in common with the best philosophical thinkers of his generation' – such as La Primaudaye, Charron, Bright and others.

The tragedies were classified as treatments of Grief (*Hamlet*), Jealousy (*Othello*), Wrath in Old Age (*King Lear*), and Fear (*Macbeth*). Some complexity was allowed for: thus Hamlet, though sanguine by complexion, suffered from adust melancholy. Othello's jealousy was a compound of envy and grief. Renaissance philosophy became a digest of commonplaces, tragedy a set of case-studies.

Others followed the psychological approach with rather more caution. Mary I. O'Sullivan[4] dwelt on the influence of Bright's *Treatise of Melancholie*, but declined to sum up Hamlet as a 'mental invalid'. His character was 'unified by the qualities of the melancholy man', yet had 'the glamor of Shakespeare's language, of youth and royalty'. J. Dover Wilson in *What Happens in Hamlet?*[5] also discussed contemporary theories of melancholy, but stressed Hamlet's uniqueness. Yet the idea of Shakespeare's tragedies as object-lessons in psychological ethics died hard. Lawrence Babb in *The Elizabethan Malady*[6] again fixed Hamlet in the category of the melancholy malcontent. Elizabethan audiences would have had no difficulty in diagnosing his case. 'Quickly and confidently' they would recognize the symptoms and perceive his tragic plight, 'because he had become passion's slave, because he had failed to master his grief'. Slaves of passion and their confident spectators were still prominent in Franklin Dickey's *Not Wisely But Too Well*,[7] which extended Campbell's analyses to *Romeo and Juliet*, *Troilus and Cressida*, and *Antony and Cleopatra*. The protagonists were all weighed and found wanting. Elizabethan audiences would deplore or despise their passion-driven weaknesses, and not, like

[1] *Philological Quarterly*, IV (1925).
[2] *Iowa Studies*, 1927.
[3] Cambridge, 1930.
[4] 'Hamlet and Dr Timothy Bright', *PMLA*, XLI (1926).   [5] Cambridge, 1935.
[6] Michigan, 1951.   [7] San Marino, 1957.

modern 'neo-Hegelians', indulge them. Yet not only 'neo-Hegelians' but some Christian critics too protested against the attitudes of the school of Campbell. 'The great dramatist', wrote Irving Ribner in his review of Dickey's book,[1] 'subjects the doctrines of his age to imaginative exploration, exposes their antitheses...the plays are based not upon outmoded ideas garnered from obsolete treatises, but upon a great artist's conscious ordering of the human life which he himself observes'.

More allowance was made for 'imaginative exploration' in studies of Shakespeare's spirit world. N. S. Bushnell's 'Natural Supernaturalism in *The Tempest*'[2] noted how a sense of the supernatural was mainly conveyed through manifestations of natural forces: not the miraculous as such, but the marvels in life on earth and human experience were the play's major concerns. Dover Wilson came to rather similar conclusions about the effect of the Ghost in *Hamlet*. In *What Happens in Hamlet?* he repeated Spalding's account of conflicting attitudes to spectres, and saw Shakespeare as concerned with setting his audience a problem. Madeleine Doran in 'That Undiscovered Country'[3] allowed for the complexity, even confusion, of sixteenth-century attitudes to the supernatural. Responses might vary from total acceptance to a qualified admission of possibility: hence in *Hamlet* and *Macbeth* what might be doubted in fact could still be accepted as fiction. Primarily the plays worked by suggestion, arousing universal apprehensions of wonder. Most ambitious of studies in this field was W. C. Curry's *Shakespeare's Philosophical Patterns*.[4] Instead of scanning popular treatises, Curry set *Macbeth* and *The Tempest* in the two main streams of Western thought, Scholasticism and Neoplatonism. Shakespeare, he claimed, had a 'comfortable and accurate knowledge' of the rudiments of both, and integrated the plays through patterns of cosmology drawn from each. Thus *Macbeth*

presented in Thomistic terms the demonic forces active in the universe and the soul, while *The Tempest* dramatised Neoplatonist concepts of the daemonic, essentially pantheistic forces of nature. Curry's expositions were lucid and often enlightening, though his approach to each play as 'a unique world' left unexplained the adoption of mutually irreconcilable systems as the frameworks of two major dramas. Nor were the primordial horror and violence of *Macbeth*, the resplendent and dissolving visions of *The Tempest*, quite tidied away by medieval demonology or quasi-pagan theurgy. Perhaps Curry's most stimulating comments were on Renaissance philosophy seen as 'in its own right a sort of poetry', absorbed by writers of the age as a 'second nature'. Such perceptions pointed the way towards new, fruitful correlations of intellect and creativity in Shakespeare's art.

But it was Shakespeare's politics that received most scholarly attention during the years that culminated in the second world war. In no other field of thought was his conformity to received ideas so often proclaimed, or his 'fixed' and 'consistent' beliefs so confidently declared. They were to be found, according to J. E. Phillips Jr, epitomised in three *topoi*: Canterbury's speech on obedience in *Henry V*, Ulysses' oration on 'the specialty of rule' in *Troilus and Cressida*, and Menenius' parable of the belly in *Coriolanus*, together making up 'a well-rounded and well-developed theory'. *The State in Shakespeare's Greek and Roman Plays*[5] followed a now widely accepted structure. More than half of its contents were given to a closely knit exposition of sixteenth-century absolutist doctrine. Order and degree, obedience to rulers, contempt for the populace

[1] *Journal of English and Germanic Philology*, LVII (1958).   [2] *PMLA*, XLVII (1932).
[3] In *Renaissance Studies in Honor of Hardin Craig*, ed. B. Maxwell and Others (Iowa, 1941).
[4] Baton Rouge, 1937.   [5] New York, 1940.

as a political factor, were taken as the triple pillar of the Renaissance state. The rest of the book was a cursory survey of two 'Greek' plays (*Troilus* and *Timon*) and the three mature Roman tragedies seen as Shakespeare's expositions of orthodoxy. Thus *Julius Caesar* demonstrated the benefits of monarchy and 'the evils of multiple sovereignty'; *Antony and Cleopatra* 'the inevitable restoration of monarchy in the process of elimination which singles out the man naturally qualified'. Drama inhered in the tragic or satiric spectacle of 'slaves of passion' unable to conform with universal laws of political or social conduct'.

Attention centred, however, on the plays of English history. These were no longer thought to depict 'inexplicable catastrophic processes' or to reflect scepticism about the ways of politicians, but seen rather as advocacies of official views. Alfred Hart's *Shakespeare and the Homilies*[1] referred to the compulsory reading in churches, during the years of Shakespeare's boyhood, of the government-inspired sermons *On Obedience* and *On Obedience and Wilful Rebellion*. A series of articles by Lucille King, Edleen Begg, and W. Gordon Zeeveld[2] stressed the influence on the Histories of Hall's Chronicle, which was said to interpret the dynastic wars as God's retribution for Bolingbroke's sinful usurpation, and the triumph of the Tudors as the mark of divine forgiveness. These studies paved the way for E. M. W. Tillyard's vastly influential *Shakespeare's History Plays*.[3] Here the 'Tudor Myth' was taken to be the informing theme of the Histories, which traced a grand epic design, sustained through two tetralogies, that brought together the teachings of the Homilies, the punitive morality of the *Mirror for Magistrates*, and, above all, 'Hall's master-theme, the working out of destiny over the stretch of history from Richard II to the Tudors'. Tillyard's gift for bland exposition made his book more celebrated than the prim, more erudite work of

Phillips, but glossed over many anomalies. Apart from an introductory flourish meant to catch the eye of Henry VIII, the body of Hall's Chronicle was in fact little more than a compilation of earlier annals, with no theory of history beyond a vaguely biblical pattern of divine tit-for-tat. The *Mirror* knew nothing of the Tudor Myth, nor did it feature in the Homilies. Hart himself had vividly described the social context of these sermons, whereby a parvenu despotism sought to bolster itself against a resentful older nobility and a turbulent populace. Thus, despite the book's elaborate 'background of ideas', Shakespeare's theory of history could only be inferred from the actual plays. Yet in his account of these Tillyard increasingly faltered. In Part 3 of *Henry VI* he found Shakespeare already 'tired by his grim and long fidelity to Hall's pattern'. *Richard III* was 'a confused affair' that lost track of preceding events. The *Henry IV* plays were hurriedly surveyed, with apologies for the nationalist fervour of *Henry V*, the unmistakable climax of the 'tetralogy'. Only a few glances were cast at the great comic role of Falstaff, whose rejection, it was said, the Elizabethans would well understand. Their England, like that of 1944, would spare no sympathy for scoffers of official values. Throughout the work, indeed, it was these values, and Shakespeare's 'official self', that Tillyard chiefly prized.

Shakespeare's History Plays became prescribed reading for a generation of students. Ribner's *The English History Play in the Age of Shakespeare*[4] broadly supported its premises;

---

[1] Melbourne, 1934.
[2] 'The Use of Hall's Chronicles in the Folio and Quarto Texts of Henry VI', *Philological Quarterly*, XIII (1934), 'Shakespeare's Debt to Hall and to Holinshed in *Richard III*', *Studies in Philology*, XXXII (1935), 'The Influence of Hall on Shakespeare's English Historical Plays,' *ELH*, III (1936).
[3] Cambridge, 1944.
[4] Princeton, 1957.

M. M. Reese in *The Cease of Majesty*[1] amplified the interpretation with a scene-by-scene analysis. Lily Campbell's *Shakespeare's 'Histories': Mirrors of Elizabethan Policy*[2] was a horse of the same stable, though differently coloured. Shakespeare's interpretation of English history was seen here as an application of the words of the Second Commandment, 'visiting the iniquity of the fathers upon the children unto the third and fourth generation'. The Histories thus followed a recurrent cycle of sin and retribution rather than traced the drawn-out consequences of a single deed. The usurper was avenged in his third heir, through another usurper, again avenged in the third heir. The cycle continued into Elizabeth's reign, with effects dramatised by Shakespeare through covert historical parallels which the audience (though not the censorship) would easily recognize. Accordingly the Histories were to be construed as 'mirrors of policy', commenting on the present in terms of the past.

Two important wartime books attempted a wider synthesis of ideas. Tillyard's *The Elizabethan World Picture*[3] was deeply indebted to Arthur O. Lovejoy's *The Great Chain of Being*,[4] which traced the ideas of cosmic plenitude and gradation from Plato to the Romantics. But what emerged in the middle ages as a manifestation of universal *caritas*, bound by infinite links of duty and interdependence, became for Tillyard a symmetrical design whose natural or metaphysical aspects served mainly to justify the social–political *status quo*. Suitable quotations were provided, from Fortescue, Elyot, Hooker and others, with Ulysses's speech on 'the specialty of rule' as the chief Shakespearian exhibit. Nothing was said of Fortescue's staunch parliamentarianism, Hooker's theory of kingship by consent, or the disparity between Ulysses's avouched principles and his devious practice. Nevertheless this reduction of 'Elizabethen thought' to an elementary chart of parallel planes appealed to most lovers of simple solutions. By comparison, Theodore Spencer's *Shakespeare and the Nature of Man*[5] was more subtle and less schematic. Traditional ideas were set forth with lucidity and learning, but their antitheses in Renaissance thought were allowed full weight. The 'ideal picture' was offset by the questionings of Copernicus, Machiavelli and Montaigne. From this interplay of 'theoretical good' and 'evil fact', universal pattern and its far-reaching negation, the intellectual preconditions for tragedy were seen to emerge. Shakespeare, Spencer affirmed, projected the interplay mainly through his characters, who mirrored in their souls the oppositions between appearance and reality, the actual and ideal. Thus Richard II was torn between his sacrosanct self-image and its nullification by the forces of history; Troilus between his vision of Cressida and Cressida in life. From such treatments of inner conflict evolved the tragic experience of an Othello and a Lear.

Spencer's acceptance of opposed principles as the dynamic of Shakespearian tragedy was a long stride away from the ready-made constructs which had turned the plays into enunciations of received ideas. There remained a perhaps too strict dichotomy between the 'optimistic' view of nature and man, supposedly typical of the middle ages, and the 'pessimism' induced by that trio of Renaissance wicked uncles, Copernicus, Machiavelli and Montaigne.[6] Guilt and original sin were not unknown to the medieval past, and the belief in man's excellence and limitless powers was very much a sixteenth-century tenet. Hiram Haydn's *The Counter-Renaissance*[7] took these

[1] 1961. [2] San Marino, 1947.
[3] 1943. [4] Cambridge, Mass., 1936.
[5] Cambridge, Mass., 1942.
[6] Ribner's *Patterns in Shakespearean Tragedy* (1960), was more sternly moralistic, viewing the tragedies as 'affirmations' against the currents of scepticism. [7] New York, 1950.

complexities into account in his detailed study of the main currents of Renaissance thought. Despite the title reflecting contemporary fashion, and some disparaging comments on the period's 'wasteland character of skepticism and uncertainty...between two highly confident and secure world-views', this long but consistently readable book offered an admirably comprehensive survey.

Spencer's opposed world-views had a special relevance in the immediate post-war years, when parallels with recent experience could hardly be missed. Edwin Muir's 1946 Ker Memorial Lecture 'The Politics of *King Lear*'[1] viewed the tragedy as grounded on 'two conceptions of history'. Lear himself embodied 'a civilization of legendary antiquity ...destroyed by...a perfectly up-to-date gang of Renaissance adventurers', whose ideology had its modern counterpart in Fascism. J. F. Danby developed the contrast with some modifications. *Shakespeare's Doctrine of Nature in 'King Lear'*[2] ranged the characters in two 'parties' representing opposed concepts of Nature: that of tradition and Hooker, with its network of reciprocal charities, and the modern, 'Hobbesian' Nature of competition and strife. After making these points the argument took a pietistic turn, with Cordelia seen as a Christ-figure, allegorised in a drama 'at least as Christian as the *Divine Comedy*'.[3] Here Danby allied himself with a doctrinal school to be returned to later. Significantly, the wheel of Eliot's comparison between Dante and Shakespeare had come almost full circle.

'Historical criticism' reached its peak of influence during the second world war; its gradual decline would proceed through the fifties and sixties. *Shakespeare's Use of Learning* by Virgil K. Whitaker[4] was indicative of the change. Much of this lengthy book was an endorsement of 'order and degree' attitudes. Absolutist politics, Aristotelean ethics, the medieval world order and traditional natural law were taken as the underlying doctrines of Shakespearian drama. This was familiar ground; but in the detailed evaluation some important divergencies cropped up. Divine right, Whitaker noted, appeared only sporadically in the earlier Histories, and was most clearly invoked by the weak Richard II and the infamous Richard III: might this not suggest a latent scepticism? Providential history was perhaps the key to Richard III, but the high points of the drama – the chorus of queens, the ghosts on the eve of Bosworth – struck a distinctly Senecan note. The 'simple fact' remained, that 'Shakespeare's mind was on character and dramatic effect'. Hence the choice of the republican Brutus as a tragic hero; hence the anomalous Ghost in *Hamlet*, by Protestant reckoning a deception of the devil, who yet revealed the play's truth. Dover Wilson too, a 'world order' critic who had reduced Falstaff to a mere foil for the official virtues of the Prince, revised many of his views in his 'New Shakespeare' editions of *Julius Caesar* and *Richard III*.[5] A long line of classical historians and Renaissance dramatists, Wilson noted, had presented Caesar as the arch-tyrant, Brutus and Cassius as liberators: following them, Shakespeare made Caesar the 'universal dictator', a type only too well known in his age and ours. The political experience of Renaissance Europe was also seen at work in *Richard III*, whose dramatic core was not providential history but the character of Richard, suggested by More's description, in turn modelled upon the reputation of the Borgias. It might seem that the 'historical criticism' of the past twenty years had ignored a great part of relevant history.

---

[1] Glasgow, 1946.   [2] 1949.
[3] Cf. R. W. Chambers: '*King Lear* is like the *Paradiso*, a vast poem on the victory of true love' (*King Lear*, Glasgow, 1940).
[4] San Marino, 1953.
[5] Cambridge, 1949 and 1954.

Schematic interpretations came increasingly under fire. Alfred Harbage in *As They Liked It*[1] suggested that Elizabethan audiences responded to the plays rather as 'foci of a quickened moral interest' than as vehicles of accepted ideas. Scholarly attempts to apply rigid frames of reference only revealed 'an imperfect correspondence, a hiatus, between the play and the scholar's explication'. In *The Dream of Learning*, D. G. James[2] stressed the 'particularity' of both Bacon's and Shakespeare's approaches. Instead of a scientific quest, Shakespeare explored experience through the imagination, a faculty which functioned 'with all the impersonality, the bleak labour of discovery, which animates the scientist or the philsopher'. Implicitly James was affirming the guidelines of Coleridge, discarded by Eliot, and returning to the concept of poetry as an autonomous pursuit of truth. 'Particularity' might sum up Robert Speaight's attitude in his 1946 Wedmore Lecture 'Shakespeare and Politics'.[3] Essentially, he declared, Shakespeare's view was that 'while all men need government, no man is fit to govern'. Politics depended not on principles but on the man; only through faith, humility and discipline might man at last become 'pure enough for power'. L. C. Knights in two papers, 'On Historical Scholarship' and 'Shakespeare's Politics',[4] likewise opposed schematic concepts and took the individual as Shakespeare's touchstone of values. Nowhere in the mature plays were the abstract and general allowed to obscure the personal and specific. *Julius Caesar* exposed 'the contradictions and illusions involved in political action'; in *Troilus and Cressida* order and authority as *a priori* concepts were dissolved; *King Lear* and *Coriolanus* exalted the organic community of particular persons above power politics. Essentially Shakespeare's political thought was 'a challenge to become imaginatively alive'. In *Angel with Horns*,[5] comprising lectures of the early fifties,

A. P. Rossiter assailed the idea that the Tudor Myth' was the shaping principle of the history plays. He noted the paradoxical, ironic technique of *Richard III*, with its 'constant inversions', 'verbal capsizings' and 'reversals to the opposite', most clearly apparent in the character of Richard himself. Activating Shakespeare's drama was a dialectic that subsumed opposed values, thus affording 'the exact correlatives of both the nature of man...and of the nature of events'. Nature was the theme of Geoffrey Bush, who also refused to believe that Elyot's and Hooker's world order lay at the basis of Shakespeare's thought. In *Shakespeare and the Natural Condition*[6] he described *Hamlet* and *King Lear* as 'pictures of natural disorder', serving as an integral component of dramatic vision. Through his protagonists Shakespeare held in focus the dual aspects of nature, both as an unchanging principle, *natura naturans*, and as *natura naturata*, the ever-changing self-contradictory face of life. J. P. Brockbank found 'pictures of natural disorder' as far back as the early histories. In 'The Frame of Disorder: *Henry VI*'[7] he summed up their theme as 'the paradoxical plight of moral man under the rule of historical and political processes'. Not the simple-minded pieties of the *Mirror for Magistrates*, but Seneca's grim vision in *Thyestes* and *Troades* provided their underlying inspiration.

The retreat from historicist attitudes went on through the next decade. In the compressed first chapter of *The Moral Vision of Jacobean Tragedy*[8] Robert Ornstein pointed out that

[1] Cambridge, Mass., 1947.
[2] Oxford, 1951.
[3] Royal Society of Literature (1946).
[4] *Sewanee Review*, LXIII (1955), and *Proceedings of the British Academy* (1957), printed in *Further Explorations* (1965).
[5] Ed. by Graham Storey (1961).
[6] Cambridge, Mass., 1956.
[7] *Stratford-upon-Avon Studies*, III (1961).
[8] Madison, Wisconsin, 1960.

'the most vital and stimulating ideas of any age are often the uncommon ones'. Machiavelli and Montaigne were 'the intellectual offspring as well as the intellectual rebels of their age', pioneers of 'the ever-increasing desire to study the purely human world'. S. C. Sen Gupta offered pungent comments on the views of Tillyard, Lily Campbell and others,[1] while A. C. Hamilton denied any moral didacticism in *Henry VI* and found the 'providential' view of history 'expressed only negatively by its inversion'.[2] H. A. Kelly subjected the Tillyard and Campbell theses to close scrutiny, concluding that 'Shakespeare's great contribution was to unsynthesize the syntheses of his contemporaries and to unmoralize their moralizations'.[3] In his essay 'Put Away the World Picture'[4] Herbert Howarth wrote a virtual epitaph to 'the Order and Chain exegesis' which for too long, he felt, had perverted the normal, human responses of teachers and students. It was time to cease applying a supposedly historical interpretation which falsified both Shakespeare and his age. The spirit of questioning was as active amongst the Elizabethans as it is now, and at its most alert in Shakespeare. Rather it was Tillyard who, dismayed at the uncertainties of the inter-war years, had 'wished on Shakespeare his own passion for order'.

A comparable passion for metaphysical assurance may explain the rise in the forties and fifties of a new school of Shakespearian exegesis, which reads the plays as repositories of Christian doctrine. That Shakespeare knew his Bible well was beyond dispute, and clearly shown in the numerous echoes listed by Richmond Noble.[5] It was plain, too, that his ethical values were deeply suffused with Christian conception of mercy and love. But a tighter, more dogmatic theology was now in demand. Like the historical critics, the doctrinal school invoked a hypothetical Elizabethan audience, nourished on sermons and tracts, wedded to the genre of the morality play. But historical assumptions were less in regard than a kind of typology that valued Shakespeare's dramas mainly as texts affording cryptic allusions to biblical truth. Hence characters were construed as archetypes, dramatic situations as parables, comic or tragic resolutions as tokens of redemption or damnation. The pioneer of this approach was not, as sometimes claimed, Wilson Knight, whose highly individual estimates of Shakespeare as a Christian artist generally eschewed doctrinal categories, but more probably Hardin Craig, who in 'The Ethics of *King Lear*' had proclaimed Shakespeare's 'thoroughgoing and interpretative conformity' to the theology of Aquinas and Hooker. Kenneth O. Myrick in 'The Theme of Damnation in Shakespearean Tragedy'[6] traced patterns of diabolical temptation in *Hamlet*, *Macbeth* and *Othello*. In each play the hero was tempted to deadly sin and damned like Faustus when he succumbed (Hamlet fortunately escaped his mouse-trap). A spate of articles and some book-length studies followed,[7] establishing to their authors' satisfaction the salvation of Lear, the damnation of Othello and sometimes of Romeo and Juliet, the identification as Christ-figures of heroines

[1] In *Shakespeare's Historical Plays* (Oxford, 1964).
[2] *The Early Shakespeare* (San Marino, Calif., 1967).
[3] *Divine Providence in the England of Shakespeare's Histories* (Cambridge, Mass.), 1970.
[4] In *The Tiger's Heart* (1970).
[5] *Shakespeare's Use of the Bible* (1935).
[6] *Studies in Philology*, XXXVIII (1941).
[7] Including O. J. Campbell, 'The Salvation of Lear', *ELH* 15 (1948), Nevill Coghill, 'The Basis of Shakespearean Comedy', *Essays and Studies*, III (1950), and 'Comic Form in *Measure for Measure*', *Shakespeare Survey 8* (Cambridge, 1955); S. L. Bethell, 'Shakespeare's Imagery: The Diabolic Images in *Othello*', *Shakespeare Survey 5* (Cambridge, 1952); Paul N. Siegel, 'The Damnation of Othello', *PMLA*, LXVIII (1953); and *Shakespearean Tragedy and the Elizabethan Compromise* (New York, 1957), J. A. Bryant Jr, *Hippolyta's View* (Kentucky, 1961); R. W. Battenhouse, *Shakespearean Tragedy: Its Art and Its Christian Premises* (Indiana, 1969) (based on earlier essays).

as diverse as Portia, Isabella, Desdemona and Cordelia, or, as Satan-figures, villains as various as Shylock, Lucio, Iago, Goneril and Regan. The epithets 'angel', 'devil', 'hell', 'heaven', were literally construed, and mention of swords, hanging, tears, blood, wine, allegorised as allusions to Gethsemane, Calvary or the Last Supper. Where the dramatic context was too flagrantly at odds with such constructions, 'disjunctive analogies' were found: Shakespeare with more than scholastic subtlety denoted likeness by unlikeness, *lucus a non lucendo*.

Such attitudes did not, of course, pass unchallenged. Clifford Leech in *Shakespeare's Tragedies*[1] and James in *The Dream of Learning* had staunchly affirmed Shakespeare's imaginative secularity. Sylvan Barnet in 'Some Limitations of a Christian Approach to Shakespeare'[2] noted that doctrinal approaches 'invariably cramp the meanings of the great plays and end with a saved hero or a damned hero rather than a tragic man'. Eschatology as applied to *King Lear*, for some the ark of Shakespeare's secular covenant, drew strong protests. Barbara Everett in 'The New *King Lear*'[3] rejected the conversion of a stark tragedy into a soothing morality: the play made its awesome impact by a yoking of 'intense physical awareness' to 'apprehension of nothingness'; intellectually it stood closer to the antinomies of Montaigne and Pascal than to the naïveties of medieval drama. Judah Stampfer's 'The Catharsis of *King Lear*'[4] and Nicholas Brooke's 'The Ending of *King Lear*'[5] found no peace of redemption but rather a state of universal disorder with intimations that man inhabited an imbecile universe. W. R. Elton in '*King Lear*' and the Gods[6] took into account the wide range of religious, anti-religious, sceptical and superstitious attitudes in the play, which he saw as interacting in an 'overall dramatic dialectic'. Robert H. West's *Shakespeare and the Outer Mystery*[7] included earlier articles on

Othello and *King Lear* which struck out at the more extreme sophistries of the 'doctrinal' critics. Less successfully, R. M. Frye had attempted a frontal attack on all the premises of what he chose to call 'the school of Knight'. *Shakespeare and Christian Doctrine*[8] brought angry, perhaps merited rejoinders from Knight and Ribner[9] – a 'Christian' critic whose moralistic bent was generally balanced by sound scholarship – for its rather jaunty tone of overall dismissal. But the trend of opinion was shifting decisively against doctrinal as well as political schematism. Wilbur Sanders in *The Dramatist and the Received Idea*[10] voiced the accumulated objections to both with some surface harshness and a genuine underlying sensibility; but for all his zealous forays against the establishment enemy, the main battle had already been fought.

As the dust settled from these conflicts, a transformed conception of Shakespeare's creative processes was beginning to take shape. In important respects it was a return to the intuitive outlook of the early years of the century. Shakespeare's humanism, his freedom from dogmas, his inherently dramatic approach, were again being affirmed. But in the rejection of a blinkered historicism some more definitive insights had been gained. With differences in terminology and stress, Rossiter, Geoffrey Bush, Everett and Elton had grasped a latent dualism, an acceptance of multiple oppositions and polarities, at the roots of Shakespeare's response to thought and experience. Marion B. Smith's *Dualities in Shakespeare*[11] and Norman

---

[1] 1950.   [2] *ELH*, 22 (1955)
[3] *Critical Quarterly*, II (1960).
[4] *Shakespeare Survey 13* (Cambridge, 1960).
[5] In *Shakespeare 1564–1964*, ed. E. A. Bloom (Providence, 1964).   [6] San Marino, 1966.
[7] Kentucky, 1968.   [8] Princeton, 1963.
[9] *Essays in Criticism*, XV (1965), repr. in *Shakespeare and Religion* (1967), *Tulane Drama Review*, X (1966).   [10] Cambridge, 1968.
[11] Toronto, 1966.

Rabkin's *Shakespeare and the Common Under-standing*[1] developed these insights into sustained expositions. In *Something of Great Constancy*[2] and *The Heart's Forest*[3] David A. Young pointed out many of the antitheses on which the comedies stood – a wide tract of drama almost ignored by the schematists.

This approach has an obvious contemporary appeal in an age of Marxism and existentialism: might it not prove to be yet another case of 'wishing on Shakespeare', this time a leaning to contraries and ambivalence? But there was confirmation in assessments of Elizabethan ideas by a newer school of historians and political theorists. Morris, Hill, Trevor-Roper, Hurstfield and Stone were pointing out the inherent duality of attitudes towards absolutism and the social hierarchy, stemming from conflicts endemic in the age. David Bevington's *Tudor Drama and Politics*[4] traced the reflections of social strife and political dissent through sixteenth-century drama. A sheaf of essays suitably entitled *Shakespeare in a Changing World*[5] brought together critical opinions from distinguished scholars of the left, both British and European. Amongst these, Zdenek Stríbrny's article found that Shakespeare's thought fused 'the advanced social thinking of the sixteenth-century European humanists...with the attitudes and feelings of the English people'. Robert Weimann saw in Shakespearian drama 'a living tradition of popular culture' promoting perspectives 'never outside history, but...beyond the historical conditions that made them possible'. Kenneth Muir, writing on Shakespeare's politics, noted the inadequacy of the older historicist accounts and the dialectic of his attitudes to order and authority, especially in the later plays. Meanwhile other studies had brought out the positive side of Machiavelli's teachings. Ribner's 'Bolingbroke, A True Machiavellian',[6] Felix Raab's *The English Face of Machiavelli*,[7] and A. D. Nuttall's '*Measure for Measure*:

Quid pro Quo?'[8] presented Machiavellian ideas not as a kind of subversive 'modernism' but as an integral part of the theory and practice of the age. Shakespeare's political drama focused the conflicting actualities of the Renaissance, projecting 'white' Machiavels as well as 'black', Bolingbroke or Vincentio as well as Edmund or Iago, avoiding total commitment to any one theory. The same seems true of Shakespeare's affinities with Montaigne, which transcended the matter of verbal borrowings. As Robert Ellrodt brought out in 'Self-consciousness in Montaigne and Shakespeare',[9] for both writers the questing individual signified more than any article of scepticism or belief. As on the personal and political planes, so in the macrocosm, commitment was avoided and faith made to subsist in contraries. Robert West's comprehensive study of sixteenth-century occultism, *The Invisible World*,[10] was followed by various essays collected in *Shakespeare and the Outer Mystery* which refused to attribute to Shakespeare a fixed set of beliefs. Spirit magic, like all aspects of the supernatural, remained 'at last darkly mysterious'. The tragedies established neither a compassionate deity, nor a demonic one, nor yet an 'outer indifference'. Confronting the supernatural, Shakespeare wove the mingled yarn of doubt and belief which issued from the exploratory thought of his time.

Ultimately, so these judgments imply, Shakespeare's thought is inseparable from his art, and the two are made one in the spirit of their age. No approach of our time has done more to validate this unity than the remarkable rehabilitation of Renaissance culture by an

[1] New York, 1967.   [2] New Haven, 1966.
[3] New Haven, 1972.
[4] Cambridge, Mass., 1968.
[5] Edited A. Kettle (1964).
[6] *Modern Language Quarterly*, IX (1948).
[7] 1964.
[8] *Shakespeare Studies*, II (1966).
[9] *Shakespeare Survey 28* (Cambridge, 1975).
[10] Athens, Georgia, 1939.

inspired group of European-born scholars. Cassirer, Kristeller, Panofsky, Wind and others have brought back to light an artistic philosophy and a philosophical art, mutually interacting, alike sustained by the willing acceptance of contraries.[1] Through paradox and irony, through antithetical images and myths, imaginative truth is shown to have broken from the grooves of scholastic logic to become an autonomous pursuit. Accordingly the way has been cleared for a new, more flexible historicism. To set Shakespeare's drama of dualities in its European context is to place him beside his peers of the Renaissance, instead of measuring him by the footrule or second-rate minds. His creations may be seen as typically informed by 'learned ignorance', projecting, to use Kolakowski's vivid metaphor, a drama not of priests but of clowns. Hence the omnipresence in Shakespeare's plays of the comic and grotesque, effecting that *discordia concors* which the best minds of his age saw as the common aim of philosophy and art. The first-fruits of this recognition may be seen in Young's two books and in Richard Cody's *The Landscape of the Mind*,[2] with its recognition in the comedies of the 'mystery of impassioned reason, the foolish wisdom of love'. For the prime embodiment of this mystery, this wisdom, we may look to the Erasmian figure of the Fool, the tight-rope walker of polarities who precariously bore the values of humanity across the abyss of tragic destruction. In Enid Welsford's pioneering study *The Fool*[3] and in William Empson's stimulating elaborations[4] this significance has been descried. It has been viewed in its Renaissance ambience in Walter Kaiser's *Praisers of Folly*,[5] where Falstaff is ranged with the creations of Erasmus and Rabelais. G. Lloyd Evans has added useful insights in 'Shakespeare's Fools'.[6] A continuing reassessment of the Renaissance Shakespeare would seem to be a main task of enlightened studies at the point where this retrospect ends.

[1] John Vyvyan's attractive studies of the influence of Renaissance Platonism in *Shakespeare and the Rose of Love* and *Shakespeare and Platonic Beauty* (1960 and 1961) unfortunately disregard this grounding in antinomies, and therefore tend to approach the plays as expositions of 'doctrine'.

[2] Oxford, 1969.   [3] 1935.

[4] See chapters 5 and 6 of *The Structure of Complex Words* (1951).

[5] Cambridge, Mass., 1963.

[6] *Stratford-upon-Avon Studies*, 14 (1972), 142–59.

© J. W. LEVER 1976

THE LETTER OF THE LAW IN
'THE MERCHANT OF VENICE'

E. F. J. TUCKER

Law, says the judge as he looks down his nose,
Speaking clearly and most severely,
Law is as I've told you before,
Law is as you know I suppose,
Law is but let me explain it once more,
Law is the Law.

> (W. H. Auden, 'Law Like Love')

In his delightful satire of post-Austinian legal philosophy, the modern poet mocks the entire notion of authoritarian Law, with its doctrines of judicial certainty and binding precedent ('as I've told you before'). For humanists like Auden, the essence of Justice is a mystery, supremely indefinable like the laws which govern the heart. The legal problems dramatised by Shakespeare in *The Merchant of Venice*, although historically different in point of judicial practice, are qualitatively similar to those explored in 'Law Like Love': how, given a universal statement of the law, sanctioned by the weight of statutory authority ('No power in Venice / Can alter a decree established'),[1] can the judge arrive at essential Justice in all individual and particular cases? In general terms, Tudor and Jacobean authorities found the ideal solution in Aristotelian *epikeia*, a concept they customarily rendered as 'Equity' and rather loosely associated with Christian conscience, judicial discretion, and the jurisdiction of the Court of Chancery. The general development of equity as a philosophical concept in the works of such writers as St Germain, Smith, Ashe, Hake, and Egerton has received so much attention that I need not

elaborate upon it here.[2] But it is necessary to recognise that many of the popularly expressed views, such as that equity mitigated the rigour of the law, that Chancery was 'a court of Conscience', and that the Chancellor's jurisdiction 'supplied' the defects of the Common Law, were no more than pious commonplaces which any Elizabethan ostler may have known. Unfortunately, such vague notions were considerably harder to translate into judicial practice, a difficulty reflected by the fact that few commentators (other than St Germain) attempted to expound a theory of equity in terms of actual litigation.[3] In suggesting that a

---

[1] *Mer. Ven.*, IV, i, 214-15. All citations are from J. R. Brown's New Arden edition of *The Merchant of Venice* (1964).

[2] The most authoritative modern studies of Chancery practice are W. J. Jones, *The Elizabethan Court of Chancery* (Oxford, 1967), and D. E. C. Yale's 'Introduction' to *Lord Nottingham's Two Treatises* (Cambridge, 1965). J. L. Barton is preparing a new edition, to appear this year, of Christopher St Germain's *Doctor and Student* for the Selden Society. Thomas Ashe's *Epeikeia* (1608), a derivative work of less importance, has not been edited in modern times, but the following editions of the other writers are reasonably available: (1) Sir Thomas Smith, *De Republica Anglorum*, ed. L. Alston (Cambridge, 1906); (2) Edward Hake, *Epeikeia, a Dialogue in Three Parts*, ed. D. E. C. Yale (New Haven, 1953); and (3) Sir Thomas Egerton, *A Discourse Upon the Exposition and Understanding of the Statutes*, ed. S. E. Thorne (San Marino, Cal., 1942).

[3] 'The only authoritative sources for the Elizabethan Chancery, the records, do not appear to provide the evidence to sustain notions of an elevated theory. All that can be said is that there was a notion

substantial theory of equitable jurisprudence had been formulated by Chancery lawyers in the late sixteenth century, recent Shakespearian criticism has presented an erroneous and distorted view of equity in such plays as *The Merchant of Venice* and *Measure for Measure*.[1] In fact, myopic concentration upon the court of Chancery has totally disregarded the fact that the judicial problems arising from a strict interpretation of the letter of the law were perfectly well understood by common lawyers. Moreover, in the absence of adequate Chancery records, it is to the Common Law that we must look in order to discover the equitable principles which explain Portia's pleadings in regard to Shylock's insistence upon the letter of the law. The purpose of this study is to present some alternative views of Elizabethan equity and to show briefly how the playwright's treatment of Justice correlates with the themes of appearance and reality which dominate the comedy.

Before proceeding to a detailed analysis of Shakespeare's use of equity, however, it is necessary to serve writs of error upon several critics who have previously ventured into the morass of Elizabethan law, all of whom (perhaps basing their views upon the now dated work of legal historians like Phelps, Haynes, and Maitland)[2] have suggested that *The Merchant of Venice* is the playwright's personal commentary upon a supposed conflict between the proponents of equity and the supporters of the common law. According to Professor McKay, Portia's pleadings reflect 'clearly a conflict between the courts of law and of equity (chancery) in Elizabethan England, a conflict which has affinity with the religious ideologies of the era and the ecclesiastical status of presiding chancellors', a dispute rendered 'all the more possible because the Chancellors were often ecclesiastics, versed in canon law, their thoughts of equitable remedies in close harmony with Christian precepts'.[3] This brief passage contains a number of glaring errors of fact and misinterpretation. First, *all* of Elizabeth's Chancellors were common lawyers,[4] except Sir Christopher Hatton who was not a lawyer at all, though he briefly attended the Inner Temple. Moreover, apart from the appointees of Mary I, common lawyers held the Great Seal continuously after the death of Wolsey, and the only ecclesiastical Chancellor thereafter was Bishop Williams who held office briefly after the fall of Bacon in 1621. The argument that Chancery procedure and theory were founded upon the canon law has not been generally entertained by modern legal historians. Furthermore, while there was indeed a dispute between the common law courts and Chancery, it was purely a jurisdictional conflict and never based upon a clash of fundamental principles.[5]

of conscience which embraced the defendant's conduct and state of mind' (Jones, *Elizabethan Chancery*, p. 420).

[1] 'This may explain why, despite St Germain, men in the fifteenth and sixteenth century failed to develop a consistent and broadly acceptable picture of the constituent elements of equity or conscience, at least in so far as this involved a definition of Chancery position in respect of the central courts of law' (*ibid.*, p. 418).

[2] Useful, but to be used with caution, are Charles E. Phelps, *Falstaff and Equity* (Boston, 1901); F. O. Haynes, *Outlines of Equity* (1880); and F. W. Maitland, *English Law and the Renaissance* (Cambridge, 1901).

[3] Maxine McKay, '*The Merchant of Venice*: A Reflection of the Early Conflict Between Courts of Law and Courts of Equity', *Shakespeare Quarterly*, XV (1964), 371, 374.

[4] See Jones, *Elizabethan Chancery*, pp. 27–99, for short biographies of Elizabeth's appointees to the Great Seal.

[5] J. H. Baker, 'The Common Lawyers and the Chancery: 1616', *The Irish Jurist*, IV, no. 2 (1969), 392: 'Equity by its very nature prevails over law in appropriate circumstances, but the difficulties which had troubled Coke and his contemporaries had been practical problems of judicial comity and personality, rather than theoretical problems of conflicting notions of justice.' Jones (*Elizabethan Chancery*, p. 491) independently comes to the same conclusion: 'The

John Dickinson[1] and Wilbur Dunkel[2] have also supported the conflict thesis in relationship to *Measure for Measure*, although it is doubly difficult to see how, since Chancery had no criminal jurisdiction whatsoever. It is crucial to a fuller understanding of these plays not to confuse equity with mercy, clemency, and prerogative rights of pardon.[3] Nor will it do for literary critics to confuse legal forms and actions. Both McKay and Dickinson, for example, employ the case of *Throckmorton v. Finch* (1598) in order to illustrate their sense of Shakespeare's use of equity, but neither has done his legal homework. This case (or series of cases) was based upon the common law action of *ejectio firmae*, which as a purely civil form has nothing to do with the criminal law and the pardoning of capital offences which form the core of *Measure for Measure*. Inasmuch as this case was briefly considered by Chancery, it has some tangential relevance to Shylock's case, although we must remember that the question raised in 1598 did not concern 'apparent matter in equity' (which both the Chancery and the common law judges recognised) so much as the right of the Chancellor to review cases which had already been adjudicated at the common law. Professor McKay must have taken her account of the case from Phelps,[4] even though she furnishes references to Coke's *Institutes* (3 Inst. 124 and 4 Inst. 86) and to 21 *English Reports* 576 (she even misreads 'Eng. Rep' as 'English Reprint' and could not have, given the evidence, consulted the cases cited).[5] Thus the report she offers is fanciful, to say the least.

The great Queen Elizabeth, in some pique or parsimony of her own, insisted upon the scarcely rational or just enforcement of a stale forfeiture. Throckmorton...had leased from the Queen certain lands formerly held by the Church, upon the condition that the lease should be void if the rent were unpaid forty days after it fell due. The robbery of Throckmorton's servant, who was on his way to pay the rent, caused an accidental default. This default was made up prior to the next date of payment, and a full acquittance was issued by the Queen's receiver. All further payments were promptly paid. Yet twenty years later, the Queen protested the stale forfeiture and sold the land to Sir Moyle Finch, who, in turn, sought to oust Throckmorton by bringing a suit for ejectment in the Court of Exchequer. The ruling of this court, affirmed in the Exchequer Chamber, favored the claim of Finch. Throckmorton's only natural appeal was to Ellesmere, the Chancellor [*sic*].[6] Although the Queen generally favored Ellesmere's right to prevent the enforcement of inequitable common law judgments, her animosity toward Throckmorton placed considerable restraint upon the usual quality of her mercy. She ordered that the case be heard before all the judges of England – the same judges who had affirmed the suit in Exchequer Chamber. Unanimously they ruled that the appeal of a judgment at law to the Court of Chancery was an improper subversion of the common law. Nevertheless the Court of Chancery, deprived of the review of judgments at law by such ruling, quietly continued to grant relief in original suits for equity.[7]

idea that the common lawyers were opposed to Chancery deserves to be dismissed.'

[1] John W. Dickinson, 'Renaissance Equity in *Measure for Measure*', *Shakespeare Quarterly*, XIII (1962), 287–97.

[2] Wilbur Dunkel, 'Law and Equity in *Measure for Measure*', *Shakespeare Quarterly*, XIII (1962), 275–85.

[3] W. Nicholas Knight, 'Equity, *The Merchant of Venice*, and William Lambarde', *Shakespeare Survey* 27 (Cambridge, 1974), pp. 95–6, makes the correct distinctions between these differing concepts but, in spite of reading Jones, perpetuates the conflict theory.

[4] See Phelps, *Falstaff and Equity*, pp. 48–9, but Professor McKay does not acknowledge her indebtedness to this source.

[5] The correct page references for this case are 21 Eng. Rep. 595–6; the entry in question is not a report but a polemical reply to the late publication of Coke's Third and Fourth *Institutes*, entitled 'Arguments Proving From Antiquity the Dignity, Power, and Jurisdiction of the Court of Chancery'. Undated, this tract appears to have been printed between 1641 and 1645. Such a source, betraying extreme bias in favour of Chancery, written almost half a century after many of the cases therein mentioned, must be used with great care.

[6] At this time, Egerton was not Chancellor, or Ellesmere, but merely Lord Keeper.

[7] McKay, 'Reflection of Early Conflict', 371–2.

Now, if Professor McKay had bothered to read cited reports,[1] she could only have concluded that Phelps's version of the case is somewhat at odds with the facts. The queen had little direct contact with her hundreds of tenants, and there is nothing in the reports to suggest that she was venting her spite upon Throckmorton, although, according to Coke, she directed an appeal to the judges,[2] which was her customary policy.[3] Contrary to McKay, that 'All further payments were promptly paid', Throckmorton 'made many Failures, which appeared upon Record',[4] before the holdings were granted away, and Finch was able to prove other defaults in 1573 and 1580. Accidental default, presumably, could only apply to the first late payment. In fact, the following account from *English Reports* seems to throw the whole story into doubt:

'But in all those Proceedings it doth not appear, that the Lord Keeper did make any Order to retain the Bill, as is alledged, nor that there was any Petition to the Queen, nor any Reference from her to the Judges, nor any Certificate of the Judges (other than Verbal) to the Lord Keeper (as is said) and by him declared in Court....'[5]

But the recently discovered MS of Coke's reports supports the edited version of the case in the *Institutes*,[6] and from J. P. Dawson's research among Chancery records, it appears that Egerton did make such a referral to the judges: 'Forasmuch as the cawse ys of greate waight and wilbe taken for a presydent heereafter in lyke case,[7] Therefore the Lo Keeper myndeth before any order be gyven for Reteyninge or dismyssinge of the Cawse to confer with the Judges and to have theyr opynions towching the same.'[8] Finally, it is quite misleading to suggest that the Chancery continued to grant relief in such cases in spite of the judges' decision in *Throckmorton v. Finch*.

Yet there is a conceivable relationship between Portia's equitable remedy against Shylock's bond and the question raised in *Throckmorton v. Finch*, for had the case been free of common law judgement, it was within the Chancellor's powers to discipline the conscience of a litigant even where he had the letter of the law on his side. The problem from the standpoint of *The Merchant of Venice* is that neither the Duke nor Portia makes any attempt to utilise such powers. Her 'quality of mercy' speech is an appeal to Shylock's conscience; it is not a Chancery decree aimed specifically at correcting the plaintiff's malice, which, as Keeton points out,[9] would have been a viable method of countering Shylock's demand for the letter of the law. If it could be so considered, then the case of *Shylock v. Antonio* would doubtless be the first successful suit, even by hypothesis, in equity of redemption. Professor Knight has recently urged such an interpretation of the trial scene, basing his thesis upon the case of *Shakespeare v. Lambert* (1598).[10]

[1] Many of the details of the case are not mentioned in Professor McKay's sources, especially those relating to Exchequer Chamber. For further details, consult the following reports: Moore 291–6, Croke Eliz. 221, and Croke Jac. 344.

[2] See 3 Inst. 124, confirmed by Coke's MS report in Brit. Mus. MS Harl. 6686, f. 227r. where the case was considered 'de graunde consequence, et semblable d'estre president a multes auters'.

[3] See Jones (*Elizabethan Chancery*, pp. 328–31) regarding Elizabeth's interventions, but clearly (in spite of Phelps) the queen was not half as meddlesome in legal affairs as her successor.

[4] 21 Eng. Rep. 595.   [5] 21 Eng. Rep. 596.

[6] MS Harl. 6686, ff. 226v.–229r. I am indebted to Dr J. H. Baker for letting me use his microfilmed copy of this report and for general help and suggestions.

[7] Egerton's sense of the term 'presydent' in this speech must not be taken as 'binding precedent' in its modern sense. Chancery was not a court of record, as Coke was fond of reiterating, and, even at the common law, the doctrine of precedent was only in its earliest stage of growth.

[8] J. P. Dawson, 'Coke and Ellesmere Disinterred', *Illinois Law Review*, XXXVI (1936), 134–5.

[9] G. W. Keeton, *Shakespeare's Legal and Political Background* (1967), p. 132.

[10] 'Equity, *The Merchant of Venice* and William Lambarde', pp. 93–104.

He argues that because Shakespeare owned a copy of William Lambarde's *Archaionomia* (1568), an antiquarian study of Anglo-Saxon law, and because of his own litigation in Chancery, the dramatist must have known Lambarde (Master of Chancery) well enough to have anticipated 'equity of redemption' by nearly three decades.[1] In other words,

William Shakespeare is not just dramatizing a generalized court scene and sentimentalizing about mercy; rather he is presenting Chancery procedure and advocating that it be used precisely along its theoretical lines of a superior court with its accompanying appellate function and humane spirit, so as not to abrogate the common law of Queen's Bench and Common Pleas, and thus become merely a rival court'.[2]

Once again, one remarks the same vague use of legal terms and looseness of definition. Chancery did not have an appellate function in regard to common law judgements, as the case of *Throckmorton v. Finch* proves,[3] and Egerton was never revered for his 'humane spirit' towards debtors.[4] Even at the height of his power, Ellesmere insisted that he had no such right of reversing common law judgements and claimed only to correct the guilty consciences of fraudulent and malicious litigants.[5]

It is also difficult to imagine in what ways Shakespeare presents and advocates Chancery procedure 'along its theoretical lines'. In the trial scene, one finds no allusions to written pleadings; there are no answers, demurrerss motions, rejoinders, surrejoinders, and surely no commissions of *dedimus potestatem* in any formal or technical sense. Is Portia supposed to be the Chancellor (she is referred to several times as a judge), a Mastery of Chancery, a Six-Clerk, or what? We must remember that Chancery officials were jealous of their tenured offices, doubtless regarded themselves as quite sufficient in matters of law, and would have regarded the intrusion of an outside authority as a serious breach of privilege and decorum. How do we account for the Duke's presence in

the court (English monarchs never sat personally in Chancery), and who are the 'Officers of the Court of Justice' mentioned in *Dramatis Personae*? What, in short, do we make of this unusual trial with its casual proceedings, in which neither party is represented by counsel or attorney? Certainly nothing remotely resembling this trial ever took place at Westminster Hall, and surely we rend the whimsical fabric of the illusion to ask such purely procedural questions. Of far greater importance, for our understanding of the trial scene, are those substantive matters of law which underlie the pleadings.

From a strictly legal point of view, the

[1] Inasmuch as it seems to indicate Chancery's acceptance of a right of redemption after a stated date regardless of such mitigating factors as misfortune, hardship, or the fraudulent conduct of mortgagees, the case of *Emmanuel College v. Evans* (1625) is usually cited as the principal case in establishing equity of redemption. As early as *Courtman v. Convers* (1601), the Chancellor was giving relief to mortgagors where money is repaid by the stated date and the mortgagee refuses to reconvey (see Monro, *Acta Cancellaria* 764). Likewise, occasional relief was awarded in cases of manifest misfortune, but no clear principles had emerged. D. E. C. Yale has compiled a schedule of Elizabethan and Jacobean cases from unprinted sources which largely clarifies this emerging doctrine. I am indebted to him and to members of his LL.B. seminar at Christ's College, Cambridge for these insights. For further discussion, see R. W. Turner, *The Equity of Redemption* (Cambridge, 1931) and J. L. Barton, 'The Common Law Mortgage', *Law Quarterly Review*, LXXXIII (1967), 229ff.

[2] 'Equity, *The Merchant of Venice* and William Lambarde', p. 95.

[3] J. H. Baker, *An Introduction to English Legal History* (1971), p. 59: 'In this modern sense, there was no such thing as an appeal at common law, and no procedure for bringing an appeal until the last century'. The only court reviewing judgements in either King's Bench or Common Pleas was the Exchequer Chamber.

[4] George Norburie, 'The Abuses and Remedies of Chancery', *A Collection of Tracts*, ed. Francis Hargrave (Dublin, 1787), I, 431–2.

[5] For Ellesmere's classic statement on the subject, see the *Earl of Oxford's Case* (1615), 1 Chancery Reports, pt. i, pp. 1–16.

judgement against Shylock is not without its serious difficulties, for the very nature of Portia's triumph at law is scarred by grave errors. Supporters of Shylock as victim of Christian prejudice, for example, have not noticed that Portia, as Bassanio's wife and therefore having a personal stake in the trial, acts not merely in fraudulent disguise of Bellario but in direct defiance of the legal principle (held dear by Coke) that no person may officiate as judge in his own cause (*iudex in propria causa*), a rule ironically broken at Angelo's expense in the trial scene of *Measure for Measure*.[1] In addition to this, abduction of an heiress (even with her consent as in Jessica's case) was a statutory felony in Elizabethan law and may have afforded Shylock a more sweeping means of revenge than the bond, not only against Lorenzo but his accessories, such as Bassanio, Gratiano, and even Portia herself. But certain lines of critical inquiry yield the right questions; others do not. In terms of the story as he received it, Shakespeare was limited by the main lines of the plot, and the objections raised above simply do not apply. It is less easy, though, to disregard the opinion of legal historians like Haynes who feel that Shylock is defeated of his bond by 'the merest of verbal quibbles',[2] even though others like Keeton propose that it is precisely in the matter of the spilling of blood that Portia discovers an equitable remedy.[3]

In referring to Chancery equity, Keeton is right for the wrong reasons; Portia does find an equitable remedy but bases her argument upon Common Law principles of equity, as applied to the interpretation of statutes. When she utters those fateful words, 'Tarry a little, there is something else' (IV, i, 301), Portia has already completed her appeal to mercy and to the plaintiff's conscience, and Shylock has stood firm upon the rights granted to him by statutory decree: 'It must not be, there is no power in Venice / Can alter a decree established

(IV, i, 214–5). And, of course, it is the statutory protection of alien merchants which renders the Duke powerless to act. As Shylock indicates in his defiance of the Duke, a legislative decree cannot be tampered with to suit individual needs: 'If you deny me, fie upon your law! / There is no force in the decrees of Venice' (IV, i, 101–2). Portia must rest her judgement upon the statute and the express wording of the bond in order to preserve the rights guaranteed by statute to alien merchants. Ironically, Shylock draws attention to the eventual solution of the case by his own persistent quibbling on the express wording of the bond.

Professor McKay comes partly to this solution when she alludes to the maxim *Expressio unius est exclusio alterius*,[4] but she loses this valuable insight by linking it with Chancery equity. In its broader terms, the maxim derives its chief importance from common law methods of interpretation, whereby the precise meanings of key terms were decided before issue was joined. This precision is typical of the exposition of statutes and the application of common law principles of equity. In Rastell's *Les Termes de la Ley*, Equity is defined as

of two sorts, and those of contrary effects; for the one doth abridge, and take from the letter of the law, the other doth inlarge, and add thereto. The first thus defined, *Aequitas est correctio legis generatim latae, quaparte deficit. Equity* is the Correction of the Law generally made in that part wherein it fails, which Correction is much used in our Law.... The other *Equity* is defined to be an extension of the words of the Law to Cases unexpressed, yet having the same reason.[5]

[1] D. E. C. Yale, '*Iudex in Propria Causa*: An Historical Excursus', *Cambridge Law Journal*, XXXIII (1974), 80–96.

[2] Haynes, *Outlines of Equity*, p. 21.

[3] *Shakespeare's Legal and Political Background*, p. 144.

[4] McKay, 'Reflection of Early Conflict', p. 374.

[5] John Rastell, *Les Termes de la Ley* (1527), *Equitie*. I quote from an edition of 1721. Note that

Given these definitions, one might have expected greater flexibility of interpretation than actually prevailed, but the judges moderated equitable latitude by adherence to such concomitant principles as that familiar from St Germain, 'Equity followeth the Law'.[1] Here, then, is the importance of *expressio unius*, for the letter of the law could not be expanded and diminished at will, and the controlling factor in all cases was the reason and intent of the law. As Portia herself points out to those who object to the provisions of the Venetian decrees, 'the intent and purpose of the law / Hath full relation to the penalty, / Which here appeareth due upon the bond' (IV, i, 243–5). The operative word in this speech is 'appeareth', for in law, as Feste observes, 'Words are very rascals', and, while the letter of the law seems to indicate only one outcome, reasoned law cannot 'intend and purpose' the judicial murder contemplated by Shylock. According to the equitable standards of Elizabethan law, Portia applies the correct tests and principles in arriving at her judgement; for, according to Plowden (in *Stradling v. Morgan*), the rigour of the law is qualified by Reason, so that judges have interpreted statutes 'quite contrary to the Letter' in order to fulfil the intent of the law.[2]

Elizabethan law reports are filled with parallel examples which demonstrate the soundness of Portia's reasoning. Two examples from Plowden seem particularly apt for our purposes. The first, *Reniger v. Fogossa* (4 Edw. VI) involves a Portuguese merchant charged with a customs default after losses of his cargo at sea. The cause of his failure to pay customs dues arises, like Antonio's default, from an act of God – a storm at sea which compels the merchant to jettison a large portion of his cargo of green woad into the sea for the safety of the ship and crew. In this case, the Privy Council intervened on Fogossa's behalf as a way of guaranteeing fair treatment of foreign merchants, but before this occurs, the defence

offers some compelling reasons in terms of the intent and purpose of the Customs Statutes, which it is said were not written to penalise innocent defaulters:

for in every Law there are some Things which when they happen a Man may break the Words of the Law, and yet they break not the Law itself; and such Things are exempted out of the Penalty of the Law, and the Law priviledges them although they are done against the Letter of it, for breaking the Words of the Law is not breaking the Law, so as the Intent of the Law is not broken. And therefore the Words of the Law of Nature, of the Law of this Realm, and of other Realms, and of the Law of God also will yield and give Way to some Acts and Things done against the Words of the same Laws, and that is, where the Words of them are broken to avoid greater Inconveniences, or through Necessity, or by Compulsion, or involuntary Ignorance.[3]

In Fogossa's defence, Portia may have found good arguments for Antonio, yet she chooses to attack the case from the standpoint of Shylock's demands, as in the case of *Eyston v. Studd* (16 Eliz.) in which the plaintiff also rests his argument upon the letter of the law. The case begins to turn against Eyston when counsel for the defendant remarks, 'Wherefore a Man ought not to rest upon the Letter of an Act, nor think that when he has the Letter on his Side, he has the Law on his Side in all Cases'.[4] The learned Plowden obviously approves and writes an extensive commentary explicating the principles of equity involved, quoting *Doctor and Student*, Aristotle's *Ethics*, Geraldus a Odo's *Commentary Upon Aristotle*, and several common law precedents. 'From this Judgment and the Cause of it', he remarks,

---

John Cowell's *Interpreter* (1607) cribs Rastell's definition verbatim.

[1] See *Doctor and Student* (1715), p. 52. For Cary's Elizabethan view of the maxim, see Jones, *Elizabethan Chancery*, p. 427.

[2] Plowden, 205. See also *Harbert's Case* (26, 27 Eliz.) in 3 Co. Rep. 13b. for a similar statement concerning the equitable construction of statutes.

[3] Plowden, 18.   [4] Plowden, 464a.

the Reader may observe, that it is not the Words of the Law, but the internal Sense of it that makes the Law, and our Law (like all others) consists of two parts, *viz.* of Body and Soul, the Letter of the Law is the Body of the Law, and the Sense and Reason of the Law is the Soul of the Law, *quia ratio legis est anima legis*.... And Equity, which in Latin is called *Equitas*, enlarges or diminishes the Letter according to its Discretion.

Any written law or statute is open to the fault of being generally worded, and for this reason,

Equity or *Epichaia* makes an Exception...from the general Words of the Text, which Exception is as strong as if it had been expressly put in the Act; so that the Sages of our Law, who have had the Exposition of our Acts of Parliament, have in these and many other Cases almost infinite restrained the Generality of the Letter of the Law by Equity, which seems to be a necessary Ingredient in the Exposition of all Laws.[1]

Notice that Plowden makes no mention of Chancery proceedings and that he thinks of equity in terms of actual cases and the readings upon the statutes, a traditional element of common law instruction at the Inns of Court. Observe, too, that Shylock makes the same error as Eyston and that Portia's judgement reflects an equitable diminishment of the letter of the law according to the reason and intent of true justice.

Haynes's objection to Portia's verbal gymnastics deserves closer attention, for he concentrates upon the *habendum* of the grant:

Considerable latitude is to be allowed to the dramatist; but when I see Antonio saved by a species of construction, according to which, if a man contracted for leave to cut a slice of melon, he would be deprived of his contract unless he had stipulated, in so many words, for the incidental spilling of the juice, one cannot help recognising in the fiction of the immortal bard an intensified representation of the popular faith, that the *law* regarded the *letter* and not the *spirit*.[2]

This argument is similar to the view expressed in *Throckmorton v. Tracy* (2, 3 Phil. & Mary) that 'where a Grant is made by any Word, the Thing included in the Word shall always pass'.[3] Counsel offers the examples of the grants of a piscary or a turbary, where it would be absurd to deny access to the water or to allow a claim against the grantee for disturbing the soil by removal of turf. But as Staunford, J. retorts, 'to pursue the Words, is *summun ius*, which the Judges ought to avoid, and rather pursue the Intent'.[4] Much depends upon the kind of grant in question. A pound of flesh, after all, is not in the same category of grants as a piscary, a turbary, or even a slice of melon, and because she recognises this vital distinction, Portia does observe the *spirit* rather than the *letter* of the *law*.

The brilliance of Portia's legal artistry provides the ultimate answer to those sceptics like Bassanio who oppugn the law:

So may the outward shows be least themselves, –
The world is still deceiv'd with ornament –
In law, what plea so tainted and corrupt,
But being season'd with a gracious voice,
Obscures the show of evil?   (III, ii, 73–7)

Portia's judgement is brilliant because she demonstrates that equity cuts through the 'outward shows' to probe and lay bare the corrupt and tainted pleas. Only fools confuse the letter (appearance) with the spirit (reality) of the Law, as Lorenzo unwittingly discovers in his verbal bout with Launcelot:

O dear discretion, how his words are suited!
The fool hath planted in his memory
An army of good words; and I do know
A many fools that stand in better place,
Garnish'd like him, that for a tricksy word,
Defy the matter.   (III, v, 59–64)

---

[1] Plowden, 465–7.   [2] Plowden, 154–5.
[3] *Outlines of Equity*, pp. 21–2 (italics not mine).
[4] Plowden, 160. Saunders amplifies this argument by citing the famous dictum of Cicero: 'And to cavil about the Words in Subversion of the plain Intent of the Parties, as Tully says in his Book *of Offices*, "Est calumnia quaedam et nimis callida sed malitiosa juris interpretatio, ex quo illud, summum ius, summa iniuria"' (161).

In relationship to the themes of appearance and reality, most incisively and satisfactorily analysed in J. R. Brown's criticism of the comedy,[1] it would be equally absurd to suppose that the letter and spirit are merely contrary and mutually exclusive principles of law. They must be understood as coextensive like body and soul, or Aristotelian accidentals and substance. Essential justice integrates them into a meaningful whole through the medium of reason, and this is why interpretations of the play based upon artificial conflicts and dichotomies do not work. In law, as in love,[2] the same words are frequently used to describe the appearances as much as the realities of life; but at the core of its meaning, the law is a mystery attainable only by those judicial minds capable of the finer distinctions between the letter and spirit of Justice. Upon these terms only, 'Law is the Law'.

[1] Read chapters 3, 6, and 7 of his *Shakespeare and His Comedies* (1957).

[2] The comedy abounds with legal allusions to love relationships: I, ii, 17–26; II, vi, 6–7; II, ix, 61–2; III, ii, 18–9; III, ii, 76–7; III, ii, 140–67; V, i, 297–303; and those already cited above.

SHAKESPEARE'S USE OF THE 'TIMON' COMEDY

JAMES C. BULMAN, Jr

Timon of Athens, fraught with inconsistencies and long regarded as unfinished, has been of particular interest to scholars who believe that finding the right source will resolve all its inherent problems. These scholars inevitably have cited either Plutarch's Life of Antony or Lucian's dialogue *Misanthropos* as the principle source through which the play ought to be approached; and their interpretations have alternated between the extremes of romantic tragedy and bitter satire.[1] In a recent article I suggested that the MS *Timon* comedy, long discounted as a source because of its academic quality and because there was no significant evidence that it was ever performed, probably was performed *c.* 1602 at the Inns of Court, where Shakespeare could easily have seen it.[2] I propose to examine in this paper, therefore, the comedy as a possible source for *Timon of Athens*, and to suggest some ideas Shakespeare may have gleaned from it.

Shakespeare had used North's translation (from the French of Amyot) of Plutarch's *Lives of the Noble Grecians and Romans*, published in 1579, as the major source for *Julius Caesar* as early as 1599, and as a minor source for even earlier plays. The fact that he used it extensively again for his two later Roman plays has encouraged critics to regard *Timon of Athens* as a play written at the same time, *c.* 1607; for he undoubtedly knew the brief sketch of Timon which comes at the end of the Life of Antony, and turned to it for details.[3] The sketch establishes that Timon's misanthropy was caused by 'the unthankfulness of those he had done good unto': Timon, as a result, tolerates the company of only one man, Alcibiades, 'a bold and insolent youth', because he believes that one day Alcibiades 'shall do great mischief unto the Athenians'.

From Timon's brief encounter with another misanthrope named Apemantus, Shakespeare picked up the name of his cynic and a bit of repartee. He also transplanted into his play Timon's invitation to desperate Athenians to hang themselves on his fig tree. Both epitaphs which appear at the end of the sketch – the first made by Timon himself; the second, by

---

[1] Francelia Butler, *The Strange Critical Fortunes of Shakespeare's 'Timon of Athens'* (Iowa State University, 1966), pp. 75–115, traces the history of interpretation of the play. The two critics who defined the lines of demarcation for our current critical warfare were G. Wilson Knight, who regarded Timon as a paragon of humanism, flawed only by being too good, in *The Wheel of Fire* (1930; Oxford, 1949), pp. 207–39; and O. J. Campbell, who explicitly refuted Knight by accusing Timon of selfish ostentation worthy of satirical scorn, in *Shakespeare's Satire* (Oxford, 1943), pp. 168–97.

[2] 'The Date and Production of "Timon" Reconsidered', *Shakespeare Survey 27* (Cambridge, 1974), 111–27.

[3] For general surveys of Shakespeare's sources, see two recent editions of the play: J. C. Maxwell's (Cambridge, 1957), pp. xiv–xxii; and H. J. Oliver's (1959), pp. xxxii–xl. Willard Farnham, *Shakespeare's Tragic Frontier* (Berkeley, 1950), pp. 50–67, traces the Timon legend from Lucian and Plutarch through its various Renaissance manifestations largely in terms of thematic development, without concentrating on Shakespeare's specific debts.

Callimachus – found their way into the play. Shakespeare probably intended to choose between them during revision.

From the Life of Alcibiades, he seems to have derived little more than Timon's cryptic prophecy that Alcibiades would humble Athens, the fact of Alcibiades's banishment, and the name Timandra; from the *Lives* in general, most of the names, oddly Latin, for characters in the play.[1] E. A. J. Honigmann has recently argued that Shakespeare not only milked dry this brief sketch of Timon, but scanned the *Lives* he is known to have used while writing the Roman plays for further ideas. Especially suggestive are his arguments that Timon's character bears the mark of Antony's liberality, and that Alcibiades's heroism is portrayed very much like that of Coriolanus, the parallel Life.[2]

All this material from Plutarch, however, far from being Shakespeare's 'main source', as Oliver suggests (p. xxxii), is only incidental to the body of the play. For the source which inspired Shakespeare to flesh out his play with an account of Timon's prosperity, bankruptcy, and exile, we must turn to Lucian's *Misanthropos*, a satire of hypocrisy, prodigality, and the decaying mythological system of religion which focuses on Timon's relationship with Jove and Plutus, the god of wealth.

It is much more difficult to establish how Shakespeare knew Lucian than how he knew Plutarch, for there is no known English translation of the *Misanthropos* before Heywood's in 1637. Critics have posited intermediary sources, such as Boiardo's *Il Timone* or a lost English play, through which Shakespeare may have derived his knowledge of Lucian; but inevitably their evidence has proved insufficient, and they have conceded that Shakespeare must have known the dialogue itself either in the original Greek or in Latin, Italian, or French translation.[3] All this is but surmise. Unless one allows that Shakespeare may have

recalled the *Misanthropos* from his school days – a distinct possibility – one must be inclined to agree with Joseph Quincy Adams, Jr, 'that Shakespeare's knowledge of the Greek story was indirect. A person who used absolutely everything in the barren Plutarch version, would certainly have drawn freely from the rich storehouse of material in *Misanthropos*. We can trace no close borrowing, no following of detail; the story must have been known to the dramatist only in its broadest outlines'.[4]

These broad outlines can be found in the *Timon* comedy, which, written by a man with substantial classical learning, follows the *Misanthropos* much more closely than *Timon of Athens* does and interpolates passages from other Lucianic satires as well.[5] It is possible that if Shakespeare saw the comedy acted at the Inns of Court, or read the MS, his knowledge of Lucian came largely, if not exclusively, through it. This is a possibility which I now

---

[1] This was first observed by W. W. Skeat, *Shakespeare's Plutarch* (1875), pp. xvii–xviii.

[2] 'Timon of Athens', *Shakespeare Quarterly*, 12 (1961), 3–8.

[3] Honigmann, pp. 8ff., cites a few verbal coincidences between *Timon of Athens* and the French translation of Lucian. R. Warwick Bond, on the other hand, in 'Lucian and Boiardo in *Timon of Athens*', *MLR*, 26 (1931), 53ff., argues that Shakespeare knew enough Italian to have been able to use *Il Timone* – and, it logically follows, the Italian translation of Lucian. T. W. Baldwin, *William Shakspere's Small Latine & Lesse Greeke* (Urbana, 1944), I, 732–5, imagines that Shakespeare may have read Lucian's dialogues in grammar school, either in Erasmus's Latin translation or in the original Greek; but there is little evidence of his ever having known much Greek.

[4] 'The Timon Plays,' *JEGP*, 9 (1910), 524.

[5] Adams, pp. 512–21, details a number of borrowings from Lucian scattered through the comedy, especially by Pseudocheus, whose traveler's tales correspond with various passages in *The True History*. The fact that the author of the comedy relies on Lucian exclusively, and shows no knowledge of the passages in Plutarch which Shakespeare uses, makes it all the more unlikely that he was imitating Shakespeare.

shall put to the test, weighing whether the material which Shakespeare is thought to have borrowed from the *Misanthropos* may in fact have been borrowed from the comedy instead.

I

Timon's legendary misanthropy, said by Plutarch to have been caused only by his friends' ingratitude, is more explicitly motivated by Lucian. Timon complains,

I have raised any number of Athenians to high position, I have turned poor men into rich, I have assisted everyone that was in want, nay, flung my wealth broadcast in the service of my friends, and now that profusion has brought me to beggary, they do not so much as know me...[1]

Wealth, then, is Lucian's addition to the legend; and in both plays, Timon's extravagant expenditure on his friends is dramatically contrasted with his friendless poverty. Lucian recalls a world of riches which the two plays capitalize on. And the flatterers who, when asked to reciprocate Timon's generosity, 'do not so much as know' him, are made the subjects of scathing satire.

Hermes, Jove's messenger in the *Misanthropos*, explains Timon's misfortune from two different points of view. 'It was kindness and generosity and universal compassion that ruined him', he charitably suggests; 'but it would be nearer the truth to call him a fool and a simpleton and a blunderer' (Fowler, pp. 33–4). From either point of view, Timon was a victim of ingratitude. But romantic critics have agreed with Hermes's first explanation, that Timon's spiritual nobility caused him to be blind of the nature of his flatterers, while more cynical critics have preferred the second explanation and have regarded Timon as a fool whose moral blindness justified his fall from fortune. Shakespeare drew Timon's character ambiguously enough to allow his critics ample scope for their argument. The ambiguity is apparent in this

remark of Flavius, who sees Timon at once as admirably kind but foolishly unwise:

> No care, no stop; so senseless of expense,
> That he will neither know how to maintain it,
> Nor cease his flow of riot. Takes no accompt
> How things go from him, nor resumes no care
> Of what is to continue. Never mind
> Was to be so unwise, to be so kind.
>
> (II, ii, 1–6)[2]

Shakespeare did not need to resort to the original dialogue to find the suggestion of this ambiguity. He could have found it in the comedy. The steward of the comedy, like Flavius, agonizes over Timon's senseless spending –

> Soe are my masters goods consum'd: this way
> Will bring him to the house of pouerty.
> O Joue, conuert him, leaste hee feele to soone
> To much the rodde of desp'rate misery...
>
> (III, ii, p. 48)[3]

– but elsewhere blames the flatterers' base ingratitude far more than Timon's foolishness, and asserts the essential nobility of Timon's nature: 'The greatnes of his spirit will not downe' (IV, iii, p. 69).

The central action of the *Misanthropos* begins when Timon is forced by Hermes to accept unwanted treasure. Timon's first impulse is to reject it as the cause of all his

[1] References are to *The Works of Lucian of Samosata*, ed., H. W. Fowler and F. G. Fowler (Oxford, 1905), I, 31–53, hereafter referred to as 'Fowler'. For the lines quoted here, see p. 32.

[2] References are to Oliver's New Arden edition. Act and scene divisions were absent from the Folio. Most modern editors follow those made by Edward Capell in his 1768 edition.

[3] References are to the Alexander Dyce edition, published by The Shakespeare Society (1842), from MS 52 of the Dyce Collection at the Victoria and Albert Museum. In the absence of line numbers, I cite page numbers instead. The play was reprinted in Hazlitt, *Shakespeare Library* (1875), VI; and extracts from it can be found in *Narrative and Dramatic Sources of Shakespeare*, ed., Geoffrey Bullough (1957–75), VI, 297–339.

misery, an impulse dramatized in both plays when Timon, digging for a root, finds gold:

He brought me countless troubles long ago – put me in the power of flatterers, set designing persons on me, stirred up ill-feeling, corrupted me with indulgence, exposed me to envy, and wound up with treacherously deserting me at a moment's notice.

(Fowler, p. 44)

Gold, in all three works, is the emblem of inconstancy, the fickle reward for which men will sell their souls. The brief appearance of Timandra and Phrynia in *Timon of Athens* has suggested to critics that Shakespeare thought gold can make whores of us all.[1] 'Well, more gold', beg the two whores; '...Believe 't that we'll do anything for gold' (IV, iii, 151–2). Callimela, the miser's daughter in the comedy, expresses the same sentiment: 'Who doth possesse moste golde shall mee possesse' (III, ii, p. 47). Plutus's complaint to Timon in the *Misanthropos* is a more universal statement of economic whoredom: 'you prostituted me vilely to scoundrels, whose laudations and cajolery of you were only samples of their designs upon me' (Fowler, p. 45). The prostitution, and Timon's unwillingness to acknowledge responsibility for it, is the same in all three; but Shakespeare's version is closer to the comedy.

As rumor spreads of Timon's newfound treasure, the flatterers flock back to him with vain hopes of cashing in: the remainder of the *Misanthropos* is devoted to Timon's repulsion of them. The comedy follows the form and detail of these encounters with reasonable accuracy, while the tragedy follows the form but not the detail – further evidence that Shakespeare may have gone to the comedy for his Lucianic material. A glance at Timon's individual encounters will illustrate my point.

Philiades, Lucian's miser whom Timon awards a farm and two talents as a dowry for his daughter, is thought to be the model for Shakespeare's Old Athenian, who forbids his daughter to marry Timon's servant Lucilius because he is poor. Timon, having satisfied himself that the couple love one another, vows to match the Old Athenian's dowry of three talents for his daughter with a like sum for Lucilius: evidence that Shakespeare may have known the Philiades episode in Lucian. But the comedy has its own old Athenian in the person of Philargurus, whose miserliness sets Timon's generosity in sharp relief. Philargurus is obsessed with finding a rich husband for his daughter, and entertains first the 'cittie heyre' Gelasimus, and then the even richer Timon:

Venus doth fauour thee aboue the rest;
A seconde person doth desire thy loue,
A golden youthe: reiecte Gelasimus;
This is farre richer, and thee, Callimele,
Will take without a dowry.   (III, ii, p. 47)

Like Philargurus, Shakespeare's Old Athenian is concerned with making a profitable match for his only daughter –

I am a man
That from my first have been inclin'd to thrift,
And my estate deserves an heir more rais'd
Than one which holds a trencher   (I, i, 120–3)

– whereas Philiades, unlike either stage miser, never expresses the slightest concern over his daughter's marriage to any man, let alone a rich one. It seems likely, then, that Shakespeare used the comedy rather than the dialogue as the source for this episode.

Gelasimus seems to have served as a model, at least in part, for Shakespeare's cardboard character Ventidius. Both of them are Athenian citizens and possessors of that audacity so peculiar to the bourgeoisie, which permits them

---

[1] E. C. Pettet, 'Timon of Athens: The Disruption of Feudal Morality,' *RES*, 23 (1947), 335, thinks that the whores are intended to be emblems of usury. Kenneth Muir, too, in *Shakespeare's Tragic Sequence* (1972), p. 191, suggests that sexual relations are bound totally to the cash nexus, and thus define the nature of society in *Timon*.

to boast of the wealth they inherited when their fathers died. There is no equivalent character in Lucian. Ventidius, in being redeemed from his creditors by Timon's payment of five talents, resembles Lucian's orator Demeas, whom Timon frees from arrest by paying a sixteen-talent bond. But the author of the comedy not only keeps the Demeas episode intact, but also adds a similar scene of his own invention in which Timon liberates another flatterer by paying a debt of the very amount Shakespeare mentions:[1]

Eutrapelus.
  Timon, lend me a litle goulden dust,
  To ffree me from this ffeind; some fower talents
  Will doe it.

Timon.
  Yea, take ffyue: while I haue gould,
  I will not see my ffreinds to stand in neede.

                                    (I, ii, p. 7)

This apparently was Shakespeare's model for Timon's response to Ventidius's request:

  I am not of that feather to shake off
  My friend when he must need me. I do know him
  A gentleman that well deserves a help,
  Which he shall haue: I'll pay the debt, and free him.

                                    (I, i, 103–6)

It is groundless to claim Lucian as the source for this scene when the details match those of the comedy alone.

Demeas does not appear at all in *Timon of Athens*; but the author of the comedy translated the character from Lucian almost verbatim. 'Almost verbatim': therein lies the crux. For what the author neglected to translate (or, more probably, the copyist neglected to transcribe) from Demeas's hyperbolic address to Timon has caused critics to conclude that Shakespeare must have referred to the original. Shakespeare mentions Timon's military service to Athens on three different occasions. Alcibiades has 'heard and griev'd / How cursed Athens, mindless of thy worth, / Forgetting thy great deeds, when neighbor states, / But for thy

sword and fortune, trod upon them –' (IV, iii, 93–6). This is a new theme, introduced late and taken up again soon by a senator who, repenting Athens's ingratitude, begs Timon 'to take / The captainship' and 'drive back / Of Alcibiades th' approaches wild' (V, i, 159–63); and it is capped by another senator who warns, 'We stand much hazard if they bring not Timon' (V, ii, 5). Shakespeare evidently wished to stress Timon's importance to the state in order to elevate him into something of a public character, in whose name Alcibiades might execute a revenge on the whole realm of Athens. If Shakespeare needed any inspiration for elevating Timon's character, he could have found it in Demeas's remarks about Timon's military glory in the *Misanthropos*:

– 'and Whereas he fought with distinction last year at Acharnae cutting two Peloponnesian companies to pieces –' . . . – 'and Whereas by political measures and responsible advice and military action he has conferred great benefits on his country...'

                                    (Fowler, p. 50)

These may be the very lines which the copyist of the comedy unwittingly omitted. The author probably supplied them, for they are clearly required in context. Their omission renders Timon's line, 'I neere as yett bore armes out of Athens', irrelevant. But the author added some new lines to Demeas's preface which imply that Timon has distinguished himself in military service and which may justify both the seemingly irrelevant line and the one which follows it, 'But thou shalt in the next warr':

Wher's Athens piller? wher's my glory? wher's Timon? Thou hast blest myne eyes, now I see thee. Joue saue thee, who art the defence of Greece, and the whole worlds delight!   (V, v, p. 92)

This suggestion of Timon's importance to Athens, even if one assumes that the omitted lines were never spoken in performance, may

---

[1] This parallel was first noticed by Ernest Hunter Wright, *The Authorship of Timon of Athens* (New York, 1910), p. 19.

have been sufficient to have sparked Shakespeare's imagination without necessitating his reference to the original source.

Another character whom Shakespeare purportedly derived from the *Misanthropos* is Apemantus, a figure 'roughly corresponding', writes Maxwell, 'to Lucian's Thrasicles as well as to the more shadowy Apemantus of Plutarch' (pp. xxi–xxii); Thrasicles, however, has almost nothing in common with Apemantus. He is the stoic who, in the morning, 'will utter a thousand maxims, expounding Virtue, arraigning self-indulgence, lauding simplicity', but who, at dinner, 'proceeds to turn his morning maxims inside out', and 'laps like a dog, with his nose in his plate, as if he expected to find Virtue there' (Fowler, p. 51). Apemantus, on the contrary, as the near-relation of Diogenes the Cynic, who rails at social vices with little regard for patience, prides himself on being consistent, on shunning the society of Timon's banquet and scorning Timon's meat. Thrasicles comes to fawn on Timon for gold; Apemantus, to flite with him. Slight evidence for claiming a correspondence, to be sure. On the other hand Speusippus and Stilpo, the 'two lying philosophers' in the comedy, are patterned directly after Thrasicles. They lecture Timon on the virtue of stoic fortitude but, in a sudden reversal, become epicureans at Timon's table. Like Thrasicles, they return to Timon in exile in order to win a share of his gold. I suspect that neither source suggested much more than the mere idea of 'the philosopher' to Shakespeare; and that idea he could have gleaned as easily from the comedy as from the dialogue.

Thrasicles, feigning disinterest, advises Timon to get rid of his newfound treasure as a sign of *contemptus mundi*: 'many is the man it has sunk in helpless misery. Take my advice, and fling it bodily into the sea' (Fowler, p. 52). This line probably influenced Timon's response to his newfound gold in the comedy:

> What, shall I hide
> My new found treasure vnderneath the earth,
> Or shall I drowne it in the ocean?
> Though all the world loue thee, Timon hates thee:
> Ile drowne thee in the seas profunditie.
>
> (v, iii, p. 84)

Shakespeare echoes the first half of this speech in Timon's response to his discovery – 'Th'art quick, / But yet I'll bury thee' (IV, iii, 45–6) – without alluding to burial at sea. Shakespeare apparently took his lead from the comedy rather than from the dialogue.

It should be noted, too, that although Timon ultimately is willing to keep the gold and live in isolated luxury according to Lucian, in both plays Timon is persuaded to keep the gold only as a means of revenge on his flatterers. The two plays are alike, and unlike the dialogue, remarks Bond, in that Timon's instinctive impulse to hide the gold is soon overborne by his sense of its mischief (pp. 65–6).

In the *Misanthropos* Timon beats back each intruder individually with his spade, and for his final assault on the whole army of flatterers retreats to a rock to pelt them with stones. The author of the comedy altered the order of Lucian's drubbings: his Timon pelts the flatterers with stones at a mock-banquet in Act IV, and so resorts to his spade to beat them off in Act v. Shakespeare adopted the sequence of the comedy. There is no stage direction in Shakespeare's mock-banquet scene to indicate that Timon pelts his guests with stones: the only explicit direction reads 'Throwing the water in their faces'; one more vague reads 'Drives them out'. But the mock-banquet scene is unique to the two plays; and the last line of the departing guests, 'One day he gives us diamonds, next day stones' (III, vi, 115), certainly indicates that Timon threw stones to drive them out and suggests that Shakespeare may have had the climactic action of this scene from the comedy so firmly in mind that he had no need to write it down. Shakespeare's Timon throws a stone at Apemantus (IV, iii) to get rid of him, and then turns to an alternate weapon (whether his spade or his bare hands is not made clear) in order to beat the Poet and the Painter off the stage (V, i) as a last act of aggression, just as Timon in the comedy drives off the flatterers with his spade at the very end.

Muriel Bradbrook believes that the comedy was written c. 1611 as a parody of *Timon of Athens* and cites the comedy's numerous references to Jove as proof of its indebtedness.[1] When Shakespeare's Timon pelts his guests with stones at the mock-banquet, she asserts, he resembles nothing so much as Jove hurling down his thunderbolts. And Shakespeare certainly would have traced this resemblance to Lucian, whose Timon frequently invokes Jove's thunderbolt as an instrument of revenge. But the author of the comedy is more explicitly Lucianic in his use of Jove imagery. During his mock-banquet scene, Timon hurls stones which have been painted to look like artichokes ('To the irreverent, Jove's thunderbolt, as depicted by such iconographers as G. Cartari, resembles nothing so much as an elongated artichoke' – Bradbrook, p. 99) while uttering a line of self-deification:

> If I Joues horridde thunderbolte did holde
> Within my hande, thus, thus would I darte it!
>
> (IV, v, p. 75)

Bradbrook attempts to justify her association of Timon of Athens with Jove by citing further evidence from Demeas's oration in Lucian: 'it is the pleasure of the Assembly and the Council the ten divisions of the High Court and the Borough Councils individually and collectively That a golden statue of the said Timon be placed on the Acropolis alongside of Athene with a thunderbolt in the hand and a seven-rayed aureole on the head' (Fowler, p. 50). But this part of Demeas's oration is included in the comedy as well. Shakespeare, in fact, refers to Jove only once by name, when

Timon is persuading Alcibiades to be his avenging deity:

> Be as a planetary plague, when Jove
> Will o'er some high-vic'd city hang his poison
> In the sick air.   (IV, iii, 110–12)

It is an invocation remarkably like one in the comedy:

> O Joue that darts't thy peircing thunderboults,
> Lett a dire comett with his blazing streames
> Threaten a deadly plauge from heau'n on earth!
>
> (V, iii, p. 80)

It is far more logical to conclude from this evidence that Shakespeare, recalling the importance of the Jove imagery in the comedy, incorporated a little of it into *Timon of Athens*, than that the author of the comedy seized upon a few scattered, veiled allusions to Jove in *Timon of Athens* and expanded them to Lucianic proportions. Lucian directly inspired the mock-heroic invocations to Jove in the comedy. His influence on Shakespeare was indirect, probably filtered through the comedy.

A great deal has been made of the beast imagery in *Timon of Athens*, and at least two recent critics have suggested that Shakespeare derived it from the *Misanthropos*, in which the flatterers are pictured as birds of prey devouring an innocent victim:[2]

...he did not realize that his protégés were carrion crows and wolves; vultures were feeding on his unfortunate liver, and he took them for friends and good comrades, showing a fine appetite just to please him. So they gnawed his bones perfectly clean, sucked out with great precision any marrow there might be in them, and went off...   (Fowler, p. 34)

[1] 'The Comedy of Timon: A Reveling Play of the Inner Temple,' *Renaissance Drama*, 9 (1966), 99–100; also *The Tragic Pageant of 'Timon of Athens'* (Cambridge, 1966), p. 19, reprinted in *Shakespeare the Craftsman* (1969), in which she claims that Lucian is the immediate source of Shakespeare's Jove imagery. For my refutation of her theory, see 'Date and Production', pp. 113ff.

[2] See Farnham, pp. 63–4; and G. R. Hibbard's edition of the play (Harmondsworth, 1970), p. 21.

Shakespeare uses beast imagery so frequently that I am reluctant to think he resorted to any specific source for it. But as critics have made claims of his indebtedness to Lucian, I feel duty-bound to point out that virtually the same imagery can be found in the comedy: 'I would not. see / My goodes by crowes devoured as they bee' (I, i, p. 4); 'They follow thee as crowes doe carrion' (v, v, p. 89); 'Yee crowes, yee vultures, yee doe gape in vaine: / I will make duckes and drakes with this my golde' (v, v, p. 91). If Shakespeare needed a source for his beast imagery, the comedy would have served as adequately as the dialogue.

A few similarities between the *Misanthropos* and *Timon of Athens*, however, cannot be accounted for by the source play. The Poet in *Timon of Athens*, for example, more closely resembles characters in the *Misanthropos* than any character in the comedy. Like Lucian's Gnathonides, who approaches Timon in exile with a new dithyramb, Shakespeare's Poet offers Timon a piece calculated to appeal to his misanthropy, 'a satire against the softness of prosperity, with a discovery of the infinite flatteries that. follow youth and opulency' (v, i, 33–5). Hermogenes, the figure in the comedy who most closely resembles Gnathonides, actually is modelled on a musician of the same name in Jonson's *Poetaster*; but he renounces musicianship the moment Timon makes him rich and never offers to sing for him in exile. Furthermore, the hypocrisy of the Poet's satire, with its implicit self-exemption, is patterned after the miser Philiades's warning of Timon against his fellow flatterers (see Fowler, p. 49). There is nothing comparable in the comedy.

In his Arden edition of 1905, K. Deighton listed what he thought were verbal parallels between *Timon of Athens* and the *Misanthropos*. All but two of them have been discounted by subsequent scholars; but those two are intriguing. The first is the stronger. Lucian's line, 'I cannot get a glance from the men who once cringed and worshipped and hung upon my nod' (Fowler, pp. 32–3), is distinctly echoed by Shakespeare's Poet: '– even he drops down / The knee before him, and returns in peace / Most rich in Timon's nod' (I, i, 61–3). The parallel, though inconclusive, is all the more suggestive because there is no corresponding line in the comedy. The nearest is spoken by a minor character with reference to himself rather than to Timon: 'I haue whole islands at my beck and nodd' (I, iv, p. 13).

The second verbal echo is not quite so striking. Timon's declaration, 'I am *Misanthropos*, and hate mankind' (IV, iii, 54), is thought to be a recasting of Lucian's 'Be the name he loves Misanthropus, and the marks whereby he may be known peevishness and spleen...' (Fowler, p. 47). But Shakespeare may as easily have borrowed the name 'Timon Misanthropus' from North's Life of Antony, where it appears three times in the margin.

Shakespeare alludes to Plutus at I, i, 275–6: 'Plutus the god of gold / Is but his steward.' As the god of riches, Plutus plays a significant part as Timon's antagonist in the dialogue. His name does not occur in the comedy.

It has been suggested by W. H. Clemons that Timon's apostrophe to gold in *Timon of Athens* was modelled on a parallel apostrophe in the *Misanthropos*.[1] The absence of such an apostrophe from the comedy is offered as further evidence that Shakespeare had direct recourse to Lucian. The two apostrophes are similar in their use of erotic imagery:

Come to me, my own, my beloved. I doubt the tale no longer; well might Zeus take the shape of gold; where is the maid that would not open her bosom to receive so fair a lover gliding through the roof?

(Fowler, p. 46)

O thou sweet king-killer, and dear divorce
'Twixt natural son and sire, thou bright defiler

[1] 'The Sources of *Timon of Athens*', *Princeton University Bulletin*, 15 (1904), 219.

Of Hymen's purest bed, thou valiant Mars,
Thou ever young, fresh, loved and delicate wooer,
Whose blush doth thaw the consecrated snow
That lies on Dian's lap!   (IV, iii, 384–9)

But they are so discrepant in tone – the one rapturous, as to a lover; the other bitter, as to a whore – that the case for direct influence remains undecided. There is, perhaps, enough evidence to indicate that Shakespeare was recalling Lucian from a firsthand acquaintance, possibly from a school text.

While these parallels prevent me from stating conclusively that Shakespeare could have derived all the Lucianic material from the comedy, they nevertheless are tenuous enough to allow me to doubt that he had recourse to the original dialogue at the time he wrote his play. The problem must go unsolved. But the the balance of evidence suggests that he gleaned all the important Lucianic material from comedy.

II

Working from Apemantus's assessment of Timon's character, 'The middle of humanity thou never knewest, but the extremity of both ends' (IV, iii, 301–2), Geoffrey Bullough states, 'Plutarch presented one extremity; Lucian indicated the previous existence of the other' (p. 247). But this statement only serves to remind us that even Lucian could not have been the ultimate source for Shakespeare's play. His narrative is the equivalent of only Acts IV and V of *Timon of Athens*, only Act V of the comedy. Lucian, says Bullough, 'indicated the previous existence' of Timon's prosperity; but if this mere indication of something gone by provided Shakespeare with enough substance to structure three acts, it must have been magic to his imagination. No other source so thin had undergone such marvelous transformation in Shakespeare's hands. For *The Life of Tymon of Athens* – and this is its Folio title – concentrates on Timon before he banishes himself from Athens, depicts how he enjoyed his fortune and how he lost it. A few critics over

the years have conceded, none too willingly, that the comedy may in some way have contributed to Shakespeare's grand design:[1] there are many correspondences unique to the two plays, to be found in no common source. Of all the possible sources for *Timon of Athens*, only the comedy depicts Timon in prosperity – and for a full three acts. I suggest that the comedy was the most significant influence on the way Shakespeare developed both the structure and the theme of *Timon of Athens*.

If we except the Jonsonian sub-plot from the comedy and narrow our focus only to those scenes in which Timon figures, we arrive at the following synopsis:

Timon enters as a magnificent prodigal, entertaining his parasitic companions and paying off their debts, revelling with them, and finally falling in love. With

[1] George Steevens, *Shakspere* (20 vols., 1788), XVII, Annotations pp. 3–4, was first to record a few similarities between the two plays. The problem at once arose, who borrowed from whom? Most critics, finding the comedy an embarrassment, have tried to circumvent the issue of Shakespeare's possible debt. G. C. Moore Smith, 'Notes on Some English University Plays', *MLR*, 3 (1907–8), 143, and Georges A. Bonnard, 'Note sur les Sources de *Timon of Athens*', *Études Anglaises*, 7 (1954), 59–69, for example, claim that the comedy was a school play, never acted in London and therefore unknown to Shakespeare; Warwick Bond (p. 66) and Geoffrey Bullough (p. 235), on the other hand, join Muriel Bradbrook in supposing that the comedy was written later than Shakespeare's *Timon*. Ernest Hunter Wright was daring enough to examine the problem without bias and, having assessed the major correspondences, to declare the comedy a significant source for Shakespeare (pp. 17–23). Tucker Brooke, *The Tudor Drama* (Boston, 1911), 410–11, acknowledged Shakespeare's probable debt without close scrutiny; and J. C. Maxwell, after more careful deliberation, was forced to the same acknowledgement (pp. xix–xxi). It is curious that no one has bothered to look any more closely for correspondences than Steevens and W. H. Clemons (p. 217) did. Perhaps critics are satisfied with the obvious few. Even Robert Hilles Goldsmith, the most recent to ask 'Did Shakespeare Use the Old Timon Comedy?', *Shakespeare Quarterly*, 9 (1958), 31–8, was far more concerned with the comedy as a source for *King Lear* than for *Timon of Athens*.

him there is a faithful steward who remonstrates against his extravagance and warns him in vain that his wealth is being rapidly depleted by riot. Timon, at the height of his fortune, suddenly loses everything: destitute, he appeals to his companions for help, only to be refused. He grows bitter and stages a mock-banquet, at which he pelts them with stones. Then, in absolute misanthropy, he banishes himself from Athens, but is followed by his steward – the one man who does not forsake him. Digging in the earth, he finds unwanted gold; and as word of his wealth spreads, he is once again approached by the old parasites, whom he drives off with his spade.

This distillation of the main plot of the comedy, which omits only a handful of details, corresponds almost exactly with the plot of *Timon of Athens*. Though ultimately Jonsonian in spirit, the comedy nevertheless is the only source which could have provided Shakespeare with the *De Casibus* tragic pattern of Timon's rise to and fall from fortune; and this pattern is reinforced throughout by an undercurrent of tragic *sententiae*: 'Base pouertie doth followe luxury' (III, v, p. 56): 'Man's like vnto the sea, that ebbes and flowes, / And all things in this world vnstable are' (IV, iii, p. 68).

In neither play does Timon adjust to his fall from fortune with patience or fortitude. In the comedy, the hypocritical philosophers instruct Timon in the virtue of stoic endurance:

> Art thou opprest with griefe? be patient.
> A heauy burthen patience makes light.
> Hath fortune left thee naked and forlorne?
> Then clothe thyselfe with vertue....
> The chiefest good in vertue doth consiste.
> Whose rage is moderate, that man is wise.
>
> (IV, iii, p. 68)

But in both plays, Timon's rage is immoderate and belies any claim that he has accommodated himself to a life of poverty. In Lucian, on the contrary, Timon accepts the allegorical figure of Poverty as 'a true teacher...of Wisdom and Toil' who has 'perfected him in virtue'; it is a stoic virtue Timon learns from Poverty, and he is content with it (see Fowler, pp. 43–4).

That this accommodation is not suggested in either play indicates a certain connection between them. A further examination of details will bolster my argument that the comedy was Shakespeare's chief source.

Feasting is the central emblem of Timon's prosperity in both plays: the lure of food and drink proves irresistible to the parasites, and is ironically turned against them in the mock-banquet. There are corresponding scenes in the two plays in which Timon, having redeemed insolvent friends and enriched others, invites them all to dine as a kind of reward for their constancy. 'Hermogenes, thou hast deseru'd thye dynner', remarks the comic Timon after he has been entertained with a song (I, v, p. 19); similarly the tragic Timon says to the Poet who has offered him a flattering verse, 'You must needs dine with me. Go not you hence / Till I have thank'd you' (I, i, 243–4). The feast itself immediately follows in *Timon of Athens*; in the comedy, however, it is postponed by the comic plot and ultimately becomes a drinking bout at a tavern.

Between these emblematic scenes of communion and the later mock-banquets fall the scenes of appeal, in which Timon wakes up to the ingratitude of his erstwhile 'friends'. Each play devotes three consecutive scenes to these trials of friendship. In the comedy Timon makes the appeals himself, while in the tragedy he remains offstage, allowing his servants to make the appeals for him – a device by which Shakespeare focuses with utmost clarity on the various modes of hypocrisy. But Shakespeare recalls the comedy at least once, in the scene in which Lucullus tries to bribe Timon's servant with 'three solidares' to 'say thou saw'st me not'. The servant's response is violent:

> Is't possible the world should so much differ,
> And we alive that lived? Fly, damned baseness,
> To him that worships thee!
> [*Throwing the money back at Lucullus.*
> (III, i, 46–8)

In the comedy, Demeas has given Timon 'this one groate', with the provision, 'thou must publish my munificence'. Timon's response is what Shakespeare echoes in his servant: 'Thus I returne it backe into thy face: / Ne're bende thy browes; proude threats I doe not feare' (IV, i, p. 60).

The mock-banquets are handled with remarkable similarity in the two plays. They come upon the heels of Timon's rejection by his friends as magnificent gestures of revenge, made all the more effective because the friends, obedient to their instinctive greed, come unsuspecting that Timon has anything up his sleeve. In the comedy they assume that the banquet is Timon's farewell gift to them; in the tragedy, that Timon's bankruptcy was only feigned. In both plays Timon is assisted by his steward. Even the wording is similar:

Timon. But it will lessen griefe: something Ile doe; / Ile not consume this day in idlenesse. / Inuite these rascals. / *Laches.* What shall they doe here? /	*Timon.* . . . Go, bid all my friends again, / Lucius, Lucullus and Sempronius: all. / I'll once more feast the rascals. *Steward.* O my lord, / You only speak from your distracted soul; / There's not so much left to furnish out / A moderate table.
Timon. I haue prepared them a worthy feaste: / Goe, call them therefore; tell them there remaines / Of soe much wealth as yet some ouerplus. (IV, iii, p. 70)	*Timon.* Be it not in thy care. / Go, I charge thee, invite them all, let in the tide / Of knaves once more; my cook and I'll provide. (III, iv, 106–14)

The friends arrive and are duly pelted; but in each play they exonerate themselves with assurances that Timon has gone mad. Timon hurls verbal abuse at them as well as stones, and concludes with a general curse on Athens – the same pattern in both plays.

In examining the influence of a rather amateur source play on a play of genius, it is always safer to look for similarities of plot and structure than for verbal echoes. Shakespeare's poetry, after all, so far transcends the verse of the comedy that it seems almost blasphemous to suggest that Shakespeare could have been inspired by certain passages from it. But inspiration can come from strange sources; and it is so likely that Shakespeare knew the comedy, and borrowed heavily from it for the form of *Timon of Athens*, that one ought not totally to disregard evidence of verbal borrowing.

Timon's great inversion of Ulysses's degree speech, indeed, contains scattered recollections of the comic Timon's curses. His speech is almost incantatory in its call for the disruption of a natural order: 'Matrons, turn incontinent! / Obedience fail in children! . . . Son of sixteen, / Pluck the lin'd crutch from thy old limping sire; / With it beat out his brains! . . . And yet confusion live! Plagues incident to men, / Your potent and infectious fevers heap / On Athens ripe for stroke!' (IV, i, 1 ff.). The curses which the comic Timon and his steward ring down on Athens in their stichomythic incantation are remarkably similar to those of the tragic Timon:

Timon. Men, woemen, children perish by the sword!
Laches. Lett ffunerall follow funerall, and noe parte
      Of this world ruyne want! . . .
Timon. Let riuers all wax drye,
      The hunger pyned parent eate the sonne!
Laches. The sonne the parent!
Timon. All plauges fall on this generacion,
      And neuer cease!   (v, iii, p. 81)

Sun imagery is central to *Timon of Athens* as a natural correlative to Timon's fortune: from Apemantus's warning, 'Men shut their doors against a setting sun' (I, ii, 141), to Timon's last line, 'Sun, hide thy beams, Timon hath done his reign' (v, i, 222), the sun is invoked as a deity of scourge: 'Thou sun, that comforts, burn!' (v, i, 130) exclaims Timon with deliberate paradox; and again, 'O blessed breeding sun, draw from the earth / Rotten humidity; below thy sister's orb / Infect the air!' (IV, iii, 1–3). Bond (p. 65) remarks that although the *Misanthropos* contains no invocations to the sun, the comedy does. 'Thee, thee, O sunne, I doe to witnesse call', cries the comic Timon at one point (IV, iii, p. 69); and at another, 'Lett neuer sunn shyne to the world againe, / Or Luna with her brothers borrow'd light!' (V, ii, p. 81). Although the author never identifies the sun as the instrument of plague, as Shakespeare does, he nevertheless juxtaposes his solar imagery with plague imagery to achieve a similar effect: 'I lothe to breathe that aire; / I grieue that these mine eyes should see that sunne' (V, v, p. 94).

The source for Timon's existential declaration in *Timon of Athens* –

> My long sickness
> Of health and living now begins to mend,
> And nothing brings me all things
>
> (V, i, 185–7)

– has long been thought to be 2 Corinthians vi. 10. But there is a curious repartee between Timon and Gelasimus in the comedy –

Gelasimus. What's this?
Timon.　　Somethinge.
Gelasimus. What's this something?
Timon.　　Nothing, I say, nothing:
　　　　　　All things are made nothing
>
> (V, ii, p. 64)

– which provides just enough ingredients for Shakespeare to have made poetic manna of it, without having to turn to its ultimate Biblical source.

The most striking parallel between the two plays is the presence of a faithful steward who follows Timon into exile. Flavius's only forebear among the known sources is Laches. Each steward is a voice of reason, trying in vain to curb the spending of his spendthrift master, grieving over the likely consequences of such blind excess. 'What will this come to?' asks Flavius:

He commands us to provide, and give great gifts,
And all out of an empty coffer;
Nor will he know his purse, or yield me this,
To show him what a beggar his heart is,
Being of no power to make his wishes good.

(I, ii, 189–94)

His sentiments directly echo those of Laches (above, p. 105), who hopes that Jove will convert Timon 'Before his chests bee emptied', and before 'hee feele...the rodde of desp'rate misery' (III, ii, p. 48).

The moving scene in *Timon of Athens* in which Flavius finally gets Timon to listen to an account of his insolvency is strategically placed before the scenes of appeal, when the tragic sequence of events has already been set in motion by the usurers' demands for repayment. This scene has no counterpart in the comedy; but Flavius's description of his earlier attempts to warn Timon, and Timon's persistent rebuffs, indicates that Shakespeare may have been recalling the opening scene of the comedy, in which Laches tries to warn an ungrateful Timon not to be so prodigal:

Timon. Laches, hast thou receau'd my rents?
Laches. Master, I haue,
　　　　And brought in sacks filled with goulden
　　　　　　talents:
　　　　Is't your pleasure that I cast them into pryson?
Timon. Into pryson! why soe?
Laches. Lett your chests be the pryson,
　　　　Your locks the keeper, and your keyes the
　　　　　　porter,
　　　　Otherwise they'le fly away, swyfter then birds
　　　　　　or wyndes.
Timon. I will no miser bee.
　　　　Flye, gould, enioye the sunn beames!...
Laches. Who beares a princelie mynd needes princelie
　　　　　　wealth,
　　　　Or ells hee'le wither like a rose in springe,
　　　　Nought wilbe left but thornes of povertie,
　　　　Master, thou art noe kinge, noe prince;...
Timon. I'st euen soe, my learned counsaylor?
　　　　...By all the gods I sweare,
　　　　Bridle thy tounge, or I will cutt it out,
　　　　And turne thee out of dores.　(I, i, pp. 3–4)

This scene may have served as the model for the experience which Flavius describes as follows:

> O my good lord,
> At many times I brought in my accompts,
> Laid them before you; you would throw them off,
> And say you found them in mine honesty.
> When for some trifling present you have bid me
> Return so much, I have shook my head and wept:
> Yea, 'gainst th'authority of manners, pray'd you
> To hold your hand more close. I did endure
> Not seldom, nor no slight checks, when I have
> Prompted you in the ebb of your estate
> And your great flow of debts.   (II, ii, 137–46)

I might add parenthetically that the comedy may have been the immediate source of Shakespeare's confusion over the value of the Attic talent. Terence Spencer has argued that Shakespeare's widely discrepant sums of talents are proof positive that *Timon of Athens* is only an author's draft.[1] Timon requests fifty talents from his friends, a thousand from the senate – absurd requests, considering that the talent today is roughly equivalent to three thousand dollars – but elsewhere, as instances of apparent largesse, pays off a friend's five-talent debt and is willing to 'strain a little' (I, i, 146) to match a three-talent dowry. Shakespeare obviously learned the value of a talent in the course of composition, Spencer concludes; and those places in III, ii in which the amount is left indefinite ('so many talents') clinches his argument for Shakespeare's uncertainty.

Oliver suggests (pp. xxvii–viii) that the uncertainty may have sprung from North's Plutarch, wherein hundreds and thousands of talents are common sums. But it seems to me that the comedy might more readily have caused the uncertainty: Laches has 'brought in sacks filled with goulden talents' – indicative of great sums; and yet, as I have noted earlier, Timon in a magnificent gesture releases Eutrapelus from a five-talent bond, the same amount with which Shakespeare's Timon frees Ventidius; and furthermore Gelasimus begs

fortune to pour down 'fyve or six talents... into my hands' (V, iii, p. 85). Here, I suggest, is the likely source of Shakespeare's confusion.

From Laches's determination to follow Timon into exile and to remain his servant 'through sword, through fire, and deathe... to the pale house of hell' (IV, v, p. 76), Shakespeare wrought a whole scene of Flavius's paying off Timon's faithful servants before going to seek his master. It resembles the poignant scene in *Antony and Cleopatra* (IV, ii) in which Antony bids farewell to his 'Servitors': and just as the servitors' loyalty favorably mirrors Antony's character, so the servants here favorably reflect Timon's inherent nobility. Left alone onstage, Flavius states his intention to follow Timon: 'I'll ever serve his mind with my best will; / Whilst I have gold I'll be his steward still' (IV, ii, 50–1). The couplet is a recasting of Laches's, 'Well, howsoeuer fortune play her parte, / Laches from Timon neuer shall departe' (III, ii, p. 48).

When the comic Timon discovers that Laches has intruded upon his isolation, he abuses him with curt language which Shakespeare appears to have adopted for a different scene in which Alcibiades confronts Timon:

Alcibiades.
> What art thou there? Speak.

Timon.
> A beast as thou art. The canker gnaw thy heart,
> For showing me again the eyes of man!

Alcibiades.
> What is thy name? Is man so hateful to thee
> That art thyself a man?

Timon.
> I am *Misanthropos*, and hate mankind.
> (IV, iii, 49–54)

---

[1] 'Shakespeare Learns the Value of Money: The Dramatist at Work on *Timon of Athens*', *Shakespeare Survey 6* (Cambridge, 1953), 75–8. Spencer refers to the work of J. M. Robertson, *Shakespeare and Chapman* (1917), p. 133, who cited the discrepancies as evidence for divided authorship.

By eliminating Shakespeare's beast imagery, we are left with lines nearly identical with those muttered by the comic Timon when he sees Laches – 'This former face I hate, detest, and flye':

Laches. What is the reason thou dost hate me thus?...
 What wickednesse doth make me soe abhor'd?:

Timon. Thou art a man, that's wickednesse enough;
 I hate that fault; I hate all humane kinde,
 I hate myselfe...   (v, ii, p. 80)

Laches is more than just a faithful servant. He is an occasional satirist who rails against the parasites during Timon's prosperity and joins Timon's invective against them in exile, something which the more compromising Flavius never does. In his latter role, Laches may, as Robert Hilles Goldsmith argues, have influenced Shakespeare's concept of Apemantus: though not a confirmed cynic, Laches makes asides which have that bitter Apemantean ring to them –

  Hee baites his hooke to gaine some of thy golde;
  I know this fellowes crafty pollicy   (v, v, p. 90)

– and, as Goldsmith notes, answers Timon, 'in language which anticipates the currish replies of Apemantus to Shakespeare's Timon' (pp. 33–4):

Timon. Thou speakest like thie selfe, and in thy kinde: / Lett those that are borne slaues beare abiect minds. / I Timon am, not Laches.
Laches. I, poore Laches, / Not Timon; yf I were, I would not see / My goodes by crowes devoured as they bee.
                    (I, i, p. 4)

Timon. If thou hadst not been born the worst of men, / Thou hadst been a knave and flatterer.
Apemantus. Art thou proud yet?
Timon. Ay, that I am not thee.
Apemantus. I, that I was / No prodigal.
                    (IV, iii, 277–80)

Apparently Laches's roles as Timon's foil were diverse enough to suggest to Shakespeare both the faithful steward and the disinterested cynic.

Not all the evidence cited above, I admit, is equally convincing. The comedy is, after all, largely an exposé of Jonsonian humourous characters; its tone, not at all akin to Shakespeare's bitter tragedy. But Timon himself, though the comedy's central character, remains oddly on the periphery of the comic action – a misfit, a railer, whose fall from fortune follows a distinctly tragic curve. The number of important correspondences between the two plays, so much larger than between *Timon of Athens* and any other supposed source, points to the inevitable conclusion: not Plutarch's *Lives*, nor Lucian's *Misanthropos*, but the academic comedy, crude though it may be, is the stuff that *Timon of Athens* was made on.

RE-ENTER THE STAGE DIRECTION: SHAKESPEARE AND SOME CONTEMPORARIES

E. A. J. HONIGMANN

The twentieth century has seen important advances in the editing of Elizabethan dramatic texts. Sir Walter Greg, the acknowledged leader of the 'new bibliography', took a very special interest in the plays' stage directions which, as he demonstrated, can tell us much about their textual origins. Yet while the diversity and significance of Elizabethan stage directions is now recognised, modern editors of Shakespeare and his contemporaries have devised no new ways of dealing with them: they reprint them in their original form or adopt eighteenth-century interpolations, or, more often than not, they conflate the two, with unhappy consequences. Here I offer some preliminary remarks on modern critical editions and their stage directions (which for the purposes of this paper I take to include speech prefixes); a more systematic study would reveal other inconsistencies and errors, and could greatly help future producers of the plays.

Misplaced stage directions. (a) Every editor of Shakespeare knows that scores of stage directions have been moved in the *textus receptus* from their position in Q and F texts, where they were inserted a line or more too early or too late. Such rearrangement elicits little comment, the usual assumption being that juggling with the text is established practice and needs no defence. What requires comment is that, in addition, many more stage directions are still printed too early or too late;

editors have merely tinkered with the problem, their *ad hoc* decisions have observed no overall policy, and much textual tidying remains to be done. Compare the following:

1. *Enter Oliuer.* | *Adam.* Yonder comes my Master (*A.Y.L.I.*, Q_3^a).
2. Heere comes Monsieur the *Beu.* | *Enter le Beau* (Q_4^a).
3. Yonder sure they are comming. Let vs now stay | and see it. | *Flourish. Enter Duke*...(Q_4^a).
4. *Enter Duke with Lords.* | 2 lines | Looke, here comes the Duke...(Q_5^a).
5. *Enter Corin and Siluius.* | *Ros.* I, be so good *Touchstone*: Look you, who comes | here...(Q_6^a).
6. *Enter Iaques.* | *1. Lord.* He saues my labor by his owne approach (R_1^a).
7. But who comes here? | *Enter Orlando* (R_1^a).
8. Heere comes yong Mr *Ganimed*... | *Enter Rosalind* (R_2^a).
9. *Enter Celia with a writing.* | *Ros.* Peace, here comes my sister reading...(R_2^a).[1]

In *As You Like It* alone there are twenty such entries, preceded by 'see where they come' or its equivalent eight times, and followed by similar words twelve times. How important are these differences? Editors usually stick to the Folio's placing of the stage directions, which could suggest that Rosalind is seen by the stage characters before the audience sees her whereas Celia is seen first by the audience (8, 9, above). If no such suggestion is intended it would surely be better to standardise

[1] Shakespeare in old spelling is cited from the Folio, unless I state the contrary.

the placing of the stage directions, either just before or just after 'see where they come': so many other stage directions are moved up or down because Shakespeare and his copyists are thought to have been careless about such matters that we must reckon with the possibility that 'see where they come' entries are further examples of carelessness.

As it happens there are some signs that a Folio editor or collator was interested in such trivialities. When the Folio copy for *Othello* was prepared many entries were moved to a later point in the text, compared with their placing in the Quarto.

1. But looke, what Lights come yond? | *Enter Cassio, with Torches.* (*Othello*, Folio, 2s₄ᵇ).

2. Here comes another Troope to seeke for you. | *Enter Brabantio...*(ibid.).

3. *1. Senator.* Here comes *Brabantio*, and the Valiant Moore. | *Enter Brabantio...*(2s₅ᵃ).

4. *Enter Desdemona, Iago, Rodorigo, and Æmilia.* | Oh behold, / The Riches of the Ship is come on shore (2s₆ᵇ).

5. Loe, where he comes. | *Enter Othello...*(2t₁ᵃ).

6. *Enter Othello.* | Looke where he comes... (2t₅ᵃ).

7. *Enter Iago, and Cassio.* | Looke you, Cassio and my Husband. (2t₆ᵃ).

Yet, though sufficiently interested to improve on his Quarto copy[1] in the placing of all these entries and many more, the Folio collator of *Othello* seems to have cared very little whether he put the stage entry first or 'see where they come'. From this I deduce that other 'Elizabethans' concerned with the transmission of texts will have cared even less, and that modern editors are free to standardise.

If we wish to standardise, however, let us note that there will be special cases. An entry accompanied not by a statement but by a question ('But who comes here...?') may be meant to suggest a greater distance between the speaker and those he fails to recognise immediately: either the full width of the stage lies between them, or the speaker sees others before they appear on the stage. In some such instances there might well be a gap of several lines between the question and entry, or the entry may have to come second even though it is normally placed first.

(*b*) Editors have been so haphazard in dealing with a very common 'entry' formula that one wonders what else they have neglected. I find it strange that they are sometimes so uninterested in the precise placing of directions, especially those that should be inserted in the middle of a verse-line.

1. By this I challenge him to single fight. | *Throwes downe his Gauntlet* (*3H6*, q₂ᵃ).

2. Downe, downe to hell, and say I sent thee thither. | *Stabs him againe* (*3H6*, q₄ᵃ).

3. I Take that, and that, if all this will not do, *Stabs him.* (*R3*, r₃ᵃ).

4. Die, die, *Lauinia*, and thy shame with thee, / And with thy shame, thy Fathers sorrow die. | *He kils her.* (*Titus*, 2e₂ᵃ).

Where a single, sudden action is concerned it would be useful to indicate the precise moment for it (namely, following *this, downe, that, die*). Most of the editors leave the stage direction where they find it in the Folio – which I mention not because it leads to serious misunderstanding but because it illustrates my general case against editorial inertia. Although they know that Elizabethan dramatists and copyists were careless about the precise placing of stage directions, although they themselves move *some* directions, when they feel they have to, editors usually prefer to leave well alone, if they think they can get away with it. Yet by moving a stage direction a line or two we can quite often improve the sense or stage-effect, and so we must ask ourselves whether there is any real need to follow the first quarto or Folio.

[1] See Alice Walker, *Textual Problems of the First Folio* (Cambridge, 1953).

5. I am husht vntill our City be afire, & then Ile
   speak a litle
          Holds her by the hand silent.
   Corio. O Mother, Mother!
   What haue you done? Behold, the Heauens do ope,
                                                    (*Cor.* 2c₂ᵇ)

When Coriolanus yields in v, 3, after listening
to his mother's long speech, the actor has the
very difficult task of conveying an overwhelming emotion without the help of words. Is that
really what Shakespeare intended? The actor's
task would be easier if he could at least begin
to express his emotion – an alternative that
involves moving the stage direction one line
down ('*Corio.* O mother! mother! *Holds her
by the hand, silent.*') Here as elsewhere we may
assume that the direction was written in the
margin and not properly aligned with the text
– a common fault in surviving MS texts of the
period. And in this instance the form of the stage
direction supports rearrangement: in *Coriolanus*,
and normally in other texts, a direction lacking a
subject refers to the previous speaker, not the
next one ('*Kneeles*', 2a₅ᵃ; '*Pushes him away
from him*', '*Beats him away*', 2b₅ᵇ; '*Kneeles*',
2c₅ᵃ; compare '*Corio. drawes his Sword*', 2b₂ᵇ,
where Brutus is the previous speaker).

6. *Duk.* Oh *Hippolito?* call treason.
   Hip.   Yes my good Lord, treason, treason,
             treason. *stamping on him.*
   Duk. Then I'me betrayde.
                       (*The Revenger's Tragedy*, 1606, F₂ᵇ)

'Then I'm betrayed' from someone who has
been stamped on sounds out-of-place. The
stage direction should be moved down, perhaps
as much as ten lines (to go with '*Vind.* T'is I,
'tis Vindici, tis I.')

7. You shall get no more children till my brothers
   Consent to be your Ghossips: haue you lost your
   tongue? 'tis welcome:
   For know whether I am doomb'd to liue, or die,
   I can doe both like a Prince.   *Ferdinand giues*
   Ferd. Die then, quickle: *her a ponyard.*
                       (*The Duchess of Malfi*, 1623, F₄ᵃ)

To print the stage direction at the end of the
Duchess' speech is to associate it with Ferdinand's command, 'Die then', but leaves ''tis
welcome' a puzzle. Editors insert another
direction after 'lost your tongue', namely '*she
turns and sees Ferdinand*', which helps to give
some sense to ''tis welcome', though the
words still sound odd. The difficulty disappears, however, if we move the direction two
lines up: and if Ferdinand 'gives her a poniard'
silently, before he tells her what to do with it,
his enigmatic gesture prefigures the later offer
of the dead man's hand (IV, 1). The direction,
of course, was added to the text while it was
being printed (in the corrected sheets of Q),
when there was no room for it where I think it
should have gone (before ''tis welcome'): all
the more reason for distrusting its placing
in Q.

Asides. Modern editions of Shakespeare
contain many more asides than are found in the
Folio and quartos, as often as not a legacy
from eighteenth-century editors who maimed
and deformed where they undertook to cure.
Some of these asides merely raise questions
about editorial consistency, while others involve interesting points of interpretation.

(1) When Romeo eavesdrops on Juliet in
the balcony-scene (II, 2), why should his
second speech be called an aside ('Shall I
hear more, or shall I speak at this?') but not
the first? The first is much longer, and perhaps
editors think that asides ought to be short; yet
as neither Q nor F indicates an aside, and
Romeo's two speeches are equally inaudible to
Juliet, why treat them differently?

(2) *Poins.* Ay, four, in buckram suits.
    Fal. Seven, by these hilts, or I am a villain else.
    Prince. [*Aside to Poins*] Prithee, let him alone;
          we shall have more anon. (*1 Hen. IV*, II, 4,
          199).
(3) [*Timon.*]...I prithee let's be provided to show
    them entertainment.

Flav. [*Aside*] I scarce know how. (*Timon*, I, 2, 175).[1]

When an editor adds '*Aside*' he often implies that the speaker would not have dared to utter the same words openly; in short, he passes judgment on the relationship of two or more dramatic characters. Clearly if the situation includes an impudent speaker or an inattentive listener the case for an aside is weakened. Hal, in fact, speaks bitingly to and of Falstaff in his presence, and to give him an aside (2, above) is to make him more considerate than is necessary; while Flavius tells Timon a little later that his previous warnings went unheeded ('You would not hear me', II, 2, 128), so there is no reason why he should not protest openly (3, above).

> (4) But now my cousin Hamlet, and my son –
> *Ham.* [*Aside*] A little more than kin, and less than kind.
> *King.* How is it that the clouds still hang on you?
> *Ham.* Not so, my lord; I am too much in the sun.

Traditionally printed as an aside (since Theobald), Hamlet's first speech expresses the riddling impudence that is characteristic of all of his exchanges with Claudius before Act 5. Are we to assume that he would not have dared to speak out loud, and that the only alternative is an aside? There is surely evidence enough in the play that Hamlet's angry contemptuousness could not be muzzled. Nevertheless, a third possibility should be considered: that Hamlet, the arch-soliloquizer, not infrequently mutters to himself and cares not a rap whether or not others catch his words. Shakespeare had earlier broken the convention of 'inaudible soliloquy' when it suited him (as in the balcony-scene in *Romeo and Juliet*); now he modifies the aside, which becomes audible or semi-audible as he chooses, so that many of Hamlet's speeches resemble an aside in being partly addressed to

himself ('These tedious old fools!', 'Marry, this is miching mallecho...'). The 'semi-aside', or aside half overheard, has an important function in *Hamlet*, and in some other plays.

> (5) *Ham.* [*Aside to Horatio*] Dost know this water-fly?
> *Hor.* [*Aside to Hamlet*] No, my good lord.
> *Ham.* [*Aside to Horatio*] Thy state is the more gracious; for 'tis a vice to know him. He hath much land, and fertile. Let a beast be lord of beasts, and his crib shall stand at the king's mess. 'Tis a chough; but, as I say, spacious in the possession of dirt. (v, 2)

To label these exchanges 'asides' is to deprive them of much of their nervy edge. Hamlet enjoys insulting those he despises to their face (Claudius, Polonius, Rosencrantz and Guildenstern), and we have no grounds for supposing that he must treat Osric differently. Hamlet may half turn away, and slightly lower his voice, still allowing Osric to 'listen in' if he wishes; and in the course of this 'semi-aside' Hamlet may suddenly raise his voice for Osric's benefit on certain phrases: '...'tis a vice to know him...spacious in the possession of dirt.' Such opportunities are lost if the editor prints '*aside*'; I think it best, therefore, to return to the Quarto and Folio texts and to omit the stage directions in this passage and in others that are similar.

'*All*' *speeches.* Many texts contain speeches assigned to '*All*', or to an indefinite number of speakers (Lords, Plebeians, etc.), which ought to be looked at as a group. When two or more dramatic characters miraculously utter the very same words in scenes that are psychologically 'realistic' I believe that this is often a result of editorial misunderstanding.

[1] Shakespeare in modern spelling is cited from P. Alexander's edition (1951), but the examples given are found in many or most modern editions.

The tradition of simultaneous speech goes back to choric passages in pre-Shakespearian drama. No one can quarrel with simultaneous speech in more 'realistic' drama where it has an obvious choric or ritual function – the incantations of the ghosts in *Richard III*, or of the Weird Sisters, or appropriate salutations or responses such as '*All*. God saue the King, God saue the King' (*2H6*, O_1^b), '*All*. Amen' (*R3*, S_2^b). And short and appropriate exclamations need no defence either ('*All*. The Troians Trumpet.' (*Tr. and Cress.*, ¶¶ $_3^b$), '*All*. Longer, longer' (*Ham.* $2n_6^a$)). But when '*All*' hit upon words that cannot be thus explained, what should be done? '*All*. Against him first: He's a very dog to the Commonalty', '*All*. Nay, but speak not maliciously' (*Cor.*, $2a_1^a$): here, and in many other places, we have '*All*' speeches that are individualised, not ritualistic, and they always sound wrong in the theatre if uttered by more than a single voice.

To get the problem into focus let us turn to the three pages in *Sir Thomas More* now generally ascribed to Shakespeare where, it seems, the dramatist wrote at such speed that he did not trouble to indicate all the minor speakers' names in a crowd-scene. Shakespeare's 147 lines include four speeches assigned not to a named person but to 'other' (i.e. another), a speech prefix that shrinks to 'oth' and even 'o';[1] and, in addition, no less than ten '*All*' speeches. A scribe concerned with the play was dissatisfied with so many vaguely assigned speeches, deleted the four 'other' prefixes and substituted more specific ones, 'GEO BETT' and 'WILLIAN'; and, significantly, he also deleted one '*All*' prefix and substituted 'LINCO' (= Lincoln).

Let us remember, too, that there are '*All*' speeches that cannot be taken to imply simultaneous speech of the kind mentioned above. '*Fairies*. Readie: and I, and I, and I. Where shall we goe?' (*M.N.D.*, Q, D_3^b); '*All People*. Teare him to peeces, do it presently: /

He kill'd my Sonne, my daughter, he kill'd my Cosine / *Marcus*, he kill'd my Father' (*Cor.*, $2c_3^b$). The dramatist clearly wanted each fairy to answer individually, and so the Quarto's single speech is usually chopped up to read '*Peaseblossom*. Ready. *Cobweb*. And I. *Moth*. And I.' etc. In *Coriolanus* it is equally certain that different individuals cry out about the death of a son, daughter, cousin and father (though editors do not identify them as individuals, as I think they should, most of them printing '...He kill'd my son. My daughter. He kill'd my cousin Marcus' etc.).

From these examples we learn that Shakespeare sometimes used the '*All*' speech prefix loosely, no doubt because he wrote in haste and thought that he could explain the details later – just as he might fall back on 'other', or on an actor's name, when he was too impatient to pause. We learn that an '*All*' prefix could be reassigned to a single speaker (*Sir Thomas More*), or could indicate that different consecutive speakers are required (*M.N.D.*). In *Coriolanus* we encounter a third possibility, simultaneous 'confused' speech, for which *Antony and Cleopatra* gives an unambiguous direction (y_4^a):

2. How now Maisters? *Speak together.*
Omnes. How now? how now? do you heare this?
1. I, is't not strange?
3. Do you heare Maisters? Do you heare?

It would be quite wrong, of course, to urge that individualised or longer '*All*' speeches must never be delivered as simultaneous 'choric' speech. Two unusual directions in *Titus Andronicus* (Quarto B_4^b, C_1^a) put this beyond doubt:

Titus two sonnes speakes.
And shall or him wee will accompanie.

they all kneele and say,
No man shed teares for Noble *Mutius*,
He liues in fame, that died in vertues cause.

[1] Compare *Timon* $2h_1^a$: '*Some other*. I know not'; *Ham.*, Q2, M_1^b ff: '*Clowne*' and '*Other*'.

On the other hand, editors have not made as much as they could or should of the fact that '*All*' speech prefixes were used more loosely than single-name prefixes and may therefore be variously interpreted.

(1) Very often an '*All*' speech in a crowd-scene may mean no more than that one person speaks while the rest howl or clamour or contribute what was known as 'confused noise':

All. That would hang vs, euery mothers sonne
(*M.N.D.*, Q, B₂ᵇ)
All. Most true, the Will, let's stay and heare the Wil.
(*J.C.*, 2l₁ᵇ)
All. We will so: almost all repent in their election.
(*Cor.* 2b₁ᵇ)

(2) Many '*All*' speeches could be divided between two or more consecutive or simultaneous speakers. '*All.* A Clifford, a Clifford, // Wee'l follow the King, and Clifford' (*2H6*, O₁ᵇ), and '*All.* It shall be so, it shall be so: // let him away: // Hee's banish'd, and it shall be so' (*Cor.* 2b₄ᵃ) could thus be assigned to two or three (new speakers indicated by //).

(3) Some short '*All*' exclamations may have been repeated more than once. '*A long flourish. They all cry, Martius, Martius, cast vp their Caps and Launces: Cominius and Lartius stand bare*' (*Cor.* 2a₄ᵃ): if caps and lances are flung up and retrieved this would take longer than the shouting of 'Marcius, Marcius'. I assume that an '*All*' speech involving the repetition of a word or phrase indicates repetition but may leave it to the actors to decide how often to repeat. '*Warwicke and the rest cry all, Warwicke, Warwicke, and set vpon the Guard, who flye, crying, Arme, Arme*' (*3H6*, p₆ᵇ). Indeed, even when an '*All*' exclamation is printed only once, repetition may have been intended in 'ritual' situations where one would normally expect it:
Cry, S. George, A Talbot (*1H6*, K₅ᵃ: compare K₅ᵇ, '*Enter a Souldier, crying, a Talbot, A Talbot*'). *Henry VI, Part 2*, perhaps confirms

when the bad quarto indicates twice that the Folio's '*All*' cry was repeated. (The bad quarto, admittedly, is not a perfect witness).

After the Beadle hath hit him once, he leapes ouer the Stoole and runnes away: and they follow, and cry, A Miracle. (Folio, m₆ᵃ)...they run after him, crying, A miracle, a miracle. *Hump.* A miracle, a miracle, let him be taken againe... (*The Contention*, C₃ᵃ)

And sometimes we find echoes in the dialogue immediately after an '*All*' cry that suggest, again, that the cry was meant to be repeated:

Within crie arme. | The word is giuen, arme, arme flies through the camp (*Sir Thomas Wyatt*, 1607, E₁ᵃ);
A great noise, follow. | *Enter Wyat...* | *Within.* Follow, follow (*ibid.*, E₄ᵇ)

'*Both*' *speeches.* Most of my remarks about '*All*' apply equally to '*Both*' speeches. While the existence of some choric '*Both*' speeches cannot be denied, we should always consider alternative possibilities.

(1) In a 'realistic' context where non-ritualistic lines are concerned it may be that there ought to be only one speaker, who indicates by a gesture that he speaks for both. ('*Both.* Why? how are we censur'd?' *Cor.* 2a₄ᵇ).[1]

(2) '*Both*' speeches may signify nothing more than the author's hasty composition. This must often be so, I think, in *Timon*, a text that includes so many other non-specific speech prefixes (an exceptional number of '*All*' speeches, as well as '*Some speake*' and '*Some other*', 2h₁ᵃ): '*Both.* Giue vs some Gold good *Timon*, hast ᵘ⁄ᵧ more?' 2h₂ᵃ); '*Both.* More counsell with more Money, bounteous *Timon*'

---

[1] It is interesting that a '*Both*' speech in *Hamlet*, Q2, was assigned to a single speaker in Q1 ('*Both*' Longer, longer.' (Q2, C₂ᵇ), '*Mar.* O longer, longer.. (Q1)), and also a '*Both*' speech in F1 (*Hor. & Mar, within.* My Lord, my Lord' (F1), '*Hor.* My lord, my lord' (Q1, D₁ᵃ)). As these passages involve the Marcellus-actor, who is thought to have been the Q1 pirate, Q1 may record what was said in the theatre.

($2h_2^b$); 'Both. What we can do, / Wee'l do to do you seruice' ($2h_4^b$), etc.

(3) When the text names two speakers, instead of using the speech prefix 'Both', it is more likely that simultaneous 'choric' speech is required. In Shakespeare such speech prefixes are usually reserved for short replies or exclamations that any two persons might well make independently, and 'choric' speech is then quite acceptable.

Cleo. Dio. All this we sweare. (*W. Tale*, $2A_6^a$)
Macb. and Lenox. What's the matter? (*Mac.* $2m_3^a$)
Hor. & Mar. within. My Lord, my Lord. (*Ham.* $2O_1^b$)
Gui. Arui. Stand, stand, and fight. (*Cym.* $3b_2^b$)

Occasionally, however, this type of 'Both' speech sounds less natural (but, occurring at moments of social or legal ritual, it stops short of the unnatural):

Ang. Esc. Happy returne be to your royall grace. (*M. for M.* G_4^a)
Gray. Scro. To which we all appeale' (*H5* h_3^b)

Crypto-directions. If editors have erred in the treatment of stage directions it could also be said that they have not helped readers as they should with Elizabethan 'crypto-directions'. I refer in particular to expletives, some of which appear to have served as short-hand directions for a great variety of noises. To take one example, the ubiquitous 'O! – o!' is sometimes described as an 'actor's vulgarisation' – as if no self-respecting dramatist would stoop to write such stuff. Yet the metre confirms that even the greatest dramatists could sometimes write 'O! – o!' etc., while the context makes it equally clear that at other times this expletive was nothing more nor less than a familiar signal, like Malory's 'ha, ha' (indicating anger) or Molière's 'Ah, ah, ah' (indicating laughter); a different kind of signal, however, since it directed the actor to make whatever noise was locally appropriate. It could tell him to sigh, groan, gasp, roar, weep.

1. all the perfumes of Arabia will not sweeten this little hand. Oh, oh, oh. Doct. What a sigh is there? (*Mac.* $2n_2^b$).

2. Oh! Lou. Why do you sigh? (*A New Way to Pay Old Debts*, 1633, F_2^a).

3. Ooh. – Within. / D'am. What groane was that? (*The Atheist's Tragedy*, 1611, K_2^b).

4. Cont. Oh. 1. Sur. Did he not groane? (*The Devil's Law Case*, 1623, F_1^b).

5. Ooh. / D'am. His gasping sighes are like the falling noise of some great building. (*The Atheist's Tragedy*, K_3^a).

6. Oh, oh! / Ver. What horrid sounds are these? (*The Changeling*, v, 3, 140)[1].

7. Oth. Oh, oh, oh. / Emil. Nay, lay thee downe, and roare (*Oth.* $2v_5^a$).

8. Ooh. / Ruf. Hell grinnes to heare this roaring (Dekker, *If It Be Not Good*, 1612, L_3^b).

9. oh- oh. / Mel. Doe not weepe, what ist? (*The Maid's Tragedy*, 1622, F_1^b).

Middleton even resorted to 'O! o! o!' to express gloating;[2] and when the immediate context gives no further explanation, the wide range of possibilities elsewhere suggests that the actor could do as he liked. Editors, I think, should deal with such crypto-directions as they deal with other private signals in Elizabethan texts: they should replace them with the appropriate equivalent (as they remove actors' names and substitute character-names). Thus 1 and 7 (above) might be printed as

1. all the perfumes of Arabia will not sweeten this little hand. [*A long sigh.*] Doct. What a sigh is there!

7. *Othello cries out in pain.* / Emil. Nay, lay thee downe, and roare.

In short, I assume that quite often what the original audience heard was not 'O! – o!', and that it will only mislead a modern reader or audience to print the dramatist's signal in this form.

[1] Quoted from the Revels edition.
[2] *A Trick to Catch the Old One*, 1608, F_1^b: 'Ha, ha, ha...Oh–o–o...True, true, true...'

Series. Almost all 'Elizabethan' stage directions resemble others in form or phrasing. As will have become clear, we are only ready to interpret stage directions when we have identified them as members of a group, or series: and awareness of a series may prompt us to question the received text in many other places, where editors have in the past looked too narrowly at a single play, or author.

> (1) *Ege*. Full of vexation, come I, with complaint
> Against my childe, my daughter *Hermia*.
> > *Stand forth Demetrius.*
> My noble Lord,
> This man hath my consent to marry her.
> > *Stand forth Lisander.*
> And my gratious Duke,
> This man hath bewitcht the bosome of my childe
> > (*M.N.D.*, A₂ᵃff., Quarto; so F)

Editors normally emend to read '/ Stand forth, Demetrius. My noble lord, / This man hath my consent to marry her. / Stand forth, Lysander. And, my gracious Duke, /'. Yet Q would scan if the italicised words are treated as stage directions, which is what one would normally expect them to be. The fact that a similar formula is found in other stage directions inclines me to believe that emendation is unjustified ('*Lucillius and Messala stand forth*', *JC* 2l₄ᵃ; '*Berowne steps forth*', *L.L.Lost*, Q, I₂ᵇ).[1]

> (2) *Ob*. Silence a while. *Robin* take off his head:
> *Titania*, musick call, and strike more dead
> > Then common sleepe; of all these, fine the sense.
> *Tita*. Musicke, ho musicke, such as charmeth sleepe.
> > *Musick still.*
> *Rob*. When thou wak'st, with thine own fooles eies peepe.
> *Ob*. Sound musick; come my Queen, take hands with me (*M.N.D.* O₁ᵃ)

It is not easy to decide when the music starts and stops. Editors normally omit '*Musick still*' and add '*Music*' after 'take hands with

me', or misinterpret '*Musick still*' as 'Still music' or 'Soft music', with Theobald, Dyce etc. Compare, however, *King Lear* 2r₂ᵃ ff.: '*Storme still*' (repeated at the beginning of three scenes, and three times in mid-scene); *Julius Caesar* 2l₅ᵃ, '*Alarum still*'; *Coriolanus* 2C₃ᵃ, '*A shout within*'...(seven lines)... '*Sound still with the Shouts*'; *Old Fortunatus*, 1600: '*Musicke sounding still*' (G₂ᵇ). '*Musick still*' must have meant something like 'the former music continues', whereas '*Music*' on its own implies something very different, 'music starts at this point'. I take it that the '*Rurall Musicke*' called for earlier in the same scene in *M.N.D.* (a stage direction added in the Folio, as was '*Musick still*') continues at Titania's command, viz. music 'such as charmeth sleep'. Puck, thereafter, speaks his one line when the rural music stops, and Oberon then calls for another kind of music (dance music).

> (3) *Officer*. It is his Highnesse pleasure, that the Queene
> Appeare in person, here in Court. *Silence*.
> *Leo*. Reade the Indictment. (*W.Tale*, 2A₅ᵇ)

Most editors print '...here in court. Silence!', changing what appears to be a stage direction into a spoken command. In this instance it is helpful to cite another stage direction where the staging, if not the phrasing, follows a similar formula – from the trial-scene in *Henry VIII* (V₂ᵇ).

> *Crier*. *Katherine* Queene of England, &c.
> *The Queene makes no answer, rises out of her Chaire, goes about the Court, comes to the King, and kneeles at his Feete. Then speakes.*

The *Henry VIII* stage direction spells out what must have happened in *The Winter's Tale*. Hermione, like Katherine, is asked to appear in

---

[1] 'Stand forth' in *M.N.D.* is more 'imperative' than in *J.C.*, but this is in line with the text's other directions: '*Ly doune*' (E₁ᵃ), '*Winde horne*' (F₄ᵃ), '*Shoute within*'(F₄ᵇ).

court, and evidently walks to her appointed place. '*Silence*' in the Folio looks like a stage direction, and should not be altered since it makes good sense as one. It tells us that a very special silence is required. Not the short 'pause' of modern play-texts, but a protracted silence at the end of which Hermione stands face to face with Leontes – stands, perhaps, not only silent but motionless, like a statue. The unusual stage direction, in short, may point forward to the statue-scene, where Leontes and Hermione once more face one another and Paulina comments '*I like your silence*, it the more shewes off / Your wonder' (my italics).

Conclusion. The last example may not qualify as one of a series, but at least it can be compared with the stage-effect in another play. Such comparisons can be illuminating, even though they will include a large element of conjecture. If a stage direction turns out to belong to a recognisable group, however, the editor is in an immeasurably stronger position: in Shakespeare alone, a systematic study would, I believe, show that many scores of stage directions and speech prefixes have been wrongly placed or wrongly interpreted.

© E. A. J. HONIGMANN 1976

THE STAIRCASES OF THE FRAME: NEW LIGHT ON THE STRUCTURE OF THE GLOBE?

NEIL CARSON

Considering the shortage of pictorial evidence relating to the Elizabethan stage and theatres, it is surprising that more attention has not been paid to the sketches included among the Alleyn–Henslowe papers at Dulwich College. The existence of these drawings was brought to the attention of scholars by W. W. Greg in his edition of some of those papers in 1907.[1] In a headnote to Article 14 of Volume I of the manuscripts (an autograph letter from Philip Henslowe to Edward Alleyn dated 28 September 1593), Greg remarked that the letter also contained 'several pen and ink sketches on the outer leaf, one apparently for some scenery in perspective'.[2] In spite of the interest of such sketches to theatre historians, the drawings were not reproduced. Nor, indeed, did Greg make further reference to them either in *Henslowe Papers* or in the much fuller commentary on Henslowe's 'diary' published a year later.[3]

It was not until 1960 that the general reader had an opportunity to judge for himself the significance of any of the pictures. In that year R. A. Foakes and R. T. Rickert published one of the sketches which they hesitantly identified as a drawing of an Elizabethan stage (Fig. 1).[4] A year later the same sketch was reproduced in their edition of *Henslowe's Diary*.[5] Their commentary on the drawing is a model of circumspection.

If the sketch reproduced is of a stage, it is not at all clear what it is intended to show. The two pillars could be the pillars supporting a canopy over the stage, such

as the Swan and Fortune theatres possessed; the lines joining the tops of the columns vaguely suggest a roof there. What is drawn between the columns might be a setting as seen from the auditorium, or the theatre as seen from the stage. The long rectangle at the bottom of the sketch could be intended to represent a flat or a vertical surface, though the latter seems more probable. Above this are shown, on either side, two tiers of steps or seats, turning in alongside the steps which lead back from the centre. These stairs end in a number of faint vertical lines, whose purpose is not clear, and some even fainter horizontal lines through and above these seem intended to close off the vista with a hint of a solid background. Three heavy lines superimposed across the bottom of the central steps and ending in tiny circles or open dots, seem to mark a barrier of some kind.[6]

This description has the merit of accuracy, but little else. The suggestion that the pillars may be those supporting the canopy seems unconvincing because of the absence of any representation of the stage itself. Equally improbable is the idea that the sketch is of a stage setting, or that any 'vista' is intended by the geometrical pattern of crudely drawn lines. Much more suggestive is the comment that a view of the auditorium from the stage might

[1] W. W. Greg (ed.), *Henslowe Papers* (1907).
[2] *Ibid.*, p. 39.
[3] W. W. Greg (ed.), *Henslowe's Diary*, vol. II (1908).
[4] R. A. Foakes and R. T. Rickert, 'An Elizabethan Stage Drawing?' *Shakespeare Survey 13* (Cambridge, 1960), pp. 111–12.
[5] R. A. Foakes and R. T. Rickert (eds.) *Henslowe's Diary* (Cambridge, 1961), p. 281.
[6] 'An Elizabethan Stage Drawing?', p. 112.

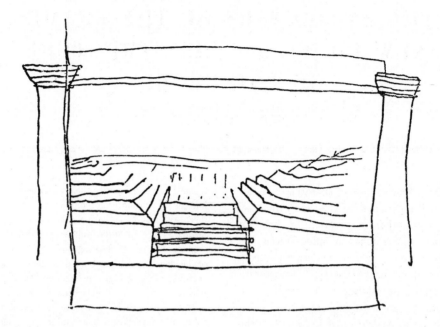

Fig. 1. Dulwich College, Henslowe papers, MSS. 1.14: letter from Phillip Henslowe to Edward Alleyn, 28 September 1593. Sketch on blank leaf.

be shown. Here again, however, the remark seems to offer a possible interpretation of the relationship of the pillars to the two rectangles, but does not convincingly illuminate the rest of the sketch.

It seems to me that Greg, Foakes, and Rickert have all been misled by recent theatrical conventions into concentrating on the frame of the picture (which bears such an obvious resemblance to a proscenium arch) rather than its central subject. A much more fruitful approach to the problem is to start with the focal point of the drawing – the short flight of stairs rising behind what appear to be three bars or ropes across an entrance. If we could determine why Philip Henslowe or Edward Alleyn might have been concerned with illustrating such an apparently ordinary structure as a staircase, we might have a clue to the picture's meaning. One possible explanation for such concern is to be found in the contract for the building of the Fortune theatre drawn

up in January, 1600. In that contract, now preserved as Muniment 22 of the Alleyn papers, there appear the following conditions:

[that] necessarie Seates...be placed and sett... througheoute all the rest of the galleries of the saide howse and w[th] suchelike steares Conveyances & divisions w[th]oute & w[th]in as are made & Contryved in and to the late erected Plaiehowse On the Banck in the saide pishe of Ste Savio[r]s Called the Globe w[th] a Stadge and Tyreinge howse to be made erected & settupp w[th] in the saide ffame...w[ch] Stadge shal be placed and sett *As alsoe the stearecases of the saide ffame in such sorte as is p[r]figured in a Plott thereof drawen.*[1]

Is it possible that we have in this drawing a sketch made by Alleyn or Henslowe on a letter written several years earlier for the instruction of their theatre carpenter? If so, it is yet another of the bitter ironies of theatrical history that this comparatively insignificant drawing should have survived while the infinitely more

---

[1] *Henslowe Papers*, p. 5. My italics.

valuable sketch of the stage perished. In any case, it seems to me that many of the details of the Alleyn–Henslowe drawing which seem puzzling when looked at as parts of the illustration of a stage setting fall into place if the sketch is regarded as the illustration of an entrance to the galleries from the yard of a public theatre.

THE SWAN THEATRE, BANKSIDE.

Fig. 2. De Witt's sketch of the Swan Theatre (c. 1596). Drawing in the Bibliotheek der Rijkuniversiteit.

The very prominent pillars, for example, instead of being connected with the stage, may represent the major supports on two sides of a single segment of the circular lower gallery. The precise disposition of these supporting columns in the Elizabethan theatre is not known. The evidence of the Swan drawing (as in so many other respects) is puzzling since it shows more uprights in the open sections of the three levels than are represented on the gallery facing or guard rail (see Fig. 2). Even

more perplexing is the fact that on either side of the theatre, one of these uprights seems to rest on what appears to be a beam across the '*ingressus*' opening. Richard Southern suggests that what the artist has attempted to show here is 'two rows of posts, one on the facade, and one within under the binding joists' half way between the inner and outer faces of the frame.[1] Ingenious as this explanation is, it does not seem altogether convincing. One reason for this is that the artist has evidently been at some pains to show all of the pillars descending to the same level, even going to the extent of continuing the line of the gallery rail across the stairway opening on either side.

Another possible explanation of this peculiar feature of the drawing is that the post does, in fact, stand in the middle of the entrance and that the stairway, instead of being flush with the gallery face, extends from the top of the railing of the first balcony down and out into the yard. This interpretation gains some support from the attention given to the sketching of the far ends of the 'steps' which on both sides of the drawing seem to be shown extending out from the gallery wall. The close spacing of the posts in the void area might have been dictated by the fact that in the Swan the weight of the building was not carried directly down through aligned pillars, but was distributed over different areas at different levels.

Whatever the structural principles employed at the Swan, it is certain that at the Hope a much more logical form of pillar construction was used than that suggested by the De Witt drawing. The contract for that theatre specifies that

the inner principall postes of the first storie be twelve footes in height and tenn ynches square.[2]

Since common sense would seem to dictate

[1] Richard Southern, 'On Reconstructing a Practicable Elizabethan Public Playhouse', *Shakespeare Survey*, *12* (Cambridge, 1959), p. 25.
[2] *Henslowe Papers*, p. 19.

such construction, commentators such as C. W. Hodges are almost certainly correct in assuming that the main posts supporting the gallery in most Elizabethan theatres ran from the ground to the floor of the second gallery, and looked very much like the pillars in the Alleyn–Henslowe drawing.[1]

Once the assumption is made that the latter drawing is not of a stage but is of the 'steare-case of the fframe', then other details of the sketch fall into place. The peculiar oblong section at the bottom of the drawing which Foakes and Rickert think represents a vertical surface of undetermined purpose may well be the brick foundation of the theatre. Once again the Fortune contract is suggestive. It specifies that the theatre must have

a good suer and stronge foundacon of pyles brick lyme and sand, both wthoute & wthin, to be wroughte one foote of assize att the leiste aboue the grounde.[2]

It is sometimes suggested in reproductions of the interior of Elizabethan public theatres that the interior brick foundation was not carried through those sections which allowed access from the yard to the galleries.[3] But this is surely an error since the cross beams support-ing the floor and the framing of the staircase would have to be protected from dampness in the same way as similar members in other parts of the theatre. That the rectangle in the drawing is indeed intended to portray a vertical surface such as would be presented by the foundation of the theatre is confirmed, to my mind, by the slight curve of the upper right hand corner. If the artist had been intending to indicate a flat surface terminating one or two feet behind the pillar, I think he would have carried the upper line straight to (or possibly beyond) the edge of the pillar (as he did with the line in the middle of the picture which intersects the top of the right pyramid).

If my hypothesis is correct, and we have in this sketch a drawing of a part of the Globe

theatre prepared for the guidance of Peter Streete when constructing the Fortune, what further can we deduce about the construction of Shakespeare's playhouse? There are two features of the picture that seem to me to be of particular interest. The first concerns the heavy lines across the opening of the staircase which Foakes and Rickert think represent a barrier of some kind. Could these be an illustration of the way in which access to the galleries was prevented during a performance when the gatherers had left their positions? The need for such a barrier between the low-priced yard and higher-priced gallery seats was generally understood. Henslowe and Alleyn insist that in their new Fortune theatre the

lower storie [should be] laide over and fenced with stronge yron pykes.[4]

The need for such protection at the Fortune implies that the conditions obtaining at the Rose (and presumably at the Globe) were not satisfactory, and that too many of the 'groundlings' were cheating the theatre owners by climbing into the galleries. Iron pikes would make scaling the gallery walls hazardous which suggests that security arrangements at the stairways were adequate.

The second feature of interest is the arrange-ment of the ramps surrounding the staircase. It would be unwise to rely very heavily on the accuracy of such crude drawing, but one or two details deserve close scrutiny. The central staircase is represented most carefully and the angles at the left of that staircase suggest that the artist intends to show five vertical risers

[1] See the reconstructions of J. C. Adams, *The Globe Playhouse*, second edition (New York, 1961) or C. W. Hodges, *The Globe Restored*, second edition (1968).

[2] *Henslowe Papers*, p. 5. My italics.

[3] For example the sketches of Hodges, *loc. cit.* pp. 149–50, and the model of Richard Southern, a photo-graph of which appears as Plate II in 'On Reconstruct-ing a Practicable Elizabethan Public Playhouse'.

[4] *Henslowe Papers*, p. 5.

and the flat surface of the brick foundation which constitutes the first tread. This, at least, is how I interpret the artist's attempts to indicate perspective by decreased width without any representation of the edges of the treads converging on a vanishing point. If we allow seven or eight inches for each riser and twelve inches for the foundation, then the height of the landing would be about four feet above the level of the yard.

Another detail that seems to be conveyed by the drawing is that the bleacher-like steps or seats flanking the staircase extend further than the stairway towards the back of the gallery, and that the lowest of these steps is therefore higher than the top landing. Since this step runs forward and along the front of the gallery, the height of this front facing would seem to be between four-and-a-half and five feet high. This point is interesting because both C. W. Hodges and J. Cranford Adams in their reconstructions show the seating in the first gallery beginning about one foot above ground level.[1] This would mean that gallery patrons sitting in the front row would have their vision of the stage blocked by spectators standing in the yard. If, however, the seating in the first gallery were raised as is suggested by the Alleyn–Henslowe drawing, then the gallery spectators would be comfortably seated well above those standing.

The drawing of the steps or seats on each side of the central opening is relatively careless and suggests that the artist was not as concerned with this part of the sketch. This means, of course, that it is correspondingly more dangerous to make deductions about details of the playhouse. Nevertheless, if this is indeed a picture of the gallery entrance of the Globe theatre, the purpose stairs might serve at this point is obvious. They would provide access to the upper levels of the adjoining seats and could at the same time serve to accommodate any spectators who could not crowd further

along. Steps here would also eliminate the necessity of any other entrance to the seats from the landing running around the theatre behind the audience.

The existence of what appear to be stairs (rather than bleacher style seats) at this point in the theatre raises the question of the nature of the seats in those bays between entrances. It has been widely assumed that spectators sat in three ranks of seats at the Globe.[2] It seems to me altogether possible that the form of seating available may have been considerably more rough-and-ready than that imagined by commentators accustomed to the standards of comfort of a later age. Is it not conceivable that the seats (throughout the lower gallery at any rate) were as suggested by the Alleyn–Henslowe drawing? Such an arrangement would permit the audience to spread out in relative comfort on days when attendance was light, but also allow for very effective crowding at other times. Indeed it may have been this very flexibility – making it impossible to define the area of a 'seat' – which contributed to inconsistent estimates of the capacity of the public theatres. It may also have necessitated the construction of the gentlemen's rooms and two penny rooms mentioned in the Fortune contract which were needed to accommodate those spectators disinclined to suffer the intimacy which such seating imposed.

If, as I suspect, the Alleyn–Henslowe drawing is not of scenery but rather of the entrance to the theatre galleries, then it will prove a disappointment to many whose interest in theatrical history might be said to stop at the stage rails. Nevertheless, while it tells us nothing about the staging of Elizabethan drama, the drawing may afford a glimpse of the auditorium, and even of the relatively uncomfortable conditions that may have

[1] See note 1, p. 129, above.
[2] See the reconstructions of Adams, Hodges and Southern.

prevailed even after the spectator had paid his admission to the galleries. It also provides further evidence of the continuing importance of the Alleyn–Henslowe papers and for the need for the reproduction of any other sketches that may be included among them.

SHAKESPEARE IN MAX BEERBOHM'S THEATRE CRITICISM

STANLEY WELLS

In May 1898 Bernard Shaw gave up his post of theatre critic of *The Saturday Review*. He was ill. His doctor, he explained, had discovered that 'for many years [he had] been converting the entire stock of energy extractable from [his] food...into pure genius'. He was 'already almost an angel', and would complete the process if he wrote any more articles. So, on 21 May, he wrote an essay headed 'Valedictory'.[1] He cannot justify the fact that he has spent four years on dramatic criticism. He has

sworn an oath to endure no more of it....Still, the gaiety of nations must not be eclipsed. The long string of beautiful ladies who are at present in the square without, awaiting, under the supervision of two gallant policemen, their turn at my bedside, must be reassured when they protest, as they will, that the light of their life will go out if my dramatic articles cease. To each of them I will present the flower left by her predecessor, and assure her that there are as good fish in the sea as ever came out of it. The younger generation is knocking at the door; and as I open it there steps spritely in the incomparable Max.

Shaw was forty-one years old; Max Beerbohm was twenty-six. *The Saturday Review* was edited with great success by Frank Harris, who was already developing an unhealthy interest in Shakespeare. He had published his essay 'The True Shakespeare' in March of this year. The following year, Oscar Wilde was to write in a letter from France, 'Frank Harris is upstairs, thinking about Shakespeare at the top of his voice'.[2] The thinking eventually bore ripe fruit in Harris's sensational book *The Man*

Shakespeare and His Tragic Life-Story, published in 1909, and its sequel, *The Women of Shakespeare*, of two years later. Max Beerbohm knew Harris, and had already contributed to *The Saturday Review* before becoming its theatre critic. Lord David Cecil tells the story of a luncheon party in 1896. 'During a moment of silence Harris's voice was heard booming out. "Unnatural vice!" he was saying, "I know nothing of the joys of unnatural vice. You must ask my friend Oscar about them. But," he went on, with a reverential change of tone, "had Shakespeare asked me, I should have had to submit!" Max went home and drew a cartoon of Harris, stark naked and with his moustache bristling, looking coyly over his shoulder at Shakespeare who shrinks back at the alarming prospect. Underneath was written, "Had Shakespeare asked..." (Plate I A). This was a very daring cartoon for 1896; and Max showed it to few people. It is not known if Harris was one of them. He is unlikely to have minded if he did see it; he was remarkably impervious to Max's teasing.'[3]

It was with no great enthusiasm that Max accepted Harris's invitation to succeed Shaw. He needed the money: £5 a week at the start. He held the post for twelve years, until two weeks before his marriage, soon after which he left England to live in Italy. It was the only

[1] Bernard Shaw, *Our Theatres in the Nineties*, 3 vols. (1932), III, 384–6.
[2] *Letters*, ed. R. Hart-Davis (1962), p. 778.
[3] David Cecil, *Max: A Biography* (1964), p. 164.

regular work he ever did; and he disliked it. In his own valedictory essay he wrote: 'Had I been told that I was destined to write about plays for twelve weeks, I should have shuddered. Had I been told that I was destined to write about them for twelve years, I should have expired on the spot, neatly falsifying the prediction.' He admits that he 'acquired a vivid interest' in the task. But the writing itself was uphill work, 'mainly because I am cursed with an acute literary conscience... And thus it is that Thursday, the day chosen by me (as being the latest possible one) for writing my article, has for twelve years been regarded by me as the least pleasant day of the week.'[1] He locked himself in his room, the household observed a nervous silence, and Max spent much of the time gloomily staring at the paper and doodling in the effort to get started.[2] Nevertheless, he fulfilled his duties with great success, and admitted that the discipline was good for him.[3] A selection of his reviews was published in two volumes in 1924 under the title of *Around Theatres*. It was reprinted as a single volume in 1953. A second selection, *More Theatres: 1898–1903* appeared in 1969, and the reprinting of his theatre criticism was completed in 1970 with the publication of *Last Theatres: 1904–1910*.[4] Between them, the volumes run to well over 1700 pages. Most of the essays are straightforward reviews of plays, but there are occasional departures in the form of reviews of books on theatrical subjects, more general essays on the theatre, and obituaries. These volumes are, of course, an invaluable commentary on the theatre of their time. Max was, he claimed, more interested in literature than in the theatre, and much of his criticism reflects this. There is, for instance, a brilliant essay on Pinero's prose style (I, 286–90). Bernard Shaw, released from the bonds of weekly composition, entered into a fruitful period of playwriting on his own account, and Max's reviews of the first productions of some of Shaw's plays include

still some of the most thoughtful criticism they have received. Max was writing at a time when the music-hall was rich in talent, and this too he was able to enjoy and to communicate in words.

Still, it was not simply out of a delight in paradox that Max headed his first essay as a dramatic critic 'Why I Ought Not to Have Become a Dramatic Critic' (I, 1–4). He admits that of the arts he loves literature best of all, and claims that he is 'not fond of the theatre.' He has not read his distinguished predecessors such as Hazlitt, Lamb, and Lewes, though he has 'a fragmentary recollection of Aristotle's fragment on the drama', on which he once wrote an examination paper for which he was awarded the mark of 'gamma-minus query'. He cannot even claim the virtue of coming fresh to the theatre, because, having been born into the theatrical world, he is over-familiar with it. He was half-brother to Sir Herbert Beerbohm Tree, one of the leading actors of the day.

One well-known player and manager is my near relative. Who will not smile if I praise him? How could I possibly disparage him?... Most of the elder actors have patted me on the head and given me sixpence when I was 'only *so* high'. Even if, with an air of incorruptibility, I now return them their sixpences, they will yet expect me to pat *them* on the head in the *Saturday Review*.[5]

In fact, Max wrote so urbanely that such considerations never have the appearance of troubling him. Reviewing his half-brother as Falstaff in *The Merry Wives of Windsor*, for instance, he was to write:

[1] *Around Theatres* (1953), p. 578.
[2] Cecil, *op. cit.*, p. 168.
[3] *More Theatres: 1898–1903* (1969), p. 12.
[4] The three collections will be referred to in the text of this article as I, II, and III.
[5] Presumably because he took this passage too seriously, Riewald mistakenly says that Max 'made it a rule never to criticize a play in which his great brother appeared' (J. G. Riewald, *Sir Max Beerbohm ...A Critical Analysis with A Brief Life and a Bibliography*, 's-Gravenhage, 1953, pp. 146–7).

It is difficult for us, to whom Mr Tree's personality is so familiar through photographs in the illustrated papers, to accept him as a perfect Falstaff. But...if we project ourselves into the state of knowing nothing whatsoever about Mr Tree as he is, we get, I think, the true impression of a fat mind in a fat body.

(II, 473)

In his first article there is a Shakespeare allusion: 'The Editor of this paper has come to me as Romeo came to the apothecary, and what he wants I give him for the apothecary's reason.' And later Max was to draw a cartoon illustrating this, with Frank Harris as a florid Romeo, and Max as the apothecary, handing him a phial marked 'Dramatic Criticisms'. The caption is 'My poverty, but not my will, consents'.[1] (Plate IB). Still, Max tries to cheer himself up:

I daresay that there are many callings more uncomfortable and dispiriting than that of dramatic critic. To be a porter on the Underground Railway must, I have often thought, be very terrible. Whenever I feel myself sinking under the stress of my labours, I shall say to myself, 'I am not a porter on the Underground Railway'.   (I, 4).

The proportion of Shakespearian comment in Max's theatre criticism is relatively small. This is not the result of any shortage of productions of Shakespeare's plays while Max was reviewing. It is because he was far more interested, in general, in the art of his own time than in that of the past, and also because he was temperamentally unresponsive to much in Shakespeare. He admits as much in the Epistle Dedicatory to *Around Theatres*. He has had to select the articles as in themselves they were. 'Whether the play I had criticised were by Shakespeare or by Mr Tomkins must not matter to me...And I fear I had always preferred Mr Tomkins, as a theme, to Shakespeare. I felt more at home with him, and wrote better about him. That is a drawback of the satiric temperament; and I deplore it.'

The 'satiric temperament' is also something of a drawback for us in so far as it makes it difficult for us always to know how seriously to take Max's statements about his lack of knowledge. He certainly had an educated person's familiarity with at least those Shakespeare plays that were in the popular repertory, and of the general background. Shakespeare allusions are scattered through his writings. There are several in *Zuleika Dobson*, for instance, including the exquisitely humorous one in which Gertrude's account of Ophelia's death introduces a description of Zuleika in her morning bath.[2] Sotheby's catalogue of the sale of Max's books in 1960 records a copy of Dowden's edition of the Sonnets in which, we are tantalizingly told, Max has supplied irreverent endings to three sonnets. It records too a collected Shakespeare containing eight limericks on the characters of Shakespeare.[3] The one on Othello is reproduced:

No doubt you have heard of Othello –
An African sort of a fellow.
     When they said 'You are black'
     He cried 'Take it back!
I am only an exquisite yellow.'

The theatre review in which Max displays most familiarity with Shakespeare scholarship is one of *Macbeth*, dating from October 1898 (I, 8–11). In this, he makes an excursus into stage history. He recalls Aubrey's account of the performance of the play at Hampton Court in 1606 from which we learn that the boy taking the part of Lady Macbeth fell sick, as a result of which 'Master Shakespeare himself did enacte in his stead.' Combating the fallacy that the play has 'hitherto been acted only in the blood-and-thunder convention of Mrs Siddons', he quotes also a passage from Pepys's diary

[1] This is reproduced as the frontispiece to *More Theatres*.

[2] Chapter XXI.

[3] These are reprinted in *Max in Verse* (ed. J. G. Riewald, Brattleboro, Vermont, 1963, pp. 31–3), with the information that they were printed in *The Mask* (Florence), July 1924, p. 119, and that there is a privately owned manuscript in California.

which seems to suggest, he feels, that Mrs Knipp's performance in the autumn of 1667 was not essentially different from Mrs Patrick Campbell's.

Methought Mrs Knipp did never play so fine, specially in the matter of the two daggers, yet without brawl or overmuch tragick gesture, the which is most wearisome, as though an actress do care more to affright us than to be approved. She was most comickal and natural when she walks forth sleeping (the which I can testify, for Mrs Pepys also walks sleeping at some times), and did most ingeniously mimick the manner of women who walk thus.

Max's use of these passages of historical evidence is impressive enough when one considers how little known they were in 1898. It is even more impressive when one realises that they are entirely of his invention. Here Max is the total ironist, employing his gifts as a parodist in a completely straight-faced manner which may easily go undetected and, indeed, appears to have done so. The spoof is a careful one; Pepys did in fact see *Macbeth* in October 1667. Max was indulging here the strange impulse that led him to spend so many hours in his later years decorating his books with incongruous but totally convincing additions, like the mock-inscription in a copy of Ibsen's *When We Dead Awaken*, which reads 'For Max Beerbohm / critic of who / the writings fills / with pleasure me. / H. Ibsen.'[1] Had there been any dishonesty in his nature, Max could have completely overshadowed Chatterton, Ireland, and Collier. He was so clever it is even possible that he has.

In a letter to his future wife, Max acknowledged his temperamental unresponsiveness to Shakespeare. 'You shall teach me to enjoy, as well as respect and bow to, Shakespeare.'[2] But at many points in the theatre reviews he shows no respect and makes no obeisances, but rather offers reasoned criticisms. Early in his career, in the notice of *Macbeth* from which I have quoted, he writes:

Shakespeare had his shortcomings. Love of him does not blind me to his limitations and his faults of excess. But, after all, the man is dead, and I do not wish to emulate that captious and rancorous spirit – inflamed, as it often seemed to me, by an almost personal animosity – in which my predecessor persecuted him beyond the grave.

Max's discussions of Shakespeare's limitations and faults are certainly not rancorous. But they are often sharp. He blames Shakespeare for pandering to his public, using 'stupid stories conceived by stupid writers as a quick means of catching a stupid public.' He censures him for his 'plagiaristic method', inviting his readers to conceive the possibility that the twentieth century should produce a dramatic poet as great as Shakespeare who nevertheless was 'so weak or so modest as to found his plays on the farces of the late Mr H. J. Byron, and on the melodramas of the late Mr Pettitt, and on the romantic dramas of the late Mr Wills and the present Mr Henry Hamilton.' The result of such a method in Shakespeare, says Max, is that 'throughout the fabric of his work you will find much that is tawdry, irrational, otiose – much that is, however shy you may be of admitting that it is, tedious' (II, 342–3).

This general criticism underlies much of Max's comment on particular plays. He is, indeed, so unappreciative of some of them that I prefer to pass over his remarks as rapidly as possible. *Henry V* as produced by Benson is 'just a dull, incoherent series of speeches, interspersed with alarums and excursions' (I, 63) (though when it was performed by Lewis Waller at the Lyceum Max enjoyed it 'very much indeed' (II, 341)); '*Coriolanus* is a bad play we all agree' (II, 366); in reading, *King John* had seemed 'insufferably tedious' (II, 193); *Richard III* 'is very tedious indeed' (II, 186); *The Merchant of Venice* 'is a particularly sad instance of the way in which Shakespeare

[1] Cecil, *op. cit.*, p. 373.
[2] Cecil, *op. cit.*, p. 296.

wasted so much of his time' (II, 343); *The Merry Wives of Windsor* 'is the wretchedest bit of hack-work ever done by a great writer' (II, 473); and even *Twelfth Night* is 'perfunctory and formless', though 'in some degree redeemed by its accessory characters' (II, 347). Once, his criticism is bodied forth in parody of one of the areas of Shakespeare which, in our bardolatrous age, it is still permissible to find tedious. Reviewing Shaw's *The Admirable Bashville*, Max laments the absence of Shakespearian comic relief, and imagines what it might have been like:

Second Policeman: Canst tell me of this prize-fight? Is't within law?
First Policeman: Aye! To't. For what does a man prize highest? A fight. But no man fights what he prizes, else is he no man, being not manly, nor yet unmannerly. Argal, if he fight the prize, then is not the prize his, save in misprision, and 'tis no prize-fight within the meaning of the Act.
Second Policeman: Marry, I like thy wit, etc., etc.
(II, 582).

An often repeated theme of Max's criticism is that Shakespeare's plays should be performed less frequently than they are. This would be a natural reaction to the plays that Max finds tedious; but he applies it even to those that he most admires. Even Shakespeare's 'best work should not be laid before us so often as to rob us of the capacity for being freshly affected by it. And his second-best and third-best work should not be laid before us at all' (II, 339). He complains that '*Hamlet* has long ceased to be treated as a play. It has become simply a hoop through which every very eminent actor must, sooner or later, jump' (I, 36). His most serious attempt to grapple with the question of how he can both enormously admire a play yet not wish to see it performed comes in a discussion of Benson's *Hamlet* written in March 1901 (II, 359–63). He admits that 'To see *Hamlet* is one of our natural functions, one of our needs'. He finds that 'every time I hear it, the language in

Hamlet seems lovelier, comes with a new thrill.' Nevertheless, 'As drama, *Hamlet* has no power to affect me at all.' His analysis of why this should be so is revealing about his own conception of drama. Partly it is expressed in those terms of light-hearted irony with which he often veils his fundamental seriousness.

I am too much at home in Elsinore. I seem to have stayed there so often, to have written so many letters on its notepaper, helped the son of the house so often with his theatricals, talked so cordially about him to his *fiancée*, tried so sympathetically to reassure his mother as to his sanity, been so very sorry when he was called away to England.

But clearly also Max finds that *Hamlet* does not conform with his view of a well-made play. 'In modern times dramaturgy has become a strict art-form. A play has to be a concise exposition and development of a theme, and to be consistent in its manner throughout.' To Shakespeare,

dramaturgy was a go-as-you-please affair, in which any amount of time might be spent in divagations from the main theme, and in which one manner of treatment might be alternated with another, and in which the characters might, from time to time, and without warning, become the mere mouthpiece of the author.

It may seem that Max here is judging Shakespeare by the standards of Pinero. But perhaps this is not an altogether false description of Shakespeare's technique. Its implicit criticism, like that which lies behind Max's scorn of the 'stupid stories' that Shakespeare uses, and his belief that Shakespeare was pandering to a 'stupid public', anticipates points that Robert Bridges was to make in his essay 'On the Influence of the Audience'[1] in 1907, and that were to be discussed also by, notably, Stoll and Schücking during the next few decades. It is not so much that the analysis of

[1] *The Works of William Shakespeare*, 10 vols. (Stratford-upon-Avon, 1904–7), X, 321–34.

Shakespeare's technique is mistaken as that, in general, our attitude has changed, and we are now encouraged to admire these features of his art as indispensable means to a higher end.

Max's views on Shakespeare's methods of composition – his 'plagiaristic method' (II, 343) – are coloured by beliefs about Shakespeare's sources that would now have to be much modified. He envisages Shakespeare working over 'crude farces and melodramas' (II, 518), letting 'his genius gallop lightly over the ready-made material, glorifying it, but leaving it, essentially, much as it was before' (II, 361). More recent scholarship suggests that there are fewer dramatic sources for Shakespeare's plays than Max seems to have believed, and that Shakespeare put far more preliminary thought into his design. Criticism may have gone too far in the opposite direction, but it is not necessary to believe that Shakespeare's normal method was to have an idea and then to embody it in character and plot – something which I think he did only quite infrequently – to feel that still he was not at all as haphazard in his methods as Max suggests.

It will be apparent that though Max could speak so disparagingly of Shakespeare as even to be able to say that 'as a dramatist, in the narrow sense of the word, Shakespeare has had his day' (II, 518), nevertheless he found much to admire in the plays. It is understandable that a play he particularly admired, The Tempest, is one in which he felt that Shakespeare was not writing in a haphazard way but to an idea. In a review published on 7 November 1903 (I, 293–7), he suggests that no sources have been found for this play because 'Shakespeare, at the close of his career, wished to write an epilogue to his work, an autobiography, in allegorical form. . . . And what more natural than that he should proceed to evolve from his own brain, now at leisure for the task, a story after his own less quickly-pulsing heart?'. For this reason, The Tempest is the only play 'that satisfies the

modern standard of art.' Max fully accepts the belief, current in his time, that the play is an allegory of Shakespeare's own career, and that 'he who impersonates Prospero impersonates also the creator of Prospero'. His view that this play is 'essentially the work of an elder', in which art has triumphed over 'impoverished vitality', seems to be approaching Lytton Strachey's view, first propounded less than three weeks after this review appeared, of the last plays as the products of boredom.[1]

It is not surprising that one possessed of the satiric temperament should respond most easily to comedies. Although by comparison with The Tempest Max found A Midsummer Night's Dream a 'debauch of uncontrolled fancy', still it was a favourite play.

Shakespeare fulminating, Shakespeare pontificating, has never been surpassed, but Shakespeare in his slippers has never been approached by any poet in his. Throughout the Midsummer Night's Dream we see him in his slippers – exquisitely embroidered slippers, which, in sheer gaiety and lightness of heart, he kicks up into the empyrean and catches again on the tip of his toe upturned. (II, 113–16)

The theme is reiterated in another notice (II, 230–3), in which he describes this as 'the most impressive of all Shakespeare's works, because it was idly done, because it was a mere overflow of genius'. As You Like It is praised in somewhat similar terms: 'It is less like a play than like a lyric that has been miraculously prolonged to the length of a play without losing its airiness and its enchantment' (I, 478).

To the tragedies Max responded less easily. Hamlet was a great favourite, and drew from him an interesting paragraph about the subtlety of character-portrayal in Hamlet himself. Finding that H. B. Irving does not give us 'a wholly

[1] Strachey's 'Shakespeare's Final Period', first published in The Independent Review in August 1906, had been delivered as a paper to the Sunday Essay Society at Trinity College, Cambridge, on 24 November, 1903 (S. Schoenbaum, Shakespeare's Lives, Oxford, 1970, p. 664).

consistent or wholly intelligible picture' of Hamlet, he says

We must blame Shakespeare. Or, rather, we must praise Shakespeare. None of us is wholly consistent or wholly intelligible – at any rate to himself, who knows most about the matter. To his acquaintances a man may seem to be this or that kind of man, quite definitely. That is only because they know so little about him. To his intimate friends he is rather a problem. To himself he is an insoluble problem. Shakespeare, drawing Hamlet, drew him from within...drew him in all his complexity and changefulness.... We must not ask of any actor that he shall explain Hamlet to us. The most we can expect is that he shall give unity to the divergent characteristics and moods. (III, 150).

In *Hamlet*, as in many of the plays, Max finds the chief interest to lie in the portrayal of the central character. So it is with *Macbeth*, *The Merchant of Venice*, and *Othello*. He writes well on Iago and the problems that he poses for the actor (II, 518–21). *King Lear* was a difficult play for him to face. The unnaturalness of behaviour in the early scenes is too much for him; there is 'too much that Shakespeare did not transmute in the crucible of his brain'. But he recognizes that 'Shakespeare's great imagination certainly did begin to work at high pressure so soon as he got Lear out upon the storm-swept heath with the clown, and in the hovel where Poor Tom gibbered' (III, 483–7).

Max's most sustained piece of analytical Shakespeare criticism comes in relation to *Julius Caesar*, and is spread over a series of reviews. Beerbohm Tree had revived the play successfully after a long period of neglect, which Max attributed to the lack of love-interest. Max reviewed the production in September 1900 (II, 285–8). He admires *Julius Caesar* as a 'man's play', ranging 'between a sphere where the appeal is merely intellectual, and a sphere where emotion is strictly divorced from sex.' In the course of his notice he suggests that 'its idea – how finely developed! – is the vanity of idealism in practical affairs'. Two weeks later, he refers at the end of a review of

another play to a 'long interesting letter' printed in the same issue by one H.H. trying 'to show that the moral drawn by me from *Julius Caesar* – the vanity of idealism in practical affairs – was never pointed by Shakespeare himself, for that his Brutus was not an idealist but a self-seeking humbug.' Max 'cannot swallow' this. Shakespeare was a professional dramatist who knew perfectly well how to guide his audience's reactions; he could and would have made Brutus's hypocrisy apparent if this was what he had intended. Max does not object to H.H.'s finding the moral elsewhere. 'A masterpiece can be seen rightly from many aspects'. But he sticks to his own point of view. There the matter rested. But five-and-a-half years later Max devotes an entire essay to comment on an article by Harold Hodge which had just appeared in *Harper's Magazine*. Mr Hodge is, of course, H.H., who had written up his views on Brutus into a 'critical comment'.[1] He was, in fact, Max's editor, having succeeded Frank Harris in 1898; he remained editor of *The Saturday Review* till 1913. So there may be more than meets the eye in this controversy. Max's article of 17 February 1906 is a developed objection to Hodge's developed version of his earlier point of view. It is an entirely serious and forcefully expressed piece of close criticism. It provoked a reply from Hodge, to which Max devotes yet another entire article the following week, replying carefully and with some warmth to each of Hodge's points. These articles reveal Max's capacity to enter whole-heartedly into a critical debate. The issue is still live. Hodge's point of view has become a powerful one; it resembles, for instance, that of T. S. Dorsch in his new Arden edition. Max's articles form a well-argued defence of Brutus and make a real contribution to the history of the criticism of *Julius Caesar*.

[1] Harold Hodge is mistakenly identified as Herbert Hodge in Max Beerbohm's *Letters to Reggie Turner* (1964), ed. R. Hart-Davis, p. 137, fn. 1.

Of the English history plays Max had a generally low opinion, though he was several times surprised to find that he enjoyed performances of them far more than he had expected. Writing about a performance of *King John* leads him into an admission that there is a difference between reading plays and seeing them.

I had never seen the play acted before, and I must confess that, reading it, I had found it insufferably tedious. I had found many beautiful pieces of poetry in it, but drama had seemed to me absolutely lacking. That was because I have not much imagination. Lengths of blank verse with a few bald directions – enter A, exeunt B and D; dies; alarums and excursions; are not enough to make me *see* a thing. (And, I take it, this is the case with most of my fellow-creatures.) Therefore, when I go to a theatre and find that what bored me very much in the reading of it is a really fine play, I feel that I owe a great debt of gratitude to the management which has brought out the latent possibilities. I can imagine that a bad production of *King John* would be infinitely worse than a private reading of it.... But a good production, as at Her Majesty's, makes one forget what is bad in sheer surprise at finding so much that is good.   (II, 193).

Max is quite clear that, if he is to see the plays performed, it should be with modern staging methods. He saw a number of William Poel's productions with the Elizabethan Stage Society, but the only one he seems to have enjoyed was of the first Quarto of *Hamlet*, and that was because it 'came almost as a new play.... The verbal and structural differences between the First and Second Quartos were just enough to create for me a new Hamlet. And so I was grateful to Mr Poel' (I, 64–5). But in general he found that the professedly 'educational' aims of the Society were fulfilled only in so far as Poel succeeded 'in teaching us to pity the poor Elizabethans and to be thankful for the realism of the modern theatre' (I, 61). He had no objections to the Society's productions 'as object lessons in a branch of archaeology' (II, 223); he respects the Society's 'enthusiastic

scholarship'; himself, he finds their activities owlish, but they enjoy themselves, so 'Long may they blink and flutter and hoot.' But he resents claims made by 'some authoritative persons' that Poel's way is 'the one and only dignified mode of presenting Shakespeare's plays' (I, 258–9). 'To compare these revivals with the ordinary modern productions is to be convinced that if Shakespeare could come to life again he would give Mr Poel a wide berth, and would hurry to the nearest commercial theatre in which a play of his happened to be running' (II, 222). 'Shakespeare wrote at a time when the science of scenic production was in its infancy, and he himself, as he has told us, was conscious and resentful of the limitations' (I, 258). Max admits that the Elizabethans must nevertheless have found the productions satisfactory, but feels that 'we, in the twentieth century, cannot project – or rather retroject – ourselves into their state of receptivity' (I, 258). In the 1970s we have to admit that this feeling still lies behind most modern productions of Shakespeare. But we might not wish to go quite so far as Max in his praise of productions in which 'everything...contributes to illusion' (II, 222). He reviewed his half-brother's famous production of *A Midsummer Night's Dream* (II, 230–3), now regarded as a notorious climax in naturalistic presentation, and thoroughly enjoyed it.[1] He found himself

really and truly illuded by the Wood near Athens. All the little fairies there gambolled in a spontaneous and elfin way; the tuition of them had been carried so far as to make us forget that they were real children, licensed by a Magistrate, and that 'at break of day' they were going to meet, not Oberon, but a certificated Board School teacher.

In this notice he makes gentle fun of Sidney Lee, suggesting that he would have been likely only to enjoy the moment in the play-scene when Quince came on 'bearing a board with

[1] He does not refer to the live rabbits alleged to have appeared in this production.

the inscription "THIS IS A WOOD".' This quip was no doubt provoked by Sidney Lee's article 'Shakespeare and the Modern Stage'[1], printed in *The Nineteenth Century* in the same month as Max wrote his review. This is a well-considered plea that 'lovers of Shakespeare should lose no opportunity of urging the cause of simplicity in the production of the plays of Shakespeare.' Max may well have regarded it as an implicit attack on his half-brother's production methods.

Max felt similar admiration for his half-brother's production of *Twelfth Night*, in reviewing which he again defended the point of view that the plays 'are not at all degraded by a setting of beauty, that they deserve such setting, and by it are made more beautiful, and that anyone who by it is distracted from their own intrinsic beauty betrays in himself a lack of visual sense' (9 February 1901; II, 346–50).

Beerbohm Tree's elaborate productions seem, from our vantage point, the last, climactic fling of scenic extravagance in Shakespeare presentation. On *A Midsummer Night's Dream*, says Odell, 'Tree lavished the very last possibilities of stage craft', and with it he produced for the last year of the century the 'utmost scenic marvels toward which that century had steadily progressed.'[2] *The Athenaeum* was even more affirmative: 'In presenting the poetic aspects of a Midsummer Night's Dream, Mr Tree has not only gone beyond precedent and record, he has reached what may, until science brings about new possibilities, be regarded as the limits of the conceivable.'[3] It is only fair to Max to remark that his insistence on visual beauty was not limited to the purely representational. He praises Charles Ricketts's pioneering designs for *King Lear* (1909; III, 485), and writes with high admiration of Gordon Craig's scenery for *Much Ado About Nothing* (1903; II, 573–6), which was quite beyond the understanding of many who saw it.

On acting-styles in Shakespeare, Max de-clared his hand in an early notice (I, 24–7) in which he discusses what he calls the new and the old schools of acting. The new school, he finds, triumphs in modern comedy or modern tragedy, but the old school comes into its own with romantic melodrama, a form which is old-fashioned, not in the sense that it is no longer popular, but that 'it is no longer a form to which any vital English dramatist devotes himself.' The old method still flourishes in the provinces, where 'one finds infinitely better acting in romantic melodrama than one ever finds in London. There, too, Shakespeare's plays are performed much better than in London, for in Shakespeare's plays the poetry and the rhetoric are of far greater importance than the psychology' (I, 27). This theme is repeated and developed in a number of notices. Max does not crudely suggest that 'the poetry' should be emphasised all the time. Shakespeare 'was both a dramatist and a poet', and 'the best Shakespearian acting is a kind of compromise between poetry and drama' (I, 72). Thus, 'the ideal interpreter of a Shakespearean part is one who effects an exactly fair compromise between the poetry and the drama, giving to the words as much of the beauty of their rhythm as is compatible with their reflection of mood and character' (I, 260). This seems very fair, though we might not always agree with its interpretation. For example, to Max 'Ophelia's mad-scene is mere poetry'. It should not be played for an effect of realistic lunacy, as Mrs Benson plays it, 'who groans and gasps, glares, shrieks and gesticulates, so indefatigably as to make havoc of every beautiful line the poet has put into her mouth' (I, 72–3). Similarly

Miss Brayton is very pleasant in the sane scenes of Ophelia; but one would hardly be surprised if at any

[1] Reprinted in Lee's *Shakespeare and the Modern Stage* (1906), pp. 1–24.
[2] G. C. D. Odell, *Shakespeare – from Betterton to Irving*, 2 vols. (New York, 1920), II, 453.
[3] qu. Odell, *loc. cit.*

mo ment she entered springing off a bicycle. In the mad scenes of Ophelia she tries hard not to be so pleasant, and manages to give a realistic representation of lunacy.

Max thinks this a mistake, and that 'The only right way for an actress to interpret these mad scenes is through her sense of beauty.' This is questionable, though his discussion in the same notice of the speaking of Gertrude's description of Ophelia's death makes admirable sense:

'There is', says lyric Shakespeare, 'a willow grows aslant a brook', and he proceeds to revel in the landscape, quite forgetting (to our eternal gain) that he speaks through the lips of an agonised lady. What is the agonised lady to do?.... She must forget that she is an agonised lady, and speak the words as beautifully and as simply as she can. Then there will be no absurdity. But what could be more absurd than to hear a lady talking, as Miss Maud Milton talks, about 'crow-flowers, nettles, daisies, and long purples' with tragic gasps and violent gestures of woe, and dwelling with special emphasis on 'long purples' as though they were quite the most harrowing thing of all? Here the passion for naturalness leads to sheer nonsense.

H. B. Irving, in the same production, is also unsatisfactory because he sacrifices 'beauty... to exact realism' (III, 149, 151).

Max explicitly dissociates himself from 'those who would have dramatic expression, in poetic plays, utterly subordinated to the rhythm of the verse' (I, 479). He does not wish meaning to be sacrificed to rhythm; but he does ask that in both prose and verse, rhythm should be 'recognisably preserved.' This did not happen in Oscar Asche's 1907 *As You Like It*, perhaps because the players ate too many apples.

According to the modern doctor, apples are a splendidly wholesome diet, and I should not like the players to risk their health by abstaining. But I suggest that two-thirds or so of the fruit consumed on the stage might with advantage be consumed in the dressing-rooms. No doubt it is very natural that Jaques, for example, should be engaged on an apple while he describes the seven ages of man. No doubt the thoughts in that speech are not so profound that their thinker

would have had to postpone his meal because of them. But I maintain that the speech is a beautifully written one, very vivid, quaint, and offering scope for great variety in enunciation. It ought to be given for all it is worth, and not in a series of grunts between mouthfuls. (I, 479–80).

Max could praise good speaking as well as make fun of bad. Lewis Waller as Henry V has 'an elocution which wrings the full value out of every syllable. His innumerable long speeches...stir one in virtue of their delivery' (II, 341). Forbes-Robertson's famous Hamlet evokes praise for a mode of speaking which shows Hamlet for the first time 'as a quite definite and intelligible being'. 'In face, and in voice, and in manner, Mr Robertson is a heaven-born Hamlet' (II, 487). But as Othello he fails, even though he so declaims the poetry 'that every phrase and cadence has its due beauty' (II, 521).

Some of the best passages in Max's theatre criticism are ones in which he writes about an actor or actress in a manner that conveys an mpression of their quality, not necessarily by direct description of their acting. His obituary of Irving (I, 396–401) provides an excellent example. It is one of the best of English essays, and a wonderful tribute to the power of personality in acting. Here, as elsewhere, Max uses the word 'beauty' quite often, and it would be easy to accuse him, with his predilection for comedy, his insistence on the need for visual beauty, his demands that verse and prose should both be spoken with a due sense of rhythm, of a shallow over-emphasis on the superficially pleasing at the expense of the serious. It would not, I think, be fair. He can write eloquently on *Othello* as well as of *A Midsummer Night's Dream*; he can appreciate the avant-garde designs of Gordon Craig as well as the traditional settings for Tree's productions; and although he finds that Irving could not declaim, could not give Shakespeare's verse its 'true music and magic', yet he could pay noble tribute to Irving's speaking, to 'the meanings that he made the verse yield to him', even though these 'subtle and sometimes profound meanings were not always Shakespeare's own'. Irving's 'prime appeal was always to the sense of beauty'. This obviously suited Max. But 'it was not...to a sense of obvious beauty. It was to a sense of strange, delicate, almost mystical and unearthly beauty' (I, 397–8).

Of course, Max's 'satiric temperament' finds its natural outlet in reviews of performances that he found less than satisfactory, and especially in those that he found positively ridiculous. He was averse to intellectual pretension, which he found very prominent in the spectacle of play-goers watching Shakespeare being performed in a language that they did not understand. A natural target was Sarah Bernhardt's Hamlet. He heads his notice 'Hamlet; Princess of Denmark' (I, 34–7), and opens it with the admission that he cannot take the performance seriously. He deploys his wit and his irony.

Sarah ought not to have supposed that Hamlet's weakness set him in any possible relation to her own feminine mind and body. Her friends ought to have restrained her. The native critics ought not to have encouraged her. The custom-house officials at Charing Cross ought to have confiscated her sable doublet and hose.

The only compliment he could pay her was that her Hamlet 'was, from first to last, *très grande dame*'. Yet even this essay, masterpiece of comic prose as it is, includes a serious and perceptive passage on the difference between the French and the English languages. No less brilliant in its satirical effect is Max's well-known essay (I, 61–3) on the Benson company in the light of their sporting interests.

Every member of the cast [of *Henry V*] seemed in tip-top condition – thoroughly 'fit'. Subordinates and principals all worked well together. The fielding was excellent, and so was the batting. Speech after speech was sent spinning across the boundary, and one was constantly inclined to shout 'Well *played*, sir! Well

played *indeed*!' As a branch of university cricket, the whole performance was, indeed, beyond praise. But, as a form of acting, it was not impressive.

The virtues displayed in passages such as these are in part those of the essayist who happens to have chosen a theatrical topic. But then, many of our best theatre critics have also been among our best essayists. The most memorable theatre criticism, it seems to me, is not that which aims at abstract discussion or displays analytical power. It is rather that which tells us what actually happened, which gives us a sense of watching the performance described. It is not purely objective description, because it may use stylistic devices to give us a sense of emotional involvement as well as simply informing us about what was seen. This is something that Lichtenberg does brilliantly in his descriptions of Garrick as Hamlet. Hazlitt does it, especially when he is writing about Edmund Kean; Leigh Hunt does it, on Kean's Timon, for instance; and Max does it, too. He does it of a real-life situation, when he tells us how he caught a glimpse of Irving on his way to Windsor to receive his knighthood (I, 400). He does it of Dan Leno in an essay (I, 349–52) that does more to convey to us what it was like to be a member of the great comedian's audience than any of Dan Leno's gramophone records or photographs. And he does it occasionally, too, in his descriptions of Shakespearian acting. The best example in the classical style is perhaps when he describes a wordless episode in Beerbohm Tree's *Twelfth Night*.

As the two topers reel off to bed, the uncanny dawn peers at them through the windows. The Clown wanders on, humming a snatch of the tune he has sung to them. He looks at the empty bowl of sack and the overturned tankards, smiles, shrugs his shoulders, yawns, lies down before the embers of the fire, goes to sleep. Down the stairs, warily, with a night-cap on his head and a sword in his hand, comes Malvolio, awakened and fearful of danger. He peers around, lunging with his sword at the harmless furniture. One thinks of Don Quixote and 'the notable adventure of the wine-skins'. Satisfied, he retraces his footsteps up the staircase. A cock crows, and, as the curtain falls, one is aware of a whole slumbering household, and of the mystery of an actual dawn. Pedants might cavil at such imaginative glosses in a production of Shakespeare. To me the question is simply whether the imagination be of a good or bad kind. In this instance the imagination seems to me distinctly good.

(II, 349).

Finally, it is worth mentioning a review in which Max uses an unusual technique with considerable success. It is closely related to that of *Twelfth Night*, but differs in that the first five hundred words or so consist of a series of what Max himself calls 'disjointed sentences' aiming to preserve his own impressions of Tree's production of *King John*. It was a characteristically elaborate production, including a spectacular interpolated tableau of the granting of Magna Carta. Max enjoyed it greatly, though, as he admits, most of what he describes is 'points of "business" and stage management.' He responds to it very much as a visual experience. Here he is on the last scene:

The dying king is borne out in a chair. He is murmuring snatches of a song. The chair is set down, and with weak hands he motions away his bearers. 'Ay, marry', he gasps, 'now my soul hath elbow-room; it would not out at windows nor at doors. There is so hot a summer in my bosom, that all my bowels crumble up to dust. . . . And none of you will bid the winter come, to thrust his icy fingers in my maw.' The bastard comes in hot haste, and the king, to receive his tidings, sits upright, and is crowned for the last time. He makes no answer to the tidings. One of the courtiers touches him, ever so lightly, on the shoulder, and he falls back. The crown is taken from his head and laid on the head of the child who is now king. The bastard rings out those words in which poetry of patriotism finds the noblest expression it can ever find . . .' (II, 192).

It is a somewhat self-conscious style. Spontaneity was not among Max's virtues as a writer. But it is an expressive and informative style which might have been valuably applied to other productions.

A survey of Max's theatre criticism reveals him as a serious critic of Shakespeare, no wider in his response than most cultured playgoers of his time, but with a capacity for thoughtful analysis and a genius for expressing his personal reactions to theatrical experience. He was not a leader of taste, but neither was he entirely reactionary. We can value him as a recorder, an observing eye, ear, mind, during a period of transition from the high naturalism of his half-brother to the symbolism of Gordon Craig. He is, of course, more to be valued as a master of English prose than as a Shakespeare critic; but it is a happy fact that Max's hard labour in his profession provided the circumstances for a fruitful reaction between his mind and the Shakespeare productions of his time. It is fortunate for us, as it was fortunate for Max, that he was not a porter on the Underground Railway.

© STANLEY WELLS 1976

IA Max Beerbohm, 'Had Shakespeare asked me . . .'. No. 720 in *A Catalogue of the Caricatures of Max Beerbohm*, compiled by Rupert Hart-Davis (1972)

IB Max Beerbohm, 'My poverty, but not my will, consents.' No. 712 in the same

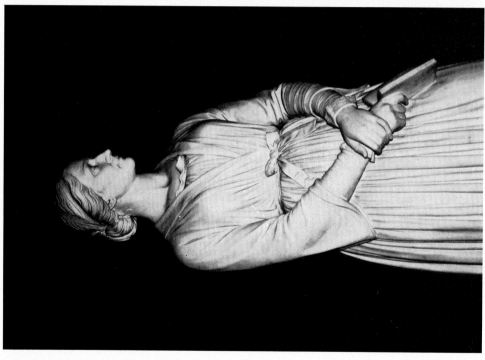

IIA   Statue of Johanne Luise Heiberg in the Royal Theatre of Copenhagen

IIB   Portrait of the same by Marstrand

III *Hamlet*, The Other Place, Stratford, 1975.
Directed by Buzz Goodbody, designed by Christopher Dyer. Ben Kingsley as Hamlet

IV *2 Henry IV*, Royal Shakespeare Theatre, 1975. Directed by Terry Hands,
designed by Farrah. Brewster Mason as Falstaff, Sydney Bromley (far left) as Shallow

V *Henry V*, Royal Shakespeare Theatre, 1975.

Directed by Terry Hands, designed by Farrah. Act III, scene i, Alan Howard as Henry at the walls of Harfleur

VI *Henry V*, act IV, scene i, the English camp before Agincourt, with Richard Moore (centre) as Pistol

VII *Henry V*, act IV, scene viii, Henry (Alan Howard) and his nobles thank God after Agincourt

VIII *The Merry Wives of Windsor*, Royal Shakespeare Theatre, 1975.
Directed by Terry Hands, designed by Timothy O'Brien and Tazeena Firth. Act II,
scene i, Barbara Leigh-Hunt (left) as Mistress Ford and Brenda Bruce as Mistress Page

A DANISH ACTRESS AND HER CONCEPTION OF THE PART OF LADY MACBETH

HENNING KRABBE

In the foyer of the Royal Theatre of Copenhagen there is a life-size statue of a woman, standing at her ease, contemplative, with no trace of passion, mild, unsmiling, a woman of the world. She is the actress Johanne Luise Heiberg. This is how she liked to see herself at the height of her fame when the statue was made, about the middle of the last century (see Plate II A).

Who was she? Even now, a hundred years after she withdrew from the theatre, she still excites our curiosity, and she has recently been the subject of a brilliant biography by the Danish stage historian, Robert Neiiendam, who has thrown much light on her personality.

For more than a generation, she dominated the Danish stage. Her beauty enchanted the sculptor, Thorvaldsen, who had her picture on his wall. Kierkegaard, the philosopher, who was a keen theatre-goer, spoke of her soulful eyes. The great of the land courted her; the ladies of Copenhagen imitated her ingenious dresses; and Lumbye, the composer, wrote a Johanne Luise Waltz, which you can still hear played in the pleasure gardens of Tivoli. Before she died she wrote the story of her life, one of the most fascinating autobiographies in our literature, and as indispensable for any student of Danish theatre history as, say, Bernard Shaw's *Our Theatres in the Nineties* to an Englishman.

Indeed, it seemed as if fortune had smiled on this woman and treated her kindly. Still, her life had not been a bed of roses, and her career was

as startling as that of Becky Sharp. She was born in poverty in 1812. Her parents had emigrated from Germany. Her father, Christian Pätges, was a Catholic, her mother a Jewess from Frankfurt. They had then settled in Copenhagen, where they kept a public house with a room for dancing; in summer they rented a tent in the pleasure garden of the Deerpark north of Copenhagen, 'Dyrehavsbakken'. This is how Johanne Luise grew up, one of nine children. She had some dancing lessons and was accepted at the ballet school of the Court Theatre (the present Theatre Museum in Copenhagen). In the same year a lank and awkward boy from Odense made his appearance at the Theatre's school of ballet and singing. His name was Hans Andersen, and he appeared at his first performance as an imp. Johanne Luise had the good fortune to come under the protection of some good people who noticed her talent, lent her books, and opened to her the world of the imagination.

Heiberg, the spirited young author, 21 years her senior, had noticed her on the stage at a performance when she was only 14, and took an interest in her. At 16, Hanne Pätges appeared as Juliet in Shakespeare's play. At 17, she was employed by the Royal Theatre, and Heiberg was writing plays for her. They became engaged.

His appearance could hardly charm a girl who was as much courted as Hanne. But he provided to an eminent degree the culture and authority she so badly needed. As nobody else he could nourish her burning ambition at the theatre, and he was passionately in love with her: 'When I sit in the stalls', he wrote to her, 'and I see you on the stage, a thrill runs through me: She is mine, she is mine!' In July 1831 they were married. The child from the public house, the daughter of a drunken cellarman from Germany, had become the leading actress of the Danish Theatre, and now Professor Heiberg's wife. She became the muse of her age. Not only was she accepted in society, but in time the Heiberg home became the model of the Copenhagen upper middle class. The Heibergs were at the same time exclusive and hospitable. Highly gifted women – such as the Swedish singer Jenny Lind – were generally less welcome than the eminent men of their time.

In the nineteenth century, Copenhagen was in fact one of the unacknowledged centres of cultural life in Europe. Authors like Hans Andersen and Kierkegaard were to achieve world fame in translation; Thorvaldsen, and the founder of Danish ballet, Bournonville, became renowned each in their field; whereas the greatest glory of intellectual life, our poetry, must remain unknown outside Denmark. In the theatre it was Johanne Luise, together with a number of good actors, who gave greatness to dramatic art. Perhaps the most striking tribute ever paid to her was the rhymed epistle which Henrik Ibsen sent her; in lofty verse he recalls unforgettable hours in the theatre, when he sat 'spell-bound by her art'.

She played a very great number of parts, 268 in all, and of all kinds. She was, generally speaking, better in comedy than in tragedy. Gaiety and beauty spiritualized through romantic longing was her true sphere. Rosalind and Viola she would play to perfection. The extraordinary thing is the care she took over every part, to make it truthful in every gesture and word, and to give a consistent and human development. Nowadays actors are in great demand in so many places outside the theatre: in television, radio, and film that they simply do not have the time to work out the characters to the same extent as the great actors of old, such as Garrick or Mrs Siddons.

Johanne Luise Heiberg's performance of Lady Macbeth took place in 1860. She was in fact no so young as she imagined the character to be, but the temptation to play Lady Macbeth was irresistible. The care she took over her parts is nowhere more apparent than in her memoirs, where she writes of Lady Macbeth:

For many years I had regarded it as a high artistic aim one day to hope to play Lady Macbeth. Confronted with this task, for years I had tried, in truth and sincerity, again and again to reach an understanding of this great female character placed in this powerfully tragical situation. . . It goes without saying that if Lady Macbeth is represented as no longer young the whole interpretation will be different from one in which she is still young. What in a young Lady Macbeth is a flare of passion will in an elderly, experienced actress appear as a deep-seated, demonic power of evil. This was the way she had always been represented, according to tradition. But this tradition, I venture to think, is a fallacious conception of the work, as I shall now try to demonstrate.

It has always seemed to me that everything in the work indicates that the poet imagined Macbeth and Lady Macbeth if not in the prime of youth, still as comparatively young, in the early years of their married life. Macbeth exclaims, when in the first scenes with him she passionately exhorts him to murder the king, 'Bring forth men-children only.' This outburst would be downright comical and unbecoming in front of an older woman. This outburst seems to me to indicate with certainty that they have not been married for long, and children are yet to be born. But if so, then we must see her as a young woman. Her beauty is mentioned several times. When the King is told that Macbeth has arrived before him and his men, he says, 'His great love, sharp as his spur, hath holp him / To his home before us'. The King addresses Lady Macbeth 'Fair and Noble hostess.' Only a beautiful woman is addressed like that – a matron is not. His gift to her is given with the words: 'Most kind hostess.' Macbeth and Lady Macbeth rush forward with all the impetuosity of youth towards their ambitious plans of life as if in a demonic intoxication which has gained firmness to spur action by the prophecy of the witches on the heath. The poison of their prophecy has mingled with their blood and confused their senses. All quiet consideration is gone, and at one stroke their whole great and honourable past is blotted out, As yet, Macbeth has no sons in his marriage, but he still hopes that they will be born to succeed him on the throne. In the heat of passion his wife has lost all patience. Before her mind's eye she sees one thing only, the golden round that will one day encircle their brows. The fear of the heart, the voice of conscience are nothing to them in the first moment of intoxication; as yet they are inexperienced in sin. After the murder, Macbeth says to his wife, 'We are yet but young in deed'. In youthful recklessness they rush forward, led on by the demons who have possessed their souls. They are beginners in sin, not a pair of hardened criminals – and therefore I think it of the utmost importance that they should both have the stamp of youth; otherwise they become loathsome devils in all their doings.

. . . Shakespeare's plays were not provided with all the notes and directions which modern authors often introduce in their works in exaggerated detail for the benefit of the actors. Actually, this often harms the actor, as it limits the freedom of his imagination. It must be added, however, that these directions prevent misinterpretations on the part of the actor. But the detailed instructions of the authors through their notes tend to make the creative work of the actor mere routine, slackening the powers instead of stimulating them. What sets a real actor at work, searching for a true interpretation of the poet's work, also fires his imagination, heightens it, and sharpens his understanding; and if he feels that he is on the right track, that he has achieved his aim, then the enthusiasm will be awakened without which no brilliant creation can appear on the stage.

. . . At Lady Macbeth's first entrance in the play, the text says, 'Enter Lady Macbeth, reading a letter.' But how is this letter to be read? It is from her husband, who tells her of his meeting with the witches on the heath, who greeted him as Thane of Cawdor, ending by 'All hail, Macbeth, that shalt be king hereafter.' One prophecy has been fulfilled, and he now believes firmly in the other. It is this belief that he imparts to his wife in the letter. Now, is this letter to be read aloud, as she enters, as if she was reading it for the first time? Obviously a letter of such curious contents must be

read with quite different accents according to whether she reads these words for the first time or goes over the letter for the twentieth time. I think that the latter conception is the right one; so I entered with the letter rolled up; only after a pause did I unroll it and read it as one who repeats word by word what has already been read, to try to fathom its meaning. For imagine that the contents of this letter are here revealed to her for the first time – what surprise, what exclamations would not pour from this passionate woman's lips. For here she would have to frame the murderous plot; but we hear nothing of this. On the contrary, she is already resolved. The plan, one feels, has already been thought out. The first surprise is past – she only reflects on her husband's gentle, weak nature, fearing he does not possess 'the illness should attend' the successful implementing of the plan. And she exclaims in jubilant passion: 'Hie thee hither, / That I may pour my spirits in thine ear, / And chastise with the valour of my tongue / All that impedes thee from the golden round / Which fate and metaphysical aid doth seem / To have thee crowned withall.' What is she referring to? To her plan to put the King out of the way, of course, the sooner to attain the promised end. But how is this to be brought about? How to find means to get the King in her power? This is as yet unclear to her, and this is why, when the messenger brings her the news that the King will arrive that night and sleep in her house, she exclaims, 'Thou'rt mad to say it' – for this message is, of course, like an answer to her secret thoughts and may well inflame her, as the means to the black deed is now found, and she exclaims, 'The raven himself is hoarse, / That croaks the fatal entrance of Duncan / Under my battlements.' It is clear from this exclamation that the whole plan of the murder has been thought through with such passion, such strength, that nobody and nothing can stop what she has thrown her entire soul into. Here Macbeth enters, and she greets him, 'Great Glamis! Worthy Cawdor! Greater than both, by the all-hail hereafter!', and she continues, 'Thy letters have transported me beyond / This ignorant present.' Now this transport, I think, must be kept up throughout the entire scene. The young, passionate woman is in ecstasies, intoxicated in the rush of her crime. We should not see in Lady Macbeth a cold, base woman, hardened in evil, but a woman distracted by her demonic ecstasy who can see nothing, hear nothing except one thing, the goal which like a fire has kindled her ambitious soul, and whose flames burn out all fear, and all conscience.

She rejoices at the royal hope before her eyes and calls to Macbeth, who vacillates and shivers in the fear of deliberation, 'Look up clear!' – By this impetuosity, this demonic ecstasy, in which we see her soul in bondage, she is kept within the limits of humanity, and nobody can tell as yet what will become of her when the intoxication disappears. – On the other hand, if she remained cool and deliberate in her evilness, she would appear an absolute devil, too low to end up in deep despair, in consuming pangs of conscience, as is shown towards the end of the play, where the ecstasy is exchanged with fear and anguish at her crime.

An actor is under an obligation at the beginning of the drawing of a character to have the end in mind, so that beginning and end may form a unity in the work.

O happy the artist who has a poet like Shakespeare to interpret! How often will poets jumble their scenes together without regard to the development of character, without any preparation of the full illusion. Not so in this play. Could anyone imagine an introduction to the sleepwalking-scene more brilliant than the quiet nightly conversation preceding it between the doctor who has been sent for and Lady Macbeth's gentlewoman. Only the highest dramatic genius would think out such an introduction to so important a scene. For the first time in the play, the audience is here prepared for Lady Macbeth's condition, how in desperate anxiety she often walks in her sleep at night, uttering words of which the gentlewoman says 'I will not repeat them after her.' This quiet, confidential talk is the most effective introduction possible to the terrible nightly scene for creation of tension and atmosphere and illusion in the audience. I know of no other poet's work to rival this for dramatic art. – Except, perhaps, for the wonderful beginning of *Hamlet* on the battlements.

The doctor, who has been watching all night to see for himself the Lady's fearful walking without this having taken place, has already made his mind up to go when the gentlewoman suddenly exclaims in terror, 'Lo you, here she comes, this is her very guise.' I would like to see the spectator who does not feel a shiver down his spine at this exclamation, and then at the sight of the unhappy woman in her night-gown, carrying the burning taper and advancing stiff, petrified, like a ghost, beneath the sombre castle vaults. What a marvellous aid the actress here receives from the poet's imagination! The whole situation – from the terrible rubbing of the blood-stained hand to every

little word wrung from the tortured soul – is elevated to supreme dramatic effect. And this scene, which seems to us a whole great drama, consists of five short speeches only! But what speeches! As if hewn in marble they remain with us, unforgettable. They fall like sharp daggers in our minds, interrupted only by the subdued whispering of the doctor and the gentlewoman behind her. It intensifies the whole situation even further that these two characters stand trembling and listening to the desolate woman's heart-rending anguish, until the doctor says, 'This disease is beyond my practice.' I say again, happy the actress whose lot it is to interpret such a poet's visions and revelations.

How intensely I have felt the power of the situation while I studied the part – how every nerve is stirred. When I rehearsed this scene in the solitary hours of the night, while the whole house slept, I was often seized with an inexplicable horror, as if the room was filled with demons moving closer and closer. My breath was taken away, and they seemed to be pressing me out of the room, so that I was as it were forced to seize the lamp and hurry away. And yet, I could only rehearse this scene at night. It seemed to me all unnatural to practise it in the clear light of day. I myself needed the dark to create the full illusion, though I was often shocked to feel to what an extent it could be produced.

An actor's imagination is – as I said above – his strength in art, his danger in life. During my rehearsal of this part my imagination was stirred so powerfully that I was horrified at it and had to struggle to quench this fire of the imagination again and again and calm it by setting about the pursuits of daily life.[1]

– This is undoubtedly a very personal account of Johanne Luise Heiberg's work with the part, except, perhaps, at one point: she might have read a German translation of some reflections made by her famous predecessor as the great Lady. Mrs Siddons writes:

On the night preceding that in which I was to appear in this part for the first time, I shut myself up, as usual, when all the family were retired, and commenced my study of Lady Macbeth. ...I went on...till I came

[1] Johanne Luise Heiberg, *A Life Relived in Memory* (Copenhagen, 1891–2). Extract translated by Anne Marie Bülow-Møller and Henning Krabbe.

to the assassination scene, when the horrors of the scene rose to a degree that made it impossible for me to get farther. I snatched up my candle, and hurried out of the room, in a paroxysm of terror. My dress was of silk, and the rustling of it, as I ascended the strait to go to bed, seemed to my panic-struck fancy like the movement of a spectre pursuing me. . . .[1]

The demons seem to have had a remarkable habit of haunting young actresses at nightly rehearsals.

[1] Thomas Campbell, *Life of Mrs Siddons* (1834), I, pp. 35–6.

© HENNING KRABBE 1976

TOWARDS A POOR SHAKESPEARE: THE ROYAL SHAKESPEARE COMPANY AT STRATFORD IN 1975

PETER THOMSON

I would be doing the late Buzz Goodbody a disservice if I called the production of *Hamlet* at Stratford in 1975 hers. Against the tide of our 'director's theatre', over which the Royal Shakespeare Company has long exercised a moon-like influence, she found the courage and the skill to release the play to the actors. The actors, for their part, responded with a performance whose alertness to the text was not only exemplary but constantly invigorating. For the second time this decade Stratford has provided us with a major theatrical exploration of a familiar text; and this *Hamlet*, unlike Brook's 1970 production of *A Midsummer Night's Dream*, is imitable.

I was once in a production of *Ironhand* which overwhelmed audiences in Manchester's small University Theatre. Transferred to the Teatro Regio in Parma it dwindled. *Hamlet* was not performed in the main auditorium, but in the bare and comfortless small studio/shack named, or unnamed, The Other Place. To call the production imitable is not to claim that it is transferable. It belonged to the physical context in which it had been rehearsed, and which it exploited. There was no sign whatsoever of the conspicuous expenditure which is still a trademark of the Royal Shakespeare Company. A student society's budget could have serviced it. The tickets are one price (70p), and you sit where you can on backless benches. For *Hamlet* an end-stage had been built opposite the auditorium's single access door. The 'scenery' was a line of screens, simply constructed of paper stretched over a wood frame. 'You can be sure somebody will come bursting through that,' I whispered to a colleague before the play began. I was wrong. The line of screens left an acting area about ten feet in depth, with the actors clearly sharing a room with the audience. On this narrow platform stood Francisco at the play's opening. Torches provided the only light, and their beams, thrown across the audience, picked out the Ghost at the back of the room. It was simple and effective, and it set the tone of a production which *never* strained for its effects. There was no deception, no trickery. It was appropriate that the door through which the Ghost vanished, on which Laertes would later batter, and through which Fortinbras would make his final portentous entrance, belonged in each interval to the audience. We were sharing with the actors a neutral space whose primitive amenities became startlingly appropriate whenever they were used. There was remarkably little sense of a performance taking place. Rather, we were silent participators in a series of events whose intense logic required that they take place here and nowhere else. We were being shown neither a case-history, nor an outlandish fable. That evening (it was 1st October when I saw it) in that place *Hamlet* was a likely story. It was likely, in large part, because the actors made it so, but also because our presence and participation guaranteed its likelihood. I wonder, too, how much was owed to the costuming. This was a modern dress *Hamlet*, but without ostentation or self-conscious ingenuity. The clothes were, in effect, gestic, expressing the gist of the characters, their gesture and their social context. Claudius, in a finely tailored blue suit with broad white stripes, was as strong and clean-cut as an industrial trouble-shooter in George Baker's authoritative performance, a formidable man whose wardrobe carries the Establishment's seal of approval. There is nothing more disheartening to one who knows the need for change than a group of reasonable men in pin-striped suits. This is not a frivolous point. Most of us must, at some time, carry our reforming fervour into the board-room, where even the preliminary task, that of persuading colleagues of the existence of those flaws which they embody, is a formidable one. What we saw clearly in this production was Hamlet's attempt to ruffle composure by flouting good form, its initial success and feckless, fumbling climax. The readier way of changing governments is vigorously presented by the brash final entrance of a cynically opportunistic Fortinbras:

> I have some rights of memory in this kingdom,
> Which now to claim my vantage doth invite me.

His costume, that of a paratrooper, and his demeanour leave no doubt of his intentions towards Denmark. Like Fielding's Fireblood, he 'would have ravished her, if she had not, by a timely Compliance, prevented him'.

The benefits of careful costuming were further illustrated by a Polonius who could follow the fashion of his monarch without a hint of competition, an Osric in impeccable jodphurs, and a Reynaldo whose city pin-stripes wittily contributed to the portrait of an ambitious civil servant who would flatter his superiors only to replace them. Laertes had a student's hair and beard, but his father's taste in clothes. Ophelia, more tendentiously (the actress, anyway, was inadequate), wore a loose,

off-white dress in pre-Raphaelite style. It might have implied her independence of courtly fashion, but the performance proved nothing conclusively. Sid Livingstone, one of those rare, composed actors who makes any line appropriate and could probably convince us that Macbeth was a Lancastrian, presented a north-country Horatio in frayed brown corduroys, loose overcoat, and long scarf; a scholarship boy. The court cold-shouldered him, and he chose not to press the point, but the friendship with Hamlet was real and attractive. The players came from the same rough world, working actors who respected the craft they practised. 'The Mousetrap' was performed in the centre of the shallow stage, with Hamlet and Ophelia stage right and the rest of the court extreme stage left. There was no attempt to make of the play-within-a-play more than an adequate pretext for the disturbance it causes. Bob Peck, who doubled as First Player and Gravedigger, is greatly talented but also wisely disciplined.

On an undecorated stage, costume is doubly telling. The actors of *Hamlet*, I surmise, had been invited to select and wear with comfort the modern clothes that best expressed their characters. Hamlet himself was smart in his original black jacket and pin-striped trousers, but the smartness was nicely mothballed and Sunday-best. The neat brown suit that replaced his mourning was both in contrast and in keeping with the grimly proper court. Ben Kingsley is a conscientious actor, devoid of flamboyance. His study of Slender for *The Merry Wives of Windsor* was built on the rational development of a single gesture – something like the awkward thrusting out of a hand to take a glass that is being offered to someone else and its convulsive withdrawal just as the glass is about to be placed in it after all. It requires strict concentration to perform every up-beat action on the down-beat. It might have become routine for Kingsley by the time I saw *The Merry*

Wives, but his Hamlet certainly had not. There were 'original' readings, the relaxed jocularity with Yorick's skull for example, but the impressive thing was the constant testing of the sound of the words against their meaning. Kingsley, sallow of complexion and primly cut, is too austere to satisfy romantic tastes, but there was great charm in the honest speaking of the lines, the charm of an actor modestly encountering a poet.

That, in all frankness, is the point. The achievement of this production is to be measured, quite simply, by the fact that the actors meant what they said. Buzz Goodbody had coaxed the play into their hands, and they respected it. It is not easy to *mean* someone else's words, nor even consistently to *sound* as if you mean your own. One tendency of those modern actors who strive most earnestly for meaning has been to draw too much of the character's life into themselves, away from the audience, draining in consequence the oral strength of the pentameter. The Other Place is small enough to be lenient to such short-comings, and it would be a mistake to suppose that what has been discovered and accomplished there can be readily transposed to the Aldwych or the Royal Shakespeare Theatre. Even so, the achievements of The Other Place over the last two years offer a vital criticism of the attitudes that still govern performances in the main house. They also provide some indication of the way that may have to be followed by an impoverished professional theatre in inflationary times. That is no council of despair. To judge by the responses I heard, poverty could not have come at a better time. *Hamlet* is not the only one of The Other Place's productions to have excited its audiences. *Perkin Warbeck* was warmly received, for *Man Is Man* there is a black market in seats, and *Richard III*, which has just opened as I write, with Ian Richardson playing the title role, promises again to upstage the costlier productions at the

Theatre. Remembering how Stanislavsky closed the Moscow Art Theatre's Studio when Meyerhold's alternative style was beginning to establish itself, I fear for the future of The Other Place. Its present scope and style seem better suited to the time than anyone (even Buzz Goodbody?) had predicted, but it is utterly dependent on its parent company. It is too small, and too inconvenient, to sustain on its own even a mediocre ensemble, yet under the cloak of the Royal Shakespeare Company it has presented in successive Octobers Nicol Williamson as Uncle Vanya and Ian Richardson as Richard III. And this *Hamlet*, perhaps the first significant synthesis of straight and crooked Shakespeare.[1]

I do not know whether Buzz Goodbody had read the splendid sixth chapter of Professor John Russell Brown's *Free Shakespeare*, but there is a passage which the production of *Hamlet* vividly illustrates:

Elizabethan performances cannot be reconstructed, but it would be possible to shift the focus back to ten or a dozen actors [*Hamlet* had thirteen] working freely and responsibly upon a stage. Such performances might be truly alive to contemporary thought and feeling, and awaken in their audience a creative response in which imagination could find stimulus and extension. No one could guess what might be discovered in such a theatre, through Shakespeare's plays, and subsequently through other plays. This alternative Shakespeare could never rival the production of Shakespeare according to our present methods; it would aim at very different effects and probably it could never be widely popular. But the present monopoly needs challenging in order to recover some excitements that are now lost to public view, and to continue our exploration of Shakespeare's plays in new ways.[2]

In her last production Buzz Goodbody offered as an imitable model her own unobtrusiveness.

[1] There is a discussion of 'straight and crooked Shakespeare' in *Shakespeare Survey 27* (Cambridge, 1974), pp. 143–54.
[2] John Russell Brown, *Free Shakespeare* (1974), p. 93.

The four main house plays, all directed by Terry Hands, illustrate the opening sentence of the same chapter in Professor Brown's important book: 'Current methods of producing Shakespeare's plays in the theatre flatly contradict the explorative and fluid engagement for which they were written. The director gives unity, the actors settle into their roles and the audience is kept in the dark to receive whatever view of the play has been chosen for them.'[1] There are, of course, advantages in such a system. No group of actors could have devised the setting for the off-stage execution of Bardolph in *Henry V*. The text had to be rejigged a little – and that is something about which actors have more compunction than directors – but the effect was fine. Fluellen's news that Bardolph 'is like to be executed for robbing a church' was conveyed to Henry as he stood among dispirited soldiers, who straggled the stage in an untidy V-shape. At the downstage apex of the V sat Falstaff's Boy, watching Henry's response to Bardolph's name. Alan Howard did not suggest that the King relished his duty at this point, but he accepted it. Back to the audience, he raised, held, and finally lowered his sword. We were allowed a moment to picture Tim Wylton's grotesque but unavoidably endearing Bardolph swinging, and then the Boy threw down his bucket and fled, whilst Pistol slumped. From the gallery you could see the water from the bucket trickling down the raked stage beside the specks of confetti with which Bardolph had showered Pistol and Mistress Quickly in II, i. The rejection of Falstaff was being poignantly re-enacted. There was, indeed, much to admire in the performance of the trilogy, staged without the frantic inventiveness that has disfigured some of Terry Hands's work.

The Merry Wives of Windsor, revived from as long ago as 1968, was too frantic. It will be remembered for Ian Richardson's tortured Ford rather than for Brewster Mason's im-

probably unruffled Falstaff, yet even Richardson, with all his comic precision (the hat that falls off when, and only when, he wants it to) strained so hard for his laughs that I could rarely find one for him. On this form, Richardson invites us to watch the actor at the possible expense of the action. *Henry V*, which opened the season, is the work of a maturer director. Like the rest of the trilogy, it was mercifully free of silliness. I wonder, though, whether it was wise to begin at the end. Alan Howard, almost inevitably, carried Henry back into Hal, thus begging the whole complex question of the relationship of play to play within the trilogy. The oats Alan Howard sowed were never very wild. If Henry knows so much from the start, how can the audience relish the spectacle of his finding out? And if he does not enjoy the games he plays with Falstaff and the gang, his pretext for participation can only be a delight in the exercise of power without responsibility. Henry V, circling the camp-fires in humble disguise, cannot resist hinting broadly at his greatness. He thinks the king is but a man, *as he is*; his name is *Harry le Roy*. Alan Howard's Hal has the same proud self-consciousness. But if Hal is *merely* mucking about, learning nothing that he does not already know, *Henry IV Part I* is a hollow play.

That is exactly what it seemed in Terry Hands's production. Brewster Mason's Falstaff is dignified, but rarely funny, always conscious of Hal, always looking to him to set the tone. If the Boar's Head Tavern *was* his castle, Hal has supplanted him there, and in how joyless and acerbic a fashion. The image of the prince as spoilsport is finally confirmed in II, iv of Part II, when the mellow, gentle exchanges of Falstaff and Doll, reinforced by soft music and warm light, are not only interrupted but wantonly vilified by Hal and Poins. Pale and sour as ever, Alan Howard in this scene is also vicious and lecherous, resisting a lust for Doll

[1] *Ibid.*, p. 82.

only because of his greater delight in destroying Falstaff's finest moment. The scene was paced and patterned with such theatrical sureness as to be utterly convincing. Director and actor, having presumably sought to discover the character, have here taken a critical attitude towards him. But is the character so single, and should the audience be so browbeaten into accepting that it is? Shakespeare is at pains to give Hal at least the ambiguity he exposes in sonnets XCV and XCVI:

> Some say thy fault is youth, some wantonness;
> Some say thy grace is youth and gentle sport;
> Both grace and faults are lov'd of more and less:
> Thou makest faults graces that to thee resort.

By making Hal graceless in his faults, Hands and Howard have removed an essential ambiguity, and *Henry IV Part I*, of course, feels the loss most strongly. Its proffered theatrical contrasts were, for the most part, rejected. Henry IV in Emrys James's nervously mannered performance was quite as quirky as Falstaff, and the staging deliberately merged Eastcheap with the Court. Henry remained in the on-stage shadows at the end of I, i, watching Hal and Falstaff, and Hal, in his turn, observed his father's initial encounter with the formidable Percy family in I, iii. The on-stage observer of a comic scene has a different relationship with the audience from that of the observer of a political argument. Whereas the first will generally increase our enjoyment, the second will tend to unsettle us. The point at which eavesdropping becomes spying (absurdly straddled, you might say, by Polonius behind the arras) is the point at which comedy ceases. The many occasions for on-stage observation of other characters had fired Terry Hands's imagination. There was a fine moment in Part II when Hal, framed by the guillotine-like structure of his dying father's bed, looked down from behind the crown at the King he believed to be dead. It echoed the scenes in which, with

sinister relish, he had observed Falstaff from behind and above. It was, as I say, a fine moment, but what did it mean? That Hal contemplated both Henry IV and Falstaff alike, that he could and did reject both? Certainly it was never our *enjoyment* of the Falstaff scenes that Hal augmented by watching them.

Brewster Mason's Falstaff was more appropriate to *Part II*. (What, for instance, are we to make of a *Part I* Falstaff who actually challenges the formidable Douglas at Shrewsbury?) Shallow's was the social milieu to which he properly belonged, a bucolic world where conversation meandered among nostalgic reminiscences. But why would such a man mix with a ragged Pistol and a Bardolph sensationally suffering from advanced syphilis and drooping boots? By restoring Falstaff to his knighthood, the production isolated his associates. A small blemish in a worthy interpretation. More upsetting, in that it seemed gratuitous, was the newly crowned Henry V's appearance in solid gold from top to toe. The golden mask was removable, and Alan Howard's pale face peered out to pronounce Falstaff's doom. He looked faintly ludicrous, as divers do, or spacemen. It was a vulgar splash on the otherwise well-conceived picture of a fat knight's downfall.

The opening chorus of *Henry IV Part II* was divided between about twenty dimly-lit, black-coated actors, flitting around the stage like the rush of rumours. *Henry V* began with actors in casual modern dress, warming up or sitting in groups until brought to attention by Emrys James's speaking of the opening chorus. The casting was not random. The actor of Henry IV re-appeared, in modern dress, to usher in the prosperity of which, as King, he had dreamed. You can push an idea too far, of course. I do not know why the Chorus attended so much of the action, why he corrected Fluellen's pronunciation of 'ambiguity', or why he spoke the Duke of Burgundy's long speech in V, ii. Were we to see him as the mediating ghost of Henry IV? Or was it an evidence of the Chorus's concern to clarify the action, further exemplified by the division and re-distribution of the long introduction to Act IV?

The playing of Act I in modern dress was an acceptable application of the 'unworthy scaffold', though I have two quibbles. The interpolated lines were not sufficient to advise an unknowing audience that the two first actors were the Archbishop of Canterbury and the Bishop of Ely, and it was over-particularising to have Alan Howard make his first appearance in unnecessary dark glasses. If Henry is a *poseur* or a cultivator of enigma, let the lines show it. It was a fair point, though, to bring Mountjoy on in costume, colourful among the plain English. The production remained faithful to its concept of a calculating King, without extravagance and with no more *panache* than is needed to win a war. The scenes in France exhibited Farrah's design at its best. The stage rose steeply to form the Harfleur wall, and sank to reveal Katharine, shyly behind it. Before Agincourt the vast canopy descended to form a grey floor-cloth, wan as a defeated army. It was a major achievement of the production to present an image of war which was an antidote to glamour. The killing of the boys, represented on stage by the toppling of a wagon and the slaughter of Falstaff's page, was all the action we saw. No subject for a patriotic sonnet. Henry, who had been angry enough in England to assault the traitor Scroop, was angry now for the second time. Even Pistol responded by slitting le Fer's throat, at the cost to himself of two hundred crowns! It was all thought out with admirable care, and yet I felt no such sense of deprivation when the play ended as I had felt after The Other Place's *Hamlet*. It is profoundly to be hoped that the Royal Shakespeare Company will continue to support an offshoot that challenges its customary style.

© PETER THOMSON 1976

THE YEAR'S CONTRIBUTIONS TO SHAKESPEARIAN STUDY

1. CRITICAL STUDIES

reviewed by D. J. PALMER

Prominent among several new studies of the artistic conventions and historical contexts in which Shakespeare worked is L. Salingar's[1] comprehensive and masterly account of the traditions of comedy. Salingar's main interest is in the plot conventions from which comedy derives its dual nature 'as performance and as representation', and he traces in detail four lines of genealogical descent that are combined in Shakespeare. The first of these involves a 'reasoned speculation' that there existed from the Middle Ages a continuous tradition of popular romance drama, secular and religious, which was Shakespeare's 'point of departure'. A full and perhaps disproportionately long discussion of the evolution of classical comedy focuses on the development of the intrigue-plot, with its 'invitation to the audience to enjoy an exhibition of some form of deceit that distinguishes comedy from romance in the theatre'. Salingar points out that in learning 'the pleasure of contrivance' and 'juggling with the complicity of the audience' Shakespeare applied the principles of classical comedy to the Elizabethan popular stage more thoroughly than any of his predecessors. The festive element, much discussed in recent criticism of the comedies, is related here to the example of Italian Renaissance comedy in its association of deception, trickery and surprise with carnival masking, 'an explosion of high spirits licensed and ratified by custom'. The final chapter considers Shakespeare's use of *novelle* plots in *The Merchant of Venice*, *Much Ado*, *Measure for Measure* and *All's Well*, suggesting that Shakespeare repeatedly turned to the 'rationality' of the *novella* for a particular kind of plot, tragic or comic, concerning 'broken nuptials and a crisis involving the law'.

This is a major contribution to the understanding of Shakespeare's comic technique, particularly in its perceptive treatment of the paradoxical relationship between theatrical artifice and the representation of life. Far from reflecting a merely imitative or derivative Shakespeare, this exploration of his antecedents affirms his originality and inventiveness. 'Shakespeare's great innovation', writes Salingar, 'was to treat comedy lyrically as an emotional and imaginative experience, an inward metamorphosis.' It is good to know that a sequel to this book is planned, which will deal more directly and continuously with the plays.

Focusing on Shakespeare's use of ideas, W. G. Zeeveld[2] finds him making dramatic capital out of some of the current issues of his day. As Zeeveld observes, the conception of Shakespeare's intellectual background as a static 'Elizabethan world picture' misrepresents the flux and tension within sixteenth-century thought. The disputed and the problematical are better suited to the dynamics of drama,

[1] *Shakespeare and the Traditions of Comedy* (Cambridge University Press, 1974).
[2] *The Temper of Shakespeare's Thought* (Yale University Press, 1974).

157

particularly if, as is argued here, the question at issue is not a philosophical abstraction but arises directly from the shifting concerns of the time. Zeeveld discusses four topics: the treatment of Ceremony in the later history plays, in relation to the vestiarian controversy within the Church, and more specifically comparing Shakespeare's 'deep-seated sense for tradition' with that of Richard Hooker; changing attitudes to the idea of Commonwealth reflected in *Julius Caesar* and *Coriolanus*, the latter play being linked with the Parliamentary challenge to the royal prerogative in 1606; the concern with Equity in *The Merchant of Venice* and *Measure for Measure* as a reflection of 'the adjustment of the common law to the practice of equity in the Court of Chancery'; and finally the reassessment in the last plays of the traditional antithesis between Civility and Barbarity in the light of contemporary reactions to the New World. 'The basic texture of Shakespeare's thought' which we are invited to recognise in this historically precise and forcefully argued book is that of a mind aware of new challenges to old verities and values. But, preferable as this is to the image of a Shakespeare secure in immutable commonplaces, the very precision of the contemporary contexts in which Zeeveld locates the play is sometimes critically confining, if not distorting. The historical evidence alone, for instance, does not compel us to regard the judgment passed on Shylock as 'equitable' or the Christianity of Isabella as 'irreproachable'.

Topical significance is also pursued by F. A. Yates,[1] who brings her interests in royal iconography and the hermetic tradition to bear on the last plays with the characteristic boldness that turns speculation into triumphant conviction. She sees in the masque-like qualities of the last plays and their concern with regeneration and reconciliation a reflection of the contemporary glorification of Prince Henry and Princess Elizabeth as future champions of the Protestant cause in Europe. 'The atmosphere of Elizabethan revival around the younger royal generation' is related, for instance, to the 'Tudor-British' themes of *Cymbeline*: the legendary British king and his two sons and daughter correspond to James and his children; the Welsh cave from which the lost princes prove their chivalrous prowess recalls the cave from which Prince Henry awakened the sleeping figure of Chivalry in a masque performed in January 1610; and the 'prophetic' ghosts of Posthumus's vision are Trojans foretelling 'the return of the British line to rule'. This is somewhat cavalier in its treatment of the plot; after all, the ghosts are neither Trojan nor prophetic, nor is it Posthumus who is promised a crown, while a parallel between James and the gullible old king who banishes his daughter's husband and needs Cloten to stiffen his patriotic nerve would seem positively treasonable. Moreover, to make everything fit, we have to suppose not only a much later date for the play than many would accept but also a 1611 version revised in 1612 before Henry's death. And if, as is suggested, Prospero represents Shakespeare's vindication of John Dee, why does the magus abjure his 'rough magic'?

An alternative King James version of *The Tempest* is proposed by G. Wickham,[2] according to whom Prospero as presenter of the masque is the King himself, Juno is the Queen, and Iris and Ceres 'figure the peace and prosperity that for the British people is the product of the Union of the Scottish and English crowns'. Shakespeare is said to be using the 'court hieroglyphics' of the masque form to comment 'in the manner fashionable at the time on the most topical and controversial issue of foreign and domestic policy', namely the anticipated nuptials of Princess Elizabeth.

[1] *Shakespeare's Last Plays: A New Approach* (Routledge & Kegan Paul, 1975).
[2] 'Masque and Anti-Masque in *The Tempest*', *Essays & Studies*, XXVIII (1975), 1–14.

Unfortunately, since it had not been decided whom she was to marry when the play was written, the identity of Ferdinand is obscure.

Referring to a broader spectrum of Renaissance iconography, J. Doebler[1] demonstrates how an understanding of traditional symbolism can often illuminate the stage-imagery and therefore the meaning of the plays. The 'Mousetrap' in *Hamlet*, the mirror in *Richard II* and the harpies' banquet in *The Tempest* are among the examples that yield richer meanings to Doebler's approach, which treads warily and sometimes uneasily around the pitfalls of allegorical interpretation. One is less convinced by his elevation of Orlando to the company of David and Hercules as an 'athlete of virtue', or by the rather tenuous grounds on which Shylock's conversion to Christianity is seen as a genuine change of heart. Doebler's historical scholarship is not always matched by critical tact, and he has not fully solved the problem of how to reconcile his adoption of the Neo-platonic concept of the visual image 'as offering instant and intuitive recognition of transcendent reality' with the different degrees of erudition and cultural adjustment needed even for an Elizabethan audience to spot an iconic allusion. Nevertheless, the book offers particular insights that could be made to work effectively in the theatre, and represents a line of enquiry still rich in possibilities.

The particular aspect of Shakespeare's relationship to tradition discussed by J. Dusinberre[2] is currently one of more than academic interest, though unlike her Victorian and Shavian predecessors (not to mention some of her contemporaries) she treats the woman-question in Shakespeare within a historical context. Indeed the title of the book is slightly misleading, since the focus of interest falls broadly upon what are seen as the feminist sympathies of the popular drama as a whole between 1590 and 1625. Her main argument is that playwrights of the public stages had much

in common with Puritan attitudes towards marriage and woman's spiritual equality, attitudes themselves deriving from the anti-courtly and anti-monastic spirit of such earlier humanists as More, Erasmus, Vives and Cornelius Agrippa. The author's researches also unearth some striking examples of sexual chauvinism and feminist polemics during the period, but as far as dramatic criticism is concerned her most suggestive chapter is probably that dealing with the boy actor and the use of disguise, stage conventions which in Shakespeare's plays serve to question the stereotypes of sexual identity, as 'disguise draws men and women together in the comedies through their discovery of the artifice of difference which social custom sustains'.

Another conventional device is the figure of the commentator, whose manipulation of audience response is studied by P. Bilton.[3] He finds that commentary is usually employed to control and direct emotional sympathies rather than to state the meaning of the play directly, a conclusion unlikely to provoke much dissension, although too many plays are treated in summary and mechanical fashion as the book pursues its unremitting course through the entire canon.

Among studies of Shakespeare's early work, R. Y. Turner[4] undertakes an elaborate and complex examination of the playwright's development from a 'didactic' to a 'mimetic' dramatic mode. This may seem merely another version of the old and questionable view that Shakespeare moved from artificial towards naturalistic drama, but Turner's approach is not so simple or rudimentary. From the rhetorical

[1] *Shakespeare's Speaking Pictures: Studies in Iconic Imagery* (University of New Mexico Press, 1974).

[2] *Shakespeare and the Nature of Women* (Macmillan, 1975).

[3] *Commentary and Control in Shakespeare's Plays* (Universitetsforlaget and Humanities Press, 1974).

[4] *Shakespeare's Apprenticeship* (University of Chicago Press, 1974).

schemes and episodic plot-structure of *1 Henry VI*, in which, it is argued, character and action are designed to exemplify a central moral thesis, a progression is traced to the emergence in other plays of characters capable of expressing inner feeling and ambiguous self-awareness through imagistic and ironic techniques, as the dramatic interest shifts from the exemplary episode to the narrative continuity of cause and effect. Turner is a perceptive analyst of the different rhetorical and dramaturgical techniques employed in the early plays, but his charting of Shakespeare's artistic evolution, which also involves some rather strained parallels between the first comedies and the tragic histories, is too intricate and systematic for the brief and uncertain chronology on which it rests.

A different view of Shakespeare's use of rhetoric and stage-convention in *1 Henry VI* is taken by J. W. Blanpied,[1] who points to elements of self-parody in the play that provide 'an ironic perspective upon the language and the characters who mouth it'. Also writing on the *Henry VI* plays, G. Williams[2] pays tribute to Shakespeare's skill in adapting and expanding his source materials to develop the liaison between Suffolk and Margaret as his 'first essay in tragic, destructive love'.

Approaching *Richard III* as a tragedy of character, W. B. Toole[3] traces a process of 'psychological attrition' in Richard, which leads from a division between private and public self to the 'psychic warfare' of self against self in his soliloquy on the eve of Bosworth. E. Jones[4] draws our attention in another direction by associating the procession of spirits on Bosworth eve both with the pagan antecedents of the feast of All Souls and with Constantine's vision of the Cross as a promise of victory in battle, parallels that combine to mark the end of Richard's ungodly reign and the divinely-sanctioned advent of the Tudors.

P. A. Jorgensen[5] also contends that victory and defeat in *Richard III* are 'fully God-controlled', whereas the emphasis in the later sequence of histories is much more upon human responsibility for events. He relates this change of emphasis, not as might be expected to Shakespeare's maturing artistry, but to a supposedly wholesale shift in the English outlook between a providential view of the destruction of the Armada in 1588 and an empirical understanding of Tyrone's rebellion in 1595. According to Z. Stríbrny,[6] on the other hand, the secularism and political realism of the second tetralogy is reflected in a dynamic sense of time as historical process which supersedes the static time of the traditional feudal order.

In a lively and well reasoned essay on *Richard II*, L. Potter[7] defends Richard against detractors who find his use of language and self-dramatisation symptomatic of his weakness. She points to the 'sharp-tongued, self-mocking' note of irony that is often present in Richard's speech, transforming weakness into dramatic authority, and she observes with good critical sense that the ineffectual Richard depicted by some commentators on the play is a character

[1] '"Art and Baleful Sorcery": The Counter-consciousness of *Henry VI, Part I*', *Studies in English Literature*, XV (1975), 213–27.

[2] 'Suffolk and Margaret: A Study of Some Sections of Shakespeare's *Henry VI*', *Shakespeare Quarterly*, XXV (1974), 310–22.

[3] 'The Motif of Psychic Division in *Richard III*', *Shakespeare Survey 27* (Cambridge University Press, 1974), 21–32.

[4] 'Bosworth Eve', *Essays in Criticism*, XXV (1975), 38–54.

[5] 'A Formative Shakespearean Legacy: Elizabethan Views of God, Fortune, and War', *Publications of the Modern Language Association of America*, XC (1975), 222–33.

[6] 'The Idea and Image of Time in Shakespeare's Second Historical Tetralogy', *Shakespeare Jahrbuch* (Deutschen Shakespeare-Gesellschaft), Band III (1975), 51–66.

[7] 'The Antic Disposition of Richard II', *Shakespeare Survey 27* (Cambridge University Press, 1974), 33–41.

deprived of any dramatic interest: 'To say that Richard is an actor giving a performance is irrelevant: all good dramatic parts allow actors to behave like actors. But to ask an actor to play the part of an actor giving an unconvincing performance is theatrical suicide.' The enigmatic quality that Potter notes in the play's opening scene is also discussed by L. S. Champion,[1] with reference to Mowbray's function in motivating the conflict between Richard and Bolingbroke.

Two essays by R. Battenhouse illustrate his remarkable aptitude for turning the accepted meaning of a play inside out by invoking spurious 'analogues'. In the first of these,[2] we are invited to regard Falstaff as 'a holy fool', whose 'inner intent is a charitable almsgiving of brotherly self-humiliation and fatherly truth-telling'. The fat knight would be the first to endorse such a view, and he would doubtless also approve the outrageous gloss on his own remark that he was 'born about three of the clock in the afternoon' as an allusion to his religious conversion, which 'reflects, probably, Mark xv, 39, where at that hour a Roman centurion, on witnessing the death of Jesus, cried out: "Truly this man was the Son of God."' The other essay,[3] in similar vein, traces in *Henry V* 'a rather widespread network of analogy' with *Tamburlaine*, in which the rejection of Falstaff corresponds to the killing of Calyphas, and Henry is pilloried as a crook and hypocrite, castigated for his 'blindly Pharisaic suppression of self-examination', and dismissed as 'basically more frivolous than Tamburlaine'. Moreover, we are given to understand that all this is Shakespeare's intended meaning.

Turning, bemusedly, to the comedies, this is perhaps the place to mention the reappearance of some previously uncollected essays by H. Granville-Barker,[4] since they include two pieces on *A Midsummer Night's Dream* and one on *Twelfth Night*, in addition to the well-known British Academy lecture, 'From *Henry V* to

Hamlet'. This gathering of fugitives, however, contains little of substance or fresh interest. There is the familiar emphasis on delivering the verse of the comedies swiftly and lightly, but Granville-Barker is not at his best in judging the last scene of *Twelfth Night* to be 'scandalously ill-arranged and ill-written', nor in his inability to enjoy Bottom's scenes with Titania and as Pyramus.

The *Prefaces*, of course, have exerted their belated and somewhat remote influence on recent critical approaches to the play-text as a script for performance, and J. Hasler's[5] study of 'theatrical notation' is a useful contribution to this growing interest in the means by which the text organises and controls physical as well as verbal expression on the stage. Within this general framework, Hasler makes a sensitive analysis of a number of different aspects of Shakespeare's technique in the comedies, including eavesdropping scenes, comic endings and visual and verbal scenery. The topics covered, however, are miscellaneous aspects that fail to add up to a unified whole, and one is left wondering why Hasler has confined to the comedies a method of approach that is equally applicable to the whole canon.

Several recent articles on the early comedies are of the critical persuasion that a play is 'about' some single topic or idea. P. Lindenbaum,[6] for instance, believes that 'the central

[1] 'The Function of Mowbray: Shakespeare's Maturing Artistry in *Richard II*', *Shakespeare Quarterly*, XXVI (1975), 3–7.

[2] 'Falstaff as Parodist and Perhaps Holy Fool', *Publications of the Modern Language Association of America*, XC (1975), 32–52.

[3] 'The Relation of Henry V to Tamburlaine', *Shakespeare Survey 27* (Cambridge University Press, 1974), 71–79.

[4] *More Prefaces to Shakespeare* (Princeton University Press, 1974).

[5] *Shakespeare's Theatrical Notation: The Comedies* (The Cooper Monographs, Francke Verlag Bern, 1974).

[6] 'Education in *The Two Gentlemen of Verona*', *Studies in English Literature*, XV (1975), 229–44.

organising principle' of *The Two Gentlemen of Verona* is 'not any intent to exalt the ideals of friendship or romantic love' but 'education in one's own nature'. *Love's Labour's Lost* is seen by N. L. Goldstien[1] as a satire on Petrarchan love-conventions, while M. Evans[2] argues that 'the English language is the hero' of the play, which turns out to be Shakespeare's declaration in favour of living speech and against written rhetoric, since 'both written words in books and rhetorical penned speech entail a psychic withdrawal from the realities which are figured in the very substance and decorum of speech'. L. Guilhamet[3] applies his understanding of Aristotle's conception of 'action' as 'psychical energy working outwards' to *A Midsummer Night's Dream*, and finds that the true 'action' of the play is 'to find the concord of discord': Aristotle, it seems, is the father of thematic criticism. A somewhat rambling essay by R. Henze[4] on *The Merchant of Venice* puts it all down to 'the moral, subtle though it is, that prejudice and mistaken trust in fortune afflict Jew and Christian alike'.

Among other discussions of the comedies, J. A. Roberts[5] writes again on *The Merry Wives of Windsor*, this time to analyse the balance of sympathies in the play's final scene with its juxtaposition of natural and civilised values. R. F. Fleissner[6] reviews previous arguments for identifying *Much Ado About Nothing* with 'Love's Labour's Won', and adds some improbable possibilities of his own about a punning link between the two titles. Arguing for the importance of sequential action in *As You Like It*, R. Wilson[7] makes heavy going out of the change in attitudes to time between the court and the forest, involving 'a shift from a public to a private standard of measurement in which the latter becomes possible only through the fading into unimportance of the former'. The reciprocal values of giving and receiving in *Twelfth Night* are explored by R. Henze,[8] who finds that Viola and Feste jointly embody the play's norms, since 'they are both careful not to intrude on someone else's free disposition'.

Three essays tackle the problems of *Troilus and Cressida*. J. Bayley,[9] in a penetrating and finely wrought piece of criticism, considers that 'the play's unique status' can be seen in terms of its characterisation. Unlike Shakespeare's other plays, Bayley argues, in which our sense of character normally involves an interaction between the cumulative impression of continuity and the 'quick, often contradictory, response to the dramatic moment', the characters of *Troilus and Cressida* lack the dimension of past and future: 'everything takes place in, and ends in, the present'. This devotion of the characters to 'the divine integrity of the extant moment' is seen to be related to the incoherence of the world they inhabit, as 'behind the glitter and coruscation of the language and the rapid charade of the language [action?] there is nothing that adds up'. And by implication at least, Bayley questions the nature of much modern critical attraction to the play: 'The play is "intellectual" in a potentially damaging sense, dealing so much in arresting and

[1] '*Love's Labour's Lost* and the Renaissance Vision of Love', *Shakespeare Quarterly*, XXV (1974), 335–50.

[2] 'Mercury Versus Apollo: A Reading of *Love's Labour's Lost*', *Shakespeare Quarterly*, XXVI (1975), 113–27.

[3] '*A Midsummer Night's Dream* as the Imitation of an Action', *Studies in English Literature*, XV (1975), 257–71.

[4] '"Which is the Merchant Here? And Which the Jew?"', *Criticism*, XVI (1974), 287–300.

[5] 'Falstaff in Windsor Forest: Villain or Victim?', *Shakespeare Quarterly*, XXVI (1975), 8–15.

[6] '"Love's Labour's Won" and the Occasion of *Much Ado*', *Shakespeare Survey 27* (Cambridge University Press, 1974), 105–10.

[7] 'The Way to Arden: Attitudes Toward Time in *As You Like It*', *Shakespeare Quarterly*, XXVI (1975), 16–24.

[8] '*Twelfth Night:* Free Disposition on the Sea of Love', *Sewanee Review*, LXXXIII (1975), 267–83.

[9] 'Time and the Trojans', *Essays in Criticism*, XXV (1975), 55–73.

stimulating moments that we shall find no deeply imagined and presented differentiation of values inside the world it offers.' The other two essays are both by R. D. Fly,[1,2] who also discusses the play's formal discontinuity and 'radical instability', but finds that it does add up to a vision of apocalyptic catastrophe, a vision which is also expressed in the language of prophecy continually heard throughout the play.

Bayley's reservations about the 'intellectual' substitute for 'deeply imagined' life in *Troilus and Cressida* might perhaps be applied to two recent discussions of *Measure for Measure*, although in this case the distinction is prompted by the critics rather than by the play. L. W. Hyman,[3] for instance, considers that *Measure for Measure* can only be understood 'if we depart from psychological realism and look for a philosophical or a thematic development, an ethical equation'. But the equations set up between virtue and death on the one hand, and vice and life on the other, provide too blunt an instrument to cope with the finer shades of charity (virtue or vice?) exercised in the play's resolution by Mariana, Isabella and the Duke. H. Fisch[4] also imposes a schematic ideology on the play by regarding Angelo as a Puritan in a way that stereotypes both the dramatic character and his supposed historical counterpart, while it leaves out of account aspects of Angelo, such as his lack of self-knowledge, that are more obvious sources of dramatic interest.

L. Danson's[5] book on the tragedies pursues a fashionable critical trend in its concern with language, not only as the medium of the plays, but as their subject as well. The tragic heroes, according to this approach, are as deeply involved in the 'search for adequate expressive modes' as they are in seeking a resolving action, since the tragic world is one in which language, gesture and ritual are equivocal. In this light, Danson diagnoses the particular condition of each of the tragedies discussed:

'the inability to achieve adequate expression for overwhelming emotional needs' in *Titus Andronicus*, the use of parody in *Troilus and Cressida*, the 'different semantics' of Iago and Othello, and the significance of metonymy in *Coriolanus* as a linguistic reflection of the relationship between the part and the whole in the state. It is less clear in what sense Hamlet 'achieves his necessary language' in death while Othello apparently remains elusive, and it is difficult to see why the chapter on *King Lear* should treat the play itself rather than its hero as travailing towards self-expression. Such oscillations between drama and metadrama are confusing, if not confused.

The dramatic use of language in *Titus Andronicus* is also studied by A. H. Tricomi,[6] who examines the witty and ironic distance between 'the euphemisms of metaphor' and the gruesome actuality of events. G. K. Hunter[7] compares the play with *Romeo and Juliet*, noting that while both plays involve conflict between two families within a single city, and while both also use the image of a tomb to reflect 'the tragic importance of family and social continuities', the contrast between these two early plays in terms of ritualism and domesticity is one that foreshadows the range

---

[1] '"Suited in Like Conditions as our Argument": Imitative Form in Shakespeare's *Troilus and Cressida*', *Studies in English Literature*, xv (1975), 273–92.

[2] 'Cassandra and the Language of Prophecy in *Troilus and Cressida*', *Shakespeare Quarterly*, xxvi (1975), 157–71.

[3] 'The Unity of *Measure for Measure*', *Modern Language Quarterly*, xxxvi (1975), 3–20.

[4] 'Shakespeare and the Puritan Dynamic', *Shakespeare Survey 27* (Cambridge University Press, 1974), 81–92.

[5] *Tragic Alphabet: Shakespeare's Drama of Language* (Yale University Press, 1974).

[6] 'The Aesthetics of Mutilation in *Titus Andronicus*', *Shakespeare Survey 27* (Cambridge University Press, 1974), 11–19.

[7] 'Shakespeare's Earliest Tragedies: *Titus Andronicus* and *Romeo and Juliet*', *Shakespeare Survey 27* (Cambridge University Press, 1974), 1–9.

of the later tragedies. J. Black[1] explores some of the effects of 'incremental repetition' in the stage-images of *Romeo and Juliet*, and F. Fergusson[2] compares Shakespeare's treatment of romantic love in the play with Dante's presentation of Paolo and Francesca. A resounding challenge to the conventional view of *Romeo and Juliet* is issued by J. Seward:[3] confident that his response to the play is authentically Elizabethan, he informs us that the love relationship is really selfish lust, that Romeo is morally no better than Tarquin though treated more sympathetically, that Juliet is 'disturbing' in 'the rawness of her sexual hunger' and that the lovers' suicide ensures their eternal damnation, regrettably.

The sceptical vein in *Hamlet* is discussed in two complementary articles. J. McLauchlan[4] sees in the play's treatment of reason a conflict between Renaissance idealism and the attitudes associated with Machiavelli and Montaigne, a somewhat loosely defined alignment of good and evil forces. F. McCombie[5] detects a more precise and pervasive indebtedness to the anti-stoical and ambivalent postures of Erasmian wise folly. D. K. C. Todd's[6] random lucubrations on the play, his personal outlook, and the state of English studies ('The tragedy, the private life, public life, the tragedy: all partially connected, without precision') use *Hamlet* to perpetrate an act of anti-criticism, abetted, rather surprisingly, by a university press.

The concept of honour in *Othello*, much discussed of late, is re-examined by J. Klene,[7] who argues that its dependence on opinion and reputation allows Iago room for manipulation, producing disasters that are 'the consequences of an unquestioning adherence to a highly questionable code'. E. K. Weedin, Jr[8] takes up another familiar topic in focusing upon the usurpation of reason by the will, first manifested in Iago, and finally evident in Othello's error. In contrast with these relatively abstract interpretations, W. Staebler[9] adopts the approach of

psychological realism in his study of Iago's abnormal sexuality, not flinching from extra-textual speculation about the ensign's early married life: 'Like other men in the army he has promiscuous encounters with easy women, not only when away on campaigns but also when stationed at home in Venice.'

King Lear is the subject of a sensible if rather sedate commentary by R. C. Sharma,[10] who sees the play as moving from a division between personal and social values towards their ultimate reconciliation in an 'inner poise and freedom of spirit'. A. R. Young,[11] on the other hand, stresses the shock of the play's conclusion by reviewing the folk-tale traditions underlying the play, and finding that, while Shakespeare retains the conventional pattern of a father who first mistakenly rejects and later understands his daughter, the tragic ending is a deliberate departure from tradition in order to produce a sense of injustice. S. J. Brown[12] focuses upon the 'mythic dimension' of the

[1] 'The Visual Artistry of *Romeo and Juliet*', *Studies in English Literature*, xv (1975), 245–56.

[2] 'Romantic Love in Dante and Shakespeare', *Sewanee Review*, LXXXIII (1975), 253–66.

[3] *Tragic Vision in 'Romeo and Juliet'* (Consortium Press, 1973).

[4] 'The Prince of Denmark and Claudius's Court', *Shakespeare Survey 27* (Cambridge University Press, 1974), 43–57.

[5] '*Hamlet* and the *Moriae Encomium*', *Shakespeare Survey 27* (Cambridge University Press, 1974), 58–69.

[6] '*I Am Not Prince Hamlet*'; *Shakespeare: Criticism: Schools of English* (University of London Press, 1974).

[7] 'Othello: "A Fixed Figure for the Time of Scorn"', *Shakespeare Quarterly*, XXVI (1975), 139–50.

[8] 'Love's Reason in *Othello*', *Studies in English Literature*, xv (1975), 293–308.

[9] 'The Sexual Nihilism of Iago', *Sewanee Review*, LXXXIII (1975), 284–304.

[10] *An Approach to 'King Lear'* (Macmillan Company of India, 1975).

[11] 'The Written and Oral Sources of *King Lear* and the Problem of Justice in the Play', *Studies in English Literature*, xv (1975), 309–19.

[12] 'Shakespeare's King and Beggar', *The Yale Review*, LXIV (1975), 370–95.

confrontation between Lear and Edgar in beggar's guise, in which he locates the play's 'focal point' and argues that while 'Lear's royal identity is cruelly tested', 'it is never yielded, only purified and transformed'. Christianising the play, R. Matthews[1] maintains that Edmund undergoes a last-minute repentance after his 'recognition of love', his 'black and miserable soul' being redeemed and atoned for by the deaths of Lear and Cordelia through some strange tergiversation of theology.

The Porter's scene in *Macbeth* receives fresh attention from F. B. Tromly,[2] in an essay suggesting that 'the ultimate function of the scene is to humanize the murderer by forcing us to recognize him in the "ordinary" Porter'. J. Whatley[3] contrasts the sensuality of Shakespeare's conception of Egypt in *Antony and Cleopatra* with the barrenness, 'echoing and void', of Judea in Racine's *Bérénice*, though both dramatists represent the Orient as 'female to Rome's male'. In an account of the stage-history of *Coriolanus*, R. Berry[4] discusses the changing interpretations of the play's political conflict as 'a touchstone to the life of the times'.

The collection of fourteen essays on the late plays, edited by R. C. Tobias and P. G. Zolbrod,[5] contains six items on *The Tempest* but none on *The Winter's Tale*. Most distinguished among the contributions are L. C. Knights'[6] approach to *The Tempest* as a play that is, for all its fairy-tale qualities, firmly rooted in a sense of everyday reality and 'the common conditions and common duties of life', and K. Muir's[7] discussion of the theophanies, which also emphasises the plays' dependence on human character and conduct rather than supernatural agency.

Among other studies of the last plays, A. C. Flower[8] explores the way in which the central characters of *Pericles* adopt different roles in changing circumstances, showing how 'conscious illusion, artfully handled, can most satisfyingly interpret reality'. A fanciful essay by L. Rockas[9] on duplicating roles in *The Winter's Tale* not only finds that 'there is one king with two faces and one queen with two faces', but also resurrects Mamillius as Florizel, Antigonus as Autolycus, and, more obscurely, the Bear as the figure of Time. 'The nature, variety, and thematic importance of language' in *The Winter's Tale* is analysed by C. T. Neely[10] in terms of the disjunction and union of speech, thought and vision throughout the play. Language is also the concern of L. T. Fitz's[11] article on *The Tempest*, which points to the contrast between the bare, sparse style used to describe the island and the more richly textured language associated with Prospero's magic: 'if the imagery of the island shows nature hostile to man, the imagery of magic shows Prospero in control of nature'. In an admirably reasoned essay on *Henry VIII*, L. Bliss[12] rebuts recent attempts to relate the conversions and reconciliations in the play to those of the late romances, and examines the 'confusing perspectives on character and action' which

[1] 'Edmund's Redemption in *King Lear*', *Shakespeare Quarterly*, XXVI (1975), 25–29.

[2] 'Macbeth and his Porter', *Shakespeare Quarterly*, XXVI (1975), 151–56.

[3] '"L'Orient désert": *Bérénice* and *Antony and Cleopatra*', *University of Toronto Quarterly*, XLIV (1975), 96–114.

[4] 'The Metamorphoses of *Coriolanus*', *Shakespeare Quarterly*, XXVI (1975), 172–83.

[5] *Shakespeare's Late Plays: Essays in Honor of Charles Crow* (Ohio University Press, 1974).

[6] '*The Tempest*', *Shakespeare's Late Plays*, ed. Tobias and Zolbrod, pp. 15–31.

[7] 'Theophanies in the Last Plays', *Shakespeare's Late Plays*, ed. Tobias and Zolbrod, pp. 32–43.

[8] 'Disguise and Identity in *Pericles, Prince of Tyre*', *Shakespeare Quarterly*, XXVI (1975), 30–41.

[9] '"Browzing of Ivy": *The Winter's Tale*', *Ariel*, VI (1975), 3–16.

[10] '*The Winter's Tale*: The Triumph of Speech', *Studies in English Literature*, XV (1975), 321–38.

[11] 'The Vocabulary of the Environment in *The Tempest*', *Shakespeare Quarterly*, XXVI (1975), 42–7.

[12] 'The Wheel of Fortune and the Maiden Phoenix in Shakespeare's *King Henry the Eighth*', *ELH*, XLII (1975), 1–25.

lend an ironic significance to the play's sub-title. According to this very cogent view of the play, it does not end with an achieved renewal of society but with a vision: Cranmer's prophecy 'is hortatory and must explode the play's framework to create a world where humanity's endless, profitless cycle of rise and fall can be translated into the more miraculous image of the death and rebirth of "the maiden phoenix"'.

There are several additions to the series of Salzburg Studies in English Literature, which despite its title seems to consist almost entirely of American graduate dissertations. R. T. Simone[1] gives an account of *Lucrece* from every angle, including its structure, its sources, its place in Shakespeare's career, its relationship to his later work and its critical reputation. L. Wilds[2] finds in the early tragedies that a character's self-awareness or ability to manipu-late others is analogous to the art of the actor or dramatist, and therefore regards Titus An-dronicus, Richard III, Richard II, Caesar and Brutus and Hamlet as examples of a single 'character-type'; no doubt if the disguised heroines of the comedies had been thrown in as well, all Shakespeare's central figures could be shown to belong to the same 'type'. W. Babula's[3] concern with what he calls 'the tragi-comic archetype' takes him, with inevitable superficiality, from the mystery plays and the moralities to *All's Well*, *Measure for Measure* and *Pericles* in an effort to show that all these plays reconcile experience of life with a provi-dential scheme. G. J. Matteo[4] ploughs through the stage-history and critical reputation of *Othello* to show how 'the interpretation of the play, both theatrical and literary, is influenced by conditions and biases outside the play itself'. T. R. Waldo[5] illustrates Shakespeare's versatile use of musical terms, in a monotonous and pedestrian commentary.

The policy and *raison d'être* of this series ought to be questioned. Its general quality

hardly merits a wide readership, even among professional scholars, and it cannot be said of the series that no university library should be without it, particularly in these days of shrink-ing budgets. The apparent arbitrariness with which the volumes mentioned above are divided between three different sub-series, 'Poetic Drama', 'Elizabethan & Renaissance Studies' and 'Jacobean Drama Studies', all under the editorship of J. Hogg, is a symptom of a more serious lack of discrimination in the enterprise as a whole. Even an outstanding graduate dissertation (which none of these can claim to be) does not necessarily make a worthwhile book.

Several works testify to the interest in Shakespeare that flourishes in Eastern Europe. The Roumanian translation of *Hamlet* by L. Leviţchi and D. Duţescu[6] is based on the New Cambridge edition but abbreviated by some thousand or more lines by C. Comorovski, who also provides a preface and commentary mainly concerned with the character of the hero. The influence of J. D. Wilson looms large, according to Ana-Maria Gligore of the University of Liverpool, who very kindly supplied me with notes on this version. The final volume of the Estonian translation by G. Meri[7] and others covers the last plays and poems, and so claims to be the first complete version of Shakespeare to appear in any of the

[1] *Shakespeare and 'Lucrece': A Study of the Poem and its Relation to the Plays* (Universität Salzburg, 1974).

[2] *Shakespeare's Character-Dramatists: A Study of a Character Type in Shakespearean Tragedy Through 'Hamlet'* (Universität Salzburg, 1975).

[3] *'Wishes fall out as they're willed': Shakespeare and the Tragicomic Archetype* (Universität Salzburg, 1975).

[4] *Shakespeare's Othello: The Study and the Stage, 1604–1904* (Universität Salzburg, 1974).

[5] *Musical Terms as Rhetoric: The Complexity of Shakespeare's Dramatic Style* (Universität Salzburg, 1974).

[6] *Hamlet* (Editura Albatros, 1974).

[7] *William Shakespeare: Kogutud Teosed VII* (Eesti Raamat, 1975).

languages of the national republics of the Soviet Union other than Russian. Meri has himself translated thirty-two of the plays, in addition to providing interpretative essays and commentaries on each of the plays and poems. The volume of essays from Georgia, edited by N. Kiasashvili,[1] represents papers delivered to the first All-Union Shakespeare Symposium held in Tbilisi in 1972. Among several discussions of style in Shakespeare is the first Soviet treatment of Shakespeare's use of traditional rhetoric; there are also contributions on Shakespeare's treatment of time, on recent Soviet productions, and on Georgian and Armenian translators.

Finally there are several items of interest that refuse to fit tidily elsewhere in this review. Most substantial of these are the second and third volumes of the documentary history of Shakespeare's critical reputation edited by B. Vickers.[2] These take us through some fairly arid territory, being largely devoted to the relative degrees of rigidity displayed by neo-classical commentators, but there are occasional glimpses of Shakespeare in the theatre and even momentary aberrations of fresh insight. The lusher pastures, however, still lie ahead, and it will be interesting to see whether Vickers represents continental criticism in his future volumes. Less monumental, but more diverting is T. M. Cranfill's[3] essay surveying Shakespeare's treatment of the disabilities of old age. R. Levin[4] and R. Weimann[5] both find certain aspects of modern criticism reprehensible. Levin protests against the tendency to regard Shakespeare's endings as inconclusive or ironic by refusing to accept 'a crucial action or event on which the resolution depends'; Levin argues that the conclusive ending is demanded by a structural 'rhythm', 'the basic dramatic fact which the refuters of the ending consistently

ignore'. Weimann, in a weighty essay on the study of Shakespearian metaphor, attacks the modern critical preoccupation with metaphorical meaning in the plays as a 'denial of the mimetic function of literature', and relates it to the tendency of modern imagist poetry to divorce tenor from vehicle. V. Chatterjee[6] makes an appraisal of Rabindranath Tagore's Shakespeare criticism and finds that while Tagore admired Shakespeare's 'powerful portrayal of infinite passion', he expressed what is perhaps a characteristically Indian preference of serenity to sound and fury. In the 1974 Jayne Lectures, A. B. Harbage[7] draws some attractive parallels between Shakespeare and Dickens, as popular writers who retained a sense of artistic integrity, comparable in their fertility of invention and in the 'kindness' of their treatment of character. As H. Levin[8] puts it in his urbane recapitulation of 'the forthrights and meanders' of Shakespeare's critical reputation (in the first Annual Lecture to the Shakespeare Association of America): 'Shakespeare's reputation has undergone all the vicissitudes save neglect.'

[1] *Georgian Shakespeariana IV* (Tbilisi University Press, 1975).

[2] *Shakespeare: The Critical Heritage*, Volume Two, 1693–1733; Volume Three, 1733–1752 (Routledge & Kegan Paul, 1974–75).

[3] 'Flesh's Thousand Natural Shocks in Shakespeare', *Texas Studies in Literature and Language*, XVII (1975), 27–60.

[4] 'Refuting Shakespeare's Endings', *Modern Philology*, LXXII (1975), 337–49.

[5] 'Shakespeare and the Study of Metaphor', *New Literary History*, VI (1974), 149–67.

[6] 'Tagore as a Shakespearean Critic', *Tagore Studies* (1972–73), 15–31.

[7] *A Kind of Power: The Shakespeare–Dickens Analogy* (American Philosophical Society, 1975).

[8] 'The Primacy of Shakespeare', *Shakespeare Quarterly*, XXVI (1975), 99–112.

2. SHAKESPEARE'S LIFE, TIMES, AND STAGE

reviewed by N. W. BAWCUTT

Pride of place in this year's review must undoubtedly go to Samuel Schoenbaum's *William Shakespeare: A Documentary Life*.[1] Schoenbaum laid the groundwork for this biography in his earlier book, *Shakespeare's Lives* (enthusiastically reviewed in *Survey 25*, 1972), where he examined the gradual growth of knowledge about Shakespeare over the centuries, and gave us many fascinating sidelights into the history of Shakespearian scholarship. It was inevitable that he should go on to produce a biography of his own, and the result is a handsome and sumptuously-produced volume, though perhaps somewhat awkward to handle because of its sheer size and weight.

The most striking feature of the book is its wealth of facsimiles of early documents. There are more than two hundred, and they include legal documents of all kinds, private letters and journals, title-pages and quotations from books, and reproductions of prints and engravings. What distinguishes this collection from the conventional kind of illustrated biography is Schoenbaum's concern for authenticity and relevance; nothing is included simply because it is picturesque or typical of the age. The result of this is to give the reader the feeling, to a degree which is true of no other biography of Shakespeare, that he has in his hands virtually all the surviving documents concerning Shakespeare, in a form as close to the original as modern techniques of reproduction will allow. It is hard, however, not to feel a twinge of regret that full transcriptions of the documents are not provided; many of the early legal records can be read only by those with a training in palaeography, and most readers will need a copy of Chambers's *William Shakespeare: A Study of Facts and Problems* near at hand if they are to derive the fullest benefit from Schoenbaum.

A further admirable feature of the book is the fullness with which the facsimiles are annotated. We are given the present location, and in the case of manuscripts a list of reliable transcriptions, the name of the first discoverer and the place where the discovery was first made public, and much other useful information. This material strikingly confirms, if any confirmation was needed, the pre-eminence of Malone and Halliwell-Phillipps as discoverers of Shakespearian records.

Of course, Schoenbaum's book is a biography, not simply a collection of facsimiles As a biography, it deals scrupulously with the facts of Shakespeare's everyday life, making no attempt to explore his inner development as a creative artist. The legends that grew up round Shakespeare after his death are affectionately dismissed, though Schoenbaum wisely feels that we should be aware of their existence as they sometimes contain a grain of truth. Where there are gaps in our knowledge Schoenbaum records the more plausible modern speculations, but sensibly does not strive after certainty where certainty is impossible. Usually he is sceptical towards the more fanciful theories about Shakespeare's relations with the Elizabethan nobility, so it comes as a slight shock when for once (on page 160) he indulgently puts forward the Earl of Essex as a model for Hamlet. But lapses of this kind are very rare, and Schoenbaum usually writes with a shrewdness and controlled sense of humour which add persuasiveness to his judgements. There can be few readers, however learned, who will not derive pleasure and profit from this book.

[1] The Clarendon Press, Oxford, and The Scolar Press, 1975.

We must also salute another splendid achievement: the eighth and final volume of Geoffrey Bullough's *Narrative and Dramatic Sources of Shakespeare*. It is subtitled *Romances*, and discusses *Cymbeline, The Winter's Tale,* and *The Tempest*.[1] This volume exhibits the qualities of balance and wise judgement that we have come to expect from the series; there are no surprises or oddities, and an admirably courteous but firm scepticism is shown towards some of the more cranky readings of this group of plays. We are made aware that in the late plays Shakespeare drew upon romance motifs that had existed throughout Western Europe for several centuries. Yet at the same time he used contemporary material such as the cony-catching pamphlets of Greene and the reports of the Virginia voyagers.

On the vexed question of which play was written first, *Cymbeline* or Fletcher's *Philaster*, Bullough is undogmatic but believes that some scraps of evidence point to Shakespeare's priority. Shakespeare seems to have combined two versions of the wager story upon which the play is based, that in Boccaccio's *Decameron* and the anonymous version known as *Frederyke of Jennen*, both of which are reprinted. Bullough admires *Cymbeline*, and ends his discussion of the play with a sensitive critical account designed to prove that Shakespeare put together the heterogeneous material of his sources with much greater skill than many critics will allow.

The Winter's Tale is clearly based on Greene's *Pandosto*, here reprinted in full except for its dedication. An account is given of the relation between play and narrative, as well as of various minor sources Shakespeare may have used. (Proponents of the theory that a live bear was used in the earliest productions are invited to put this theory to the test on the modern stage.) Bullough is willing to accept that the play has topical allusions (though within carefully-defined limits), but he rejects religious and allegorical interpretations.

The section on *The Tempest* deals, as we might expect, with two main areas of interest – the pamphlets on the shipwreck of the Virginia voyagers, and the various romance tales (analogues rather than direct sources) containing magicians with beautiful daughters and log-bearing princes. The romances throw surprisingly little light on Shakespeare's play, and it is hard to believe that he needed to consult any particular one of them before constructing his plot. The voyagers' pamphlets are a different matter; Bullough skilfully shows us that besides providing spectacular accounts of a storm and shipwreck, they deal with problems of human behaviour that are of deep concern in the play.

The book ends with a sixty-page essay in which Bullough looks back over his work. He notes, among other things, how Shakespeare's treatment of sources altered as he matured artistically, how the use of multiple sources produces special effects, and how the imagery of the plays is modified by source material. It is a worthy conclusion to what will surely be regarded as one of the major efforts of modern scholarship.

Max Bluestone's *From Story to Stage* discusses a number of Elizabethan plays which derive from prose narratives.[2] Several of Shakespeare's plays are mentioned, notably *Othello* and *The Winter's Tale*. We are not, however, given separate chapters on individual plays; Bluestone's aim is to work out a general theory of adaptation, and his book is divided up into sections which consider the various ways in which the effect of a narrative is altered when it is transferred to the stage. Bluestone has a strong feeling for the vitality of live theatre, and argues that such factors as gesture and movement play an essential part in transforming a source. It is perhaps true that most scholars in handling a dramatist's use of sources have concentrated too narrowly on detailed

[1] Routledge and Kegan Paul, 1975.
[2] Mouton, 1974.

alterations of plot and character, and Bluestone does well to remind us that (for example) our sense of space and time will not necessarily be the same when we are watching a play as it is when we read fiction.

Bluestone's book claims to work at a deeper theoretical level than any previous discussion of sources, but it is precisely at this deeper level that the book is unsatisfactory. Much of it is concerned with the basic differences between drama and fiction as genres, and at times there seems to be an assumption that because drama is live – we see and hear the actor in front of us – it must always make more impact on us than words on a page as we sit reading. Obviously this would not be true of the great novels of the nineteenth century, and Bluestone seems to generalise too readily from a restricted period in which drama was highly developed but fiction relatively unsophisticated. His attitude towards the prose sources is one of barely-disguised contempt, and it is symptomatic of his bias that his bibliography does not contain one of the various recent attempts that scholars have made to look at Elizabethan prose fiction, especially Sidney's *Arcadia*, more sympathetically than in the past.

A further complication is that Bluestone uncritically accepts the arguments put forward in Alfred Harbage's *Shakespeare and the Rival Traditions*, and uses terms like 'coterie' and 'popular' as though they referred to clear and unquestionable divisions of audience. He prefers the 'popular' dramatists – apparently on moral rather than aesthetic grounds – and as a consequence playwrights like Dekker and Heywood are sometimes praised for adaptations of their sources which display little imaginative genius, while Jonson, Chapman, Marston, Tourneur, and Fletcher are treated with a lack of sympathy which occasionally borders on open hostility. We end the book feeling that Bluestone has a lively intelligence and is trying to discuss a variety of issues which

are well worth attention. But he fails to develop his arguments into an ordered synthesis, partly because he is insufficiently critical of his own basic assumptions.

Various scholars have treated the sources of individual plays. G. Harold Metz has tried to refute Marco Mincoff's theory that the late chap-book version of *Titus Andronicus* derives from Shakespeare, via the ballad version, and that Shakespeare devised his own plot for the play.[1] John B. Harcourt explores the theological and literary significance of Richard III's frequent references to Saint Paul.[2] Peter Mortensen and Jo Ann Davis suggest an influence of Greene's *Friar Bacon and Friar Bungay* on the patriotic and prophetic speeches in *Richard II*.[3] W. G. van Emden argues (not perhaps fully convincingly) that Shakespeare's handling of the Pyramus and Thisbe legend in *A Midsummer Night's Dream* owes more to Old French versions of the story than has been generally recognised.[4] Malone suggested that there is an echo of Marlowe's *Edward II* in I, iii of *Henry IV, Part I*; Richard S. M. Hirsch now argues that there is a second echo later in the same scene.[5] J. W. and S. C. Velz discuss the allusion, historically inaccurate, to 'Publius' at IV, i, 4 of *Julius Caesar*, and suggest that it derives from the references to Publius Silicius in Plutarch's *Life of Brutus*.[6] Another link with Plutarch is put forward by

[1] '*The History of Titus Andronicus* and Shakespeare's Play', *Notes and Queries*, n.s. XXII (1975), 163–6.

[2] '"Odde Old Ends, Stolne...": King Richard and Saint Paul', *Shakespeare Studies*, VII (1974), 87–100.

[3] 'A Source for *Richard II*, II, i, 40–68', *Notes and Queries*, n.s. XXII (1975), 167–8.

[4] 'Shakespeare and the French Pyramus and Thisbe Tradition, or Whatever Happened to Robin Starveling's Part?', *Forum for Modern Language Studies*, XI (1975), 193–204.

[5] 'A Second Echo of *Edward II* in I, iii of *1 Henry IV*', *Notes and Queries*, n.s. XXII (1975), 168.

[6] 'Publius, Mark Antony's Sister's Son', *Shakespeare Quarterly*, XXVI (1975), 69–74.

James A. Freeman, who considers that the device of catching the conscience of the king by means of a play in *Hamlet* was inspired by an anecdote about the tyrant Alexander of Pherae in Plutarch's *Life of Pelopidas*.[1] Also on *Hamlet*, A. P. Stabler attempts to demolish the arguments of Yngve B. Olsson[2] that the versions of the Hamlet story by Saxo Grammaticus and Albert Krantz provided plot-details for *Hamlet* which cannot be found in Belleforest's version.[3] Alan R. Young looks at the main plot of *King Lear*, and shows that behind Geoffrey of Monmouth's *History* is a widespread folk-tale in which a king or rich man asks his children to declare their love for him; the youngest gives an honest answer and is angrily rejected. But in all these tales the father comes to recognise his mistake and is happily re-united to the child. Shakespeare has deliberately altered this conclusion, and Young speculates that the original audience, probably aware of the folk-tale, would have found the conclusion of *King Lear* as difficult and un-expected as many later critics have done.[4]

Finally, two notes on *Pericles*, one suggesting yet another borrowing from Plutarch. M. P. Jackson believes that the name 'Escanes' in the play is a variant on the name of the Athenian orator Aeschines, mentioned three times in the *Life of Pericles* and in other places also.[5] Joseph Kau feels that the device of the Fourth Knight in II, ii is closer to an emblem in Samuel Daniel's translation of Paulus Giovius' book of *imprese* than it is to one in Whitney's *Choice of Emblemes*.[6] (He also sees the same image at work in Sonnet 73, though this is denied in the article by A. T. Bradford mentioned below.)

This review does not normally attempt to cover studies of medieval or early sixteenth-century drama; an exception must be made, however, in the case of Robert Potter's *The English Morality Play*.[7] Potter sees the basic pattern of the morality not as a psychomachia or struggle between good and evil, but rather as a movement from innocence to corruption followed by repentance and salvation. He traces this pattern through the drama of the sixteenth century, and sees it as underlying several of the great plays of the Elizabethan period, including Shakespeare's *Henry IV* and *Henry V*, *Hamlet*, and *King Lear*, though he is careful to stress that these late plays are infinitely richer and more complicated than their predecessors.

When it is completed in eight volumes, *The Revels History of Drama in English*, under the general editorship of Clifford Leech and T. W. Craik, will cover the whole history of English and American drama from the beginnings to the present day. Volume III is the first to appear, and covers the period 1576–1613 – from the building of The Theatre to the end of Shakespeare's career as a professional dramatist.[8] It is a collaborative venture: J. Leeds Barroll writes on the social and literary context, Alexander Leggatt on the companies and actors, Richard Hosley on the playhouses, and Alvin Kernan on the plays and playwrights.

This four-fold division of material is logical enough, but there seem to be some curious anomalies in the way it works out in practice. (Incidentally, the general editors do not provide any statement of what the series is intended

[1] 'Hamlet, Hecuba, and Plutarch', *Shakespeare Studies*, VII (1974), 197–201.

[2] 'In Search of Yorick's Skull: Notes on the Background of *Hamlet*', *Shakespeare Studies*, IV (1968), 183–220.

[3] 'More on the Search for Yorick's Skull; or, The Goths Refuted', *Shakespeare Studies*, VII (1974), 203–8.

[4] 'The Written and Oral Sources of *King Lear* and the Problem of Justice in the Play', *Studies in English Literature*, XV (1975), 309–19.

[5] 'North's Plutarch and the Name "Escanes" in Shakespeare's *Pericles*', *Notes and Queries*, n.s. XXII (1975), 173–4.

[6] 'Daniel's Influence on an Image in *Pericles* and Sonnet 73: An *Impresa* of Destruction', *Shakespeare Quarterly*, XXVI (1975), 51–3.

[7] Routledge and Kegan Paul, 1975.

[8] Methuen, 1975.

to achieve.) There are, for example, striking discrepancies in the space allotted to each contributor. Leeds Barroll has nearly a hundred pages, though much of this is taken up with a detailed (and very useful) calendar of surviving records of performances. Leggatt has a mere twenty pages, whereas Hosley has over a hundred. Kernan's critical section fills more than two hundred pages (half the book).

Partly because of this, there are noticeable differences of emphasis. Through sheer lack of space, Leggatt is unable to do more than provide an introductory sketch of his subject at a fairly elementary level. Hosley, in what is probably the most solid and useful section of the book, gives a general survey of modern theories concerning the origins of the Elizabethan playhouse, and attempts to reconstruct in some detail the Swan, the Globe, and the Second Blackfriars theatres. Much of his argument is necessarily conjectural, but it is always based on a thorough examination of the surviving evidence. Leeds Barroll's contribution is puzzling; despite its title, it has nothing to say about the literary context of Elizabethan drama, and deals with the social context in a very specialised way. His first chapter, for example, has some interesting speculations on the way in which the fortunes of acting companies were linked to the fortunes of their noble patrons; these speculations will appeal to a scholar, but are so detailed and complicated that they may well prove baffling to a reader who knows nothing of the subject and innocently starts reading the book at the beginning.

It is perhaps inappropriate here to consider Kernan's critical section in detail; he works in terms of selected plays by the major dramatists, including several by Shakespeare, and tends to lay most stress on the drama as reflecting the intellectual and philosophical pressures of the time. A brief summary of the whole volume is hard to make; the separate sections contain much valuable material, but do not finally come

together into a unity (and there is even some overlap between Leeds Barroll's contribution and Alexander Leggatt's).

In an important paper Ann Jennalie Cook reconsiders the composition of Shakespeare's audience.[1] She challenges Harbage's conclusions (in his *Shakespeare's Audience*, 1941) that the majority of theatregoers came from the working class, and that the price structure was designed to encourage them. She shows that it is very difficult to assess the social pattern of the population of Shakespeare's London, and that some modern assumptions have been too easily made. In the same journal John Shaw discusses the symbolic and iconographic significance of the staging of the brief scene in *Antony and Cleopatra* in which Hercules abandons Antony.[2] Francis Berry considers what he calls the 'geometry' of Shakespeare's stage.[3] This article looks at the 'vertical' element of the plays, their concern with high and low status and with rising and falling. For the most part it does not deal with technical problems of staging, but it clearly demonstrates that concepts and metaphors of height and depth permeate the plays, and it is reasonable to assume that some attempt was made to show this pictorially on the stage.

Little has been done lately on problems of attribution. Eliot Slater uses statistical vocabulary-tests in order to argue that *A Lover's Complaint* is authentically Shakespearian.[4] Slater also uses the same techniques to establish that *The Merry Wives of Windsor* has vocabulary links with *Henry IV, Parts 1 and 2*, and *Henry V*, and was probably written at about

[1] 'The Audience of Shakespeare's Plays: A Reconsideration', *Shakespeare Studies*, VII (1974), 283–305.
[2] '"In Every Corner of the Stage": *Antony and Cleopatra*, IV, iii', *ibid.*, pp. 227–32.
[3] 'Shakespeare's Stage Geometry', *Deutsche Shakespeare-Gesellschaft West Jahrbuch 1974*, pp. 160–71.
[4] 'Shakespeare: Word Links Between Poems and Plays', *Notes and Queries*, n.s. XXII (1975), 157–63.

the same time as they were.[1] Hanspeter Born considers that the second and third parts of *Henry VI* were written in 1592, not 1591 as is usually argued.[2]

Frances Yates's *Astraea: The Imperial Theme in the Sixteenth Century* is a fascinating exploration of a pattern of ideas linking symbolism, iconography, and political theory.[3] For most students of English literature the most interesting part will be the chapter called 'Queen Elizabeth I as Astraea', which examines allusions to the queen by a number of writers, with particular emphasis on Spenser. The book includes a small amount of material from Shakespeare's plays, though Miss Yates does not perhaps fully convince us that he was deeply interested in the concepts she elucidates.

Ronald Broude relates Shakespeare to his contemporaries in a thoughtful discussion of revenge tragedy.[4] He shows the ambiguity of terms like 'revenge' and 'vengeance', which were often used to refer to punishments by God, and he does not accept that there was a clear-cut distinction between public and private vengeance in an age when justice was administered largely by unprofessional magistrates and constables. He concludes that Elizabethan revenge tragedy is rarely didactic, but more often mirrors the harshness and confusion of real life.

Jarold Ramsey has taken a fresh look at the diary of John Manningham, including some mildly obscene stories omitted by Bruce in his edition of 1868.[5] He suggests that in the famous account of *Twelfth Night* we should read 'prescribing his gesture in suiting' rather than 'gesture in smiling', the normal reading.

The renaissance volumes of the Salzburg Studies in English Literature, published by the University of Salzburg under the general editorship of Dr James Hogg, continue to appear in large numbers. They include several critical studies of Jacobean dramatists like Webster and Middleton which are not relevant

to this review, which will concentrate on books referring specifically to Shakespeare or throwing light on the Elizabethan period. Indeed, it must be said that some of the critical books are disappointingly pedestrian, and it could be suggested that the series performs its most useful function in printing works which would have difficulty in finding a commercial market – specialised studies of particular topics or editions of minor writers.

The following volumes are all from the series called 'Elizabethan and Renaissance Studies'; unfortunately pressure of space does not allow for a detailed review of each book. *The Iconography of the English History Play* (1974), by Martha Hester Fleischer, deals with the visual emblems used in Elizabethan history plays, including Shakespeare's. In *The Words of Mercury: Shakespeare and English Mythography of the Renaissance* (1974), Noel Purdon examines the sources of Elizabethan mythography and relates them to Shakespeare, with a detailed chapter on *A Midsummer Night's Dream*. Cay Dollerup's *Denmark, Hamlet, and Shakespeare* (2 vols., 1975) is, as its sub-title indicates, 'A Study of Englishmen's Knowledge of Denmark towards the End of the Sixteenth Century with Special Reference to *Hamlet*'. In *Dido, Queen of Infinite Literary Variety: The English Renaissance Borrowings and Influences* (1974), Adrianne Roberts-Baytop looks at sixteenth-century portrayals of Dido, and has a chapter discussing Shakespeare's allusions to her. In *The Drama as Propaganda; A Study of 'The Troublesome Raigne of King John'* (1974),

---

[1] 'Word Links with *The Merry Wives of Windsor*', *ibid.*, pp. 169–71.

[2] 'The Date of 2, 3 *Henry VI*', *Shakespeare Quarterly*, XXV (1974), 323–34.

[3] Routledge and Kegan Paul, 1975.

[4] 'Revenge and Revenge Tragedy in Renaissance England', *Renaissance Quarterly*, XXVIII (1975), 38–58.

[5] 'The Importance of Manningham's *Diary*', *Shakespeare Studies*, VII (1974), 327–43.

Virginia Mason Carr argues that *The Trouble-some Raigne* is an independent anonymous play which deserves study in its own right, though of course it is inevitable that we should make comparisons with Shakespeare's play.

Philip C. Kolin's *The Elizabethan Stage Doctor as a Dramatic Convention* (1975) has a chapter on *Macbeth*; he finds Shakespeare's doctor rather more admirable than Elizabethan stage doctors usually are. Esther Yael Beith-Halahmi's *Angell Fayre or Strumpet Lewd: Jane Shore as an Example of Erring Beauty in 16th Century Literature* (2 vols., 1974) surveys historical and literary attitudes to Jane Shore, and of course touches upon Shakespeare's *Richard III*. In *Daniel's Cleopatra: A Critical Study* (1974), Russell E. Leavenworth examines Daniel's play in detail; he believes that 'Shake-speare's debt to Daniel in *Antony and Cleopatra* has been much larger than anyone has so far seen fit to recognize'.

A group of scholars including William E. Mahaney and Walter K. Sherwin has edited *Two University Latin Plays: Philip Parsons' Atalanta and Thomas Atkinson's Homo* (1973), and A. Harriette Andreadis has edited Lyly's *Mother Bombie* (1975). H. F. Lippincott has reprinted *A Shakespeare Jestbook, Robert Armin's Foole upon Foole (1600): A Critical, Old-spelling Edition* (1973), and Arthur F. Kinney has usefully put together an edition of Gosson's writings about drama in *Markets of Bawdrie: The Dramatic Criticism of Stephen Gosson* (1974).

Three works from the series of 'Jacobean Drama Studies' should be mentioned here. Robert E. Morsberger's *Swordplay and the Elizabethan and Jacobean Stage* (1974) devotes a chapter to the duel in *Hamlet*. In *A Critical Edition of Love's Hospital by George Wilde* (1973) Jay Louis Funston provides us with the first reprint of a Caroline play surviving only in manuscript. Finally, James T. Henke's *Renaissance Dramatic Bawdy (Exclusive of Shakespeare): An Annotated Glossary and Criti-cal Essays* (2 vols., 1974) examines the use of bawdy in a small group of Jacobean plays, and then gives an alphabetical glossary of bawdy terms drawn from twenty-eight Elizabethan and Jacobean plays.

Many explanatory or linguistic notes on Shakespeare's plays have been published in the last year or so. Two articles are concerned with general points: Peter J. Gillett considers the social connotations of the 'ethic dative' *me* and the 'indefinite' use of *your* (e.g. in *Hamlet*, IV, iii, 20–5),[1] while Robert D. Eagleson notes Shakespeare's use of the infinitive in such soliloquies as Hamlet's 'To be, or not to be' and Claudio's 'Ay, but to die, and go we know not where'.[2]

We may turn now to individual plays. James A. Riddell argues that 'foot-cloth', in the phrase 'foot-cloth horse' (*Richard III*, III, iv, 86), did not refer simply to the richly-em-broidered cloth placed over a horse, but had come, by extension, to refer to the kind of horse that would be used to carry such a cloth.[3] Virgil Lee thinks that Puck's 'tailor' in *A Midsummer Night's Dream*, II, i, 54, has various meanings but is basically sexual in its implications.[4] A. S. Cairncross suggests that 'spinner', in *A Midsummer Night's Dream*, II, ii, 21, and *Romeo and Juliet*, I, iv, 59, is the crane-fly, or 'daddy-long-legs', not the spider.[5] In a note on *As You Like It*, V, ii, 109, Winifried Schleiner gives quotations from sixteenth-century authors to show that wolves were not extinct in Ireland, as they were in England, and that the Irish were

[1] 'Me, U, and Non-U; Class Connotations of Two Shakespearian Idioms', *Shakespeare Quarterly*, XXV (1974), 297–309.
[2] 'Eschatological Speculation and the Use of the Infinitive', *ibid.*, XXVI (1975), 206–8.
[3] 'Hastings' "Foot-cloth Horse" in *Richard II*', *English Studies*, LVI (1975), 29–31.
[4] 'Puck's "Tailor": A Mimic Pun?', *Shakespeare Quarterly*, XXVI (1975), 55–7.
[5] '"Spinner" (*M.N.D.*, II, ii, 21, *Romeo*, I, iv, 59)', *Notes and Queries*, n.s. XXII (1975), 166–7.

held by some to be moon-worshippers and subject to lycanthropia.[1]

D. Allen Carroll looks at the name 'Fabian' in *Twelfth Night*, and suggests that it may mean 'reveller', or may contain an allusion to a certain John Fabian who became notorious in the sixteenth century.[2] Annotating 'villainous saffron' in *All's Well That Ends Well*, IV, v, 3, Nicholas Jacobs puts forward evidence indicating that saffron was used in cures for venereal disease.[3] A. T. Bradford believes that 'with' in line 12 of Sonnet 73 does not mean 'by', as most commentators argue, but is equivalent to 'together with'.[4]

Three articles on *Hamlet* can be grouped together. Mother M. Christopher Pecheux, O.S.U., relates 'this fell sergeant Death', v, ii, 328, to the medieval Dance of Death, available to Shakespeare pictorially, or in such poems as Lydgate's 'Dance of Death'.[5] Jon R. Russ thinks that the evidence put forward to identify the mole in the phrase 'old mole', I, v, 162, as Satan is inadequate and unconvincing. He feels that the word is a pun; Hamlet's companions would take it as a simple reference to the animal, but Hamlet himself alludes to the classical god Tmolus, referred to by Ovid (*Metamorphoses*, XI).[6] Horst Breuer has three points to make: 1. Hamlet is unlike Hercules (I, ii, 153) not because he is small of stature or irresolute, but because he would have been slim and well-shaped, as a prince and courtier should be, unlike the huge and brawny Hercules; 2. Hamlet's speech at I, iv, 17–38, provoked by the drunkenness of the Danish court, is a general meditation which should not be applied to Hamlet himself (and is, according to Breuer, not very distinguished as verse); 3. Hamlet's soliloquy in the prayer-scene (III, iii, 73–96) should be taken at its face-value; Hamlet *does* wish to damn Claudius as well as kill him.[7]

Shakespeare's influence on other writers has been explored in various ways. To begin with his contemporaries, Jerome W. Hogan has noticed echoes of lines by Shakespeare in three minor writers of the early seventeenth century,[8] and John Feather quotes and discusses a passage from *Henry IV, Part 2*, which is printed in the 1628 edition of a conversation manual called *A Help to Discourse*.[9] Richard E. Barbieri finds an echo of *Richard II* in Donne's *Devotions*.[10] Cathryn A. Nelson notes Shakespearian echoes in *Wit's Triumvirate* (1635),[11] and Christopher R. Reaske finds an extensive influence of II, iv of *Henry IV, Part 1* on Dryden's *MacFlecknoe*.[12]

Margaret Lamb looks at Shakespeare's influence on Romantic comedy, in terms of plays by de Musset and Büchner.[13] Helmut G. Asper considers Ludwig Tieck's imaginary production of *Twelfth Night* in his novelle *Der junge Tischlermeister*, published in 1836.[14] Günther Klotz has written on Edward Bond's

[1] '"'Tis Like the Howling of Irish Wolves Against the Moone"; A Note on *As You Like It*, v, ii, 109', *English Language Notes*, XII (1974), 5–8.

[2] 'Fabian's Grudge Against Malvolio', *Shakespeare Quarterly*, XXVI (1975), 62–6.

[3] 'Saffron and Syphilis: *All's Well That Ends Well*, IV, v, 1–3', *Notes and Queries*, n.s. XXII (1975), 171–2.

[4] 'A Note on Sonnet 73, Line 12', *Shakespeare Quarterly*, XXVI (1975), 48–9.

[5] 'Another Note on "This Fell Sergeant, Death"', *Shakespeare Quarterly*, XXVI (1975), 75–6.

[6] '"Old Mole" in *Hamlet*, I, v, 162', *English Language Notes*, XII (1975), 163–8.

[7] 'Three Notes on *Hamlet*', *English Studies*, LVI (1975), 20–8.

[8] 'Three Shakespearian Echoes', *Notes and Queries*, n.s. XXII (1975), 175.

[9] 'A Shakespeare Quotation in 1628', *ibid.*, pp. 175–6.

[10] 'John Donne and *Richard II*: An Influence?', *Shakespeare Quarterly*, XXVI (1975), 57–62.

[11] 'Echoes of *1 Henry IV*, *King Lear* and *Macbeth* in *Wit's Triumvirate* (1635)', *ibid.*, xxv (1974), 357–8.

[12] 'A Shakespearian Backdrop for Dryden's *MacFlecknoe*?', *ibid.*, p. 358.

[13] 'That Strain Again: "Shakespearian" Comedies by Musset and Büchner', *Educational Theatre Journal*, XXVII (1975), 70–6.

[14] 'Ludwig Tieck inszeniert *Was ihr wollt*. Beschreibung und Analyse einer Fiktion', *Deutsche Shakespeare-Gesellschaft West Jahrbuch 1974*, pp. 134–47.

Lear[1] and Wolff-Rainer Wilberg on the Charles Marowitz version of *Hamlet*.[2]

Gāmini Salgādo's *Eyewitnesses of Shakespeare* is a collection of first hand accounts of performances from 1590 to 1890.[3] Those from 1590 to 1700 are grouped together in roughly chronological order; from 1700 onwards each play is given a separate section to itself. The earlier material can hardly be said to provide eyewitness accounts of performances, and its main value is probably to make unmistakably clear the fact that we shall never be able to reconstruct the original productions of Shakespeare's plays. The case is of course very different for the eighteenth and nineteenth centuries, and Salgādo has compiled a well-chosen and often highly entertaining anthology of reviews of performances.

It is possible to illuminate a play by comparing different productions of it; Ralph Berry does this for *Coriolanus*,[4] Marvin Rosenberg for *King Lear*.[5]

Discussions of historical performances can be put in roughly chronological order. Albert E. Kalson notes that Colley Cibber not only adapted *Richard III* but also repeatedly played the title-role himself, though with conspicuous lack of success.[6] John W. Velz points out that in the Nuffield Library of the Shakespeare Centre, Stratford-upon-Avon, there is a manuscript cast-list for *Julius Caesar* which seems to relate to the Drury-Lane performance of the play on 24 April 1719.[7] Maarten Van Dijk offers a detailed account of Kemble's treatment of the role of King John, with special emphasis on the scene with Hubert (III, iii) and the death-scene.[8] Verner Arpe throws light on Swedish productions of Shakespeare in the eighteenth century.[9] Mary M. Nilan describes Charles Kean's 1857 production of *The Tempest*, which apparently made spectacular attempts at realism.[10]

The 1974 volume of the *Deutsche Shakespeare-Gesellschaft West Jahrbuch* contains a series of articles describing productions in terms of their staging and costumes. Sybil Rosenfeld tells us what happened when Irving commissioned Alma-Tadema to design a production of *Coriolanus*;[11] Edmund Stadler describes Adolphe Appia's sketches for *Hamlet*;[12] Timothy O'Brien reflects on some of his own work for the Royal Shakespeare Company;[13] Rolf Badenhausen examines Caspar Neher's designs for *Hamlet*;[14] Rüdiger Joppien assesses Philippe Jacques de Loutherbourg as a stage-designer;[15] Peter Loeffler gives an account of Gordon Craig's 1912 production of *Hamlet* in Moscow;[16] and Russell Jackson describes E. W. Godwin and Wilson Barrett's *Hamlet* of 1884.[17]

[1] 'Erbezitat und zeitlose Gewalt. Zu Edward Bonds *Lear*', *Shakespeare Jahrbuch 1974*, pp. 44–53.

[2] 'Ein "zersplitterter" *Hamlet*. Bemerkungen zur Kollage von Charles Marowitz', *ibid.*, pp. 54–9.

[3] Sussex University Press, 1975.

[4] 'The Metamorphoses of *Coriolanus*', *Shakespeare Quarterly*, XXVI (1975), 172–83.

[5] 'Characterizations of *King Lear*', *Deutsche Shakespeare-Gesellschaft West Jahrbuch 1974*, pp. 34–47.

[6] 'Colley Cibber Plays Richard III', *Theatre Survey*, XVI (1975), 42–55.

[7] 'An Early Eighteenth-Century Cast List for Shakespeare's *Julius Caesar*', *Theatre Notebook*, XXIX (1975), 18–20.

[8] 'John Philip Kemble as King John: Two Scenes', *ibid.*, pp. 22–32.

[9] 'Seuerling startet Shakespeare schwedisch. Ein deutscher Student macht schwedische Theatergeschichte', *Shakespeare Jahrbuch 1974*, pp. 146–52.

[10] 'Shakespeare Illustrated: Charles Kean's 1857 Production of *The Tempest*', *Shakespeare Quarterly*, XXVI (1975), 196–204.

[11] 'Alma-Tadema's Designs for Henry Irving's *Coriolanus*', pp. 84–95.

[12] 'Regieskizzen von Adolphe Appia zu Shakespeares *Hamlet*', pp. 96–110.

[13] 'Designing a Shakespeare Play: *Richard II*', pp. 111–20.

[14] 'Caspar Nehers Bühnenbauten und Kostüme für *Hamlet* (1926) unter Leopold Jessner', pp. 121–33.

[15] 'Philippe Jacques de Loutherbourg und Shakespeares *Sturm*', pp. 148–59.

[16] 'Gordon Craig und der Moskauer *Hamlet* von 1912', pp. 172–85.

[17] 'Designer and Director: E. W. Godwin and Wilson Barrett's *Hamlet* of 1884', pp. 186–200.

Two articles contribute to the history of Shakespeare criticism. Ursula Klein surveys the earlier Romantic critics of Shakespeare,[1] while Joan Coldwell considers Lamb as a Shakespeare critic, noting that his attitudes were deeply influenced by the productions he saw.[2]

David M. Bergeron's *Shakespeare: A Study and Research Guide* provides a useful annotated bibliography of modern studies of all aspects of Shakespeare.[3] There are perhaps some reservations to be made; only books dealing exclusively with Shakespeare are included, so that (for example) there is no mention of William Empson as a Shakespeare critic. There is also too much concentration on books published in the last fifteen years, some of which may prove to be of less permanent value than some older books which have been excluded.

Stanley Wells has now edited a companion volume to his *Shakespeare* in the 'Select Bibliographical Guides' series.[4] It is called *English Drama (excluding Shakespeare)*, and covers the whole history of drama in England. The various contributors assess modern scholarship and criticism on the dramatists assigned to them, and the chapters on Elizabethan drama will obviously be of great interest to students of Shakespeare.

This review will conclude with some pleasant sidelights on Shakespeare's influence on art and music. Babette Craven shows that there are three different versions of the Derby pottery figure of Richard III, and argues that they do not all represent Garrick, but rather Garrick, Kemble, and Kean.[5] Johanna Rudolph reconsiders Mendelssohn's incidental music to *A Midsummer Night's Dream*,[6] and Hans Henning reproduces and briefly discusses Picasso's sketches of the grave-scene in *Hamlet*.[7]

[1] 'Die frühromantische Kritik und Shakespeare', *Shakespeare Jahrbuch 1974*, pp. 153–63.

[2] 'The Playgoer as Critic: Charles Lamb on Shakespeare's Characters', *Shakespeare Quarterly*, XXVI (1975), 184–95.

[3] St Martin's Press, 1975.

[4] Oxford University Press, 1975.

[5] 'Derby Figures of Richard III', *Theatre Notebook*, XXIX (1975), 17–18.

[6] 'Mendelssohns *Sommernachtstraum*-Musik im Konzertsaal', *Shakespeare Jahrbuch 1974*, pp. 112–28.

[7] 'Pablo Picassos Zeichnungen zur Totengräberszene des *Hamlet*', *ibid.*, pp. 60–1.

© N. W. BAWCUTT 1976

3. TEXTUAL STUDIES

reviewed by RICHARD PROUDFOOT

This year has been marked by the publication of two of the major comedies in the New Arden Shakespeare,[1] *As You Like It* edited by Agnes Latham and *Twelfth Night* completed by T. W. Craik on the basis of work nearly finished by J. M. Lothian at the time of his death in 1970. The circumstances of their completion may be reflected in the different characters of these two excellent editions. *As You Like It* is flavoured throughout by its editor's dry wit and pon-

dered wisdom, reflected in an economy of statement which is more often informed with ironic implication than a casual reading may reveal: the edition is clearly the product of a long and deep affection for the play. It is perhaps in part the accident of juxtaposition which gives *Twelfth Night* the air of a less fully integrated piece of work, but for all its solid virtues, its style lacks the poise and pointedness

[1] Methuen, London, 1975.

of *As You Like It* and its different sections give less sense of being pervaded by a clear and subtle awareness of the play's integrity and individuality.

Miss Latham's introduction to *As You Like It* deals in its five sections with the play's text, date, sources, 'people and themes' and stage history. An emphasis on humanity and human affairs distinguishes the three central sections, greatly to the benefit of a view of the play in which Arden is seen as the setting of 'a life-enhancing and not self-deluding interlude', if somewhat to the detriment of, for instance, Fortune, Nature and Time, to name only three of the main topics of thematic criticism. Jaques and Touchstone are firmly delineated, the former as a dignified figure whose 'railing against the wicked ways of the world keeps before us the truth that, outside the charmed circle, the ways of the world are wicked', the latter as more fool than wise commentator on folly. That the name of Jaques is dissyllabic is well demonstrated, though the contention that he is thereby immunized against the 'jakes' joke may smack of pious optimism rather than carrying full conviction. The suggestion that Touchstone owes his name not to any vatic function but to the original casting in the role of Robert Armin, who 'had written the part of Tutch [in his *The Two Maids of Moreclack*], played the part of Tutch, and was by trade a goldsmith' has much to recommend it. The editor of the poems of Sir Walter Raleigh is predictably penetrating on Shakespeare's transmutations of pastoral and handles with precision the placing of this most literary of his comedies in its Elizabethan literary context. Small issues which have in their time generated more heat than light, such as the relative heights of Rosalind and Celia, or the naming of the two Dukes, are reduced to size with a common-sense that is never merely reductive. That the stage history should seem rather a bleak chronicle is partly the effect of a sense of anti-climax.

The discussion of the text, while generally illuminated by the editor's critical alertness, shows one or two moments of confusion. The note that the clerk of the Stationers' Company scribbled on a flyleaf of his register of copyrights on 4 August 1600, to the effect that *As You Like It* and three other plays were 'to be staied', is pressed too hard, in view of real doubts which persist about its significance. The most that can be affirmed with any degree of confidence is that some stationer tried on that date to enter for his copy a manuscript of the play, perhaps a 'prompt-book', if the clerk used 'booke' in its most technical sense, and that the clerk had reason to refuse to enter it and to employ delaying tactics. The fact that no publication ensued might appear to imply that his doubts were justified, at least in respect of this one play. It is therefore misleading to refer to the note as 'an assertion of copyright' (p. x) or to infer from it that the projected publication was authorized and would have occasioned the preparation of an authoritative scribal fair-copy of the play 'specifically for the press' (p. xi). It is also stretching the evidence to introduce the incompatible hypothesis that the Chamberlain's men played a direct role in preventing publication of *As You Like It* in 1600, and to use this notion as presumptive proof of its popularity (p. lxxxvi). Equally, the full act and scene divisions of the F text argue strongly against the suggestion, made, tentatively, on p. xi, that the transcript of prompt-copy from which it was printed 'may have been made about 1600', rather than in or about 1622. A footnote on p. xvii, on the division of the F text between Jaggard's compositors B, C and D, oddly includes folio Q2, the final recto page of *The Merchant of Venice*, nor is there much evidence that knowledge of the compositors has served as a control in handling details of the text. For example, B's possible double error in misreading '*hir*' as '*his*' at v, iv, 113–14, is discussed without reference to his certain perpetration of the same misreading at III, ii, 142, which might have clinched the already substantial argument against retention of 'his' in line 113. Elsewhere, the conservatism which is the only responsible attitude to this text is seldom open to serious question and most often leads to the restoration and vindication of correct F readings: an exception is the unnecessary, if logical, rejection of F at v, ii, 107, in favour of Rowe's improvement, 'Who [F Why] do you speak to [F too] "Why blame you me to love you?"?'. The record of interesting F spellings in the footnotes is inconsistent, omitting 'cheerely' (II, vi, 14), which bears on Malone's emendation, and 'Gundello' (IV, i, 36), which is by any standards noteworthy. Modernization is thorough, consistent and sensitive (e.g. 'hussif' for 'housewife', I, ii, 30) and distinctions between verse and prose are convincingly clarified in many places. Mishaps and oversights include the assigning to Rosalind of Celia's speech at IV, iii, 78; a duplication of the textual footnotes on II, iv, 60–1; failure to collate F 'by' for 'be' at I, iii, 122; italic for roman in *seeks* in the note on v, ii, 60; a wrong cross reference at v, ii, 44 to 'III. i. 253', where 'III. ii' is meant; and an inconsistency between text ('deserve') and footnote ('deserves') at v, iv, 186.

The annotation is among the best features of this edition, bringing wide and exact knowledge of Elizabethan life and language to bear on many words and phrases often ignored by commentators, such as 'caught' (II, vii, 68) or 'history' (II, vii, 164), as well as clarifying more obvious difficulties. Further notes might have been helpful on, for example, the Duke's shift from 'Thou' to 'You' in addressing Celia at I, iii, 76 and 83, or 'bounds of feed' (II, iv, 81). Cross references to v, iv, 184, in the note on 'matter' (II, i, 68), and to Orlando's complaint about the neglect of his education, in that on III, ii, 29–30, would strengthen both.

The editors of *Twelfth Night*, whose indi-

vidual contributions are not distinguished in the finished work, have dealt conservatively with a text they believe to have been printed in F from a transcript of Shakespeare's 'foul papers', in which act and scene divisions and act endings were introduced by the scribe. Their text seldom raises any question about the correctness of their conservative approach, original suggestions being limited to matters of punctuation and of stage directions, notably the plausible exit for the Clown proposed at II, iii, 118. At I, iii, 98, F's 'we' for 'me' is not collated; at I, v, 144, 'afore knowledge' or 'aforeknowledge' might be preferred to 'a foreknowledge' on the grounds of the frequency with which prefixed 'a-' is separated in Elizabethan hands; the rejection of Theobald's 'credent' (IV, iii, 6) and 'thrust' (v, i, 370), though reasonably defended, leaves some doubts, as no other instance has yet been found of 'credit' in the required sense of 'report' and F's anomalous 'thrown' is surely as likely to result from the carelessness of either the scribe or compositor B as from Shakespeare's own. The notes, which are generally full and helpful, especially on details affecting performance (such as the need for emphasis on 'I'll' in the final speech of Malvolio), spend more time than is justifiable on the refutation of error and the deflation of conjecture, much of it originating with J. Dover Wilson and Leslie Hotson. A few more notes are needed; for instance, on the tense of 'see' (I, iii, 81); on the possible allusion to hanging in 'turned away' (I, v, 17); on 'important' (I, v, 193), 'havoc' (v, i, 200) and the significance of Orsino's 'Give me thy hand' (v, i, 270). No suggestion is made about stage business at I, iii, 68, where the dialogue implies the need for some. The note on 'carpet consideration' (III, iv, 238) omits cross reference to 'carpet-mongers' at *Much Ado*, v, ii, 32, and that on 'sweet and twenty' misses the allusive use of the phrase in *The Wit of a Woman* (1604), (fol. F1., l.753).

The introduction deals briefly with the text, rejecting as unnecessary Dover Wilson's theories of revision, argues convincingly for a date of composition in the second half of 1601 and gives a full account of alleged sources and analogues, concluding that Shakespeare need have known no other version of his story than that which he read in Barnabe Riche's *Farewell to Military Profession* (reprinted as Appendix II). The hardy perennial error of naming the source of *The Two Gentlemen of Verona*, Montemayor's *Diana*, after its sequel, *Diana Enamorada* by Gil Polo, crops up in a footnote on page l. The criticism of *Twelfth Night* is treated in two sections, of which the first surveys its history, revealing a partiality for thematic analysis and for a festive reading of the play rather than for the darker view instanced in Auden's comment on it 'not merely as a farewell to comedy but as a positive rejection of mirth and romance'. The editors' own reading is supplied in a 'Critical Analysis by Acts and Scenes', whose admirable intention of recreating the experience of the play and of revealing the means whereby it operates on the expectations of an audience is not achieved without some labouring of the obvious and some surprising oversights – little is said, for example, of the ways in which thematic and linguistic details assert the unity of the various parallel actions. The lengthy stage history has much to say of the various unhappy adaptations from which *Twelfth Night* has suffered but makes no mention (perhaps because it was too recent) of John Barton's distinguished production for the Royal Shakespeare Company.

A Selective Bibliography of Shakespeare,[1] compiled by James G. McManaway and Jeanne Addison Roberts, provides a fair survey of its various topics, though revealing a distinct bias towards periodical articles as against books of more general import. Random checking revealed that the section on the 'Canon' lists no edition or discussion of *A Lover's Complaint* (although this work is listed separately); omits the Malone Society reprint of *Arden of Feversham*; misdates Tucker Brooke's *Shakespeare Apocrypha* '1918' for '1908' and ignores its corrected reissues; and credits Baldwin Maxwell with *Studies in the Shakespeare Apochrypha* (*sic*). Perhaps the present reviewer's eye has been unduly sharpened by finding himself misprinted on p. 181 – where a lapse of some significance is the omission of E. A. Armstrong's 1964 revised second edition of *Shakespeare's Imagination*. Altogether, the book seems better suited to the needs of the harassed teacher than to those of the serious researcher, though he too may be enabled by it to cut a few corners. It would be churlish to dismiss *An Index of Characters in English Printed Drama to the Restoration*, by Thomas L. Berger and William C. Bradford, Jr,[2] as merely a reference book we do not need: clearly its compilers felt a need for it or they would hardly have bothered to compile it. What use it might have had is reduced by the imposition of such arbitrary decisions as the omission of all plays in manuscript (even the three dozen available in good modern editions), and a procrustean system of dealing with variant forms of names (which has led to the inclusion of not a few misprints under separate headings, but only if they were found in the stage directions, not the text, of the play in question, so that, from *The London Prodigal* (1605), GREENSHOOD – for Greenshield – gets in, while SPURROCK – for Spurcock, does not). The separate listing of christian names and the surnames to which they belong makes the game even more difficult. Some comic and curious facts can, nonetheless, be gleaned from the book: that early English drama is richer in Bawds than Bishops, or that Doctors, Merchants and Widows far outnumber both. New

[1] University Press of Virginia, Charlottesville, 1975.
[2] Microcard Editions Books, Indian Head Inc., 1975.

parents desperate for names should handle this book with extremest care.

Compositor analysis continues to be the most frequent subject of articles bearing on the text of Shakespeare, of which, once more, several concern themselves with Jaggard's compositors in the First Folio. S. W. Reid[1] draws from an extended analysis of compositor B's spelling of rhyme-words in six F plays set from quarto copy the conclusion that such words, when so spelt as to create what he calls 'literal rhyme' (e.g. *art/hart*; *see/bee*), should be recognized as a special class of preferential spellings affected by their context and therefore to be omitted from spelling counts designed to establish B's normal preferences. John O'Connor[2] draws his harrow over the well-ploughed field of compositor analysis in the folio comedies, in an attempt, largely effective, to break up a few of the remaining hard clods. In a closely-argued essay, he sharpens discrimination between the two compositors, D and F, revealed when the blades of T. H. Howard-Hill and A. S. Cairncross bisected Hinman's original A. F is now held to have set twenty-two pages or part-pages, D forty-one: F's latest work was on quire G; D joined the Folio crew in quire F, to vanish again after V. O'Connor's findings advance positions previously suggested (on occasion) by Cairncross or (more often) substantially demonstrated by Howard-Hill. His criticisms of their work are precise and his acknowledgement of their conclusions justly appreciative. His own argument generally bears out his contention that qualitative evidence is less likely to mislead than statistical totals, but his article is afflicted by misprints and some unnerving errors of detail. The spacing of the initial speech prefix of a play cannot be evidence in discriminating between D (who set none) and F (who set one) (p. 88); 'y^t' is an abbreviation of 'that', not of 'yet' (p. 92); the form 'shee'll' is offered as evidence against assigning G2^{r}b to F and for assigning G6^v to

him (p. 104); the form '*don*' on 13^v (*Much Ado*, 1.197 – not 198) might be evidence for composition of the page by D if it were a spelling of 'done', but it is in fact part of the name '*don Iohn*'. MacD. P. Jackson[3] reviews Alice Walker's characterization of the work of Folio compositors A and B in the light of the more recent reassignments of pages she attributed to A before passing to the question of the reliability of B, C and D in setting Folio *Much Ado* from the quarto of 1600. His analysis, based on Dover Wilson's list of errors in the folio text, reveals C, 'on this occasion at any rate', as strikingly unfaithful to copy and especially given to the omission of 'words, phrases, and even whole lines' and to verbal substitutions. D is notable for his large number of literal errors. He concludes: 'I am convinced that conservatism is no virtue in editing Folio plays set by Compositors B or C, and that the editor who emends nothing but obvious nonsense will perpetuate many readings that are purely compositorial in origin.' And thus the whirligig of time brings in his revenges! This conclusion, though irrefutable, will not be of much practical help to editors in detecting the errors of B and C which they should purge.

Turning his attention from the much-canvassed questions of the Folio, Jackson[4] brings to bear on the *Sonnets* (1609) both knowledge of the habits of the same two compositors in George Eld's shop who set *Troilus and Cressida* in the same year and a wider range of information about Eld's printing methods. The regularity of Shakespeare's

[1] 'Compositorial Spelling and Literal Rhyme: The Example of Jaggard's B', *Library*, xxx (1975), 108–15.

[2] 'Compositors D and F of the Shakespeare First Folio', *Studies in Bibliography*, 28 (1975), 81–117.

[3] 'Compositor C and the First Folio Text of *Much Ado About Nothing*', *Papers of the Bibliographical Society of America*, 68 (1974), 414–18.

[4] 'Punctuation and the Compositors of Shakespeare's *Sonnets*, 1609', *Library*, xxx (1975), 1–24.

sonnet form allows him to compare, with a precision impossible in dramatic texts, the methods of punctuation favoured by the two men, of whom one shows a strong predilection for colons at the end of quatrains and the other an equally clear, though less consistent, preference for commas. Other differentiating characteristics, including spellings, forms of catchword and the lateral position of the numbers at the head of the poems and of signatures, allow him to divide the Quarto between Eld's Compositors A and B with some degree of confidence, except for about a dozen pages, five of them in *A Lover's Complaint*. The pattern of composition, with B as the main type-setter, helped out from time to time by A (a division of labour not uncommon in Eld's quartos), is tentatively related to the pattern of presswork sugges..u by the sequence of use of five skeleton formes. The evidence is displayed in full and the findings verified to a high degree of statistical probability. Jackson's conclusions, that although B was the less accurate compositor, A's errors, where they occur, are of a more damaging and substantial kind, and that the variation between the two in matters of punctuation demonstrates that 'If one compositor reproduced the punctuation of his copy for the *Sonnets*, the other obviously did not; perhaps neither did' (p. 8), are shown to be as important for subtle verbal critics in search of Shakespeare's *ipsissima puncta* as for future editors of the *Sonnets*.

Alan E. Craven has been among the most active of recent investigators of the Shakespeare quartos of the late 1590s. In his latest article, on 'Proof-Reading in the Shop of Valentine Simmes',[1] he proposes to survey the extent and character of proof-reading revealed by press-variants in some of the twenty-seven quartos Simmes printed between 1597 and 1611. Instead, the article reveals serious inadequacies in the methods and assumptions of its author and in the range of evidence considered. His aim, which is to encourage editorial freedom with texts set by Simmes's compositor A, (whom he has elsewhere characterized, on quite inadequate evidence, as prone to frequent and serious error), is urged by a statistical account of the variants in a mere eight plays and of the corrections marked (as he supposes by Simmes himself) in two surviving proof-sheets. His conclusion that careful proof-reading was the exception in Simmes's shop finds some measure of support from the evidence, but his inference from the large number of invariant formes, that only about half of the formes were proofed at all, is untenable, at least without much more corroboration in each particular case from the fullest possible analysis of composition and presswork. In any case, the small number of surviving copies affords an insufficient basis for such general conclusions: notoriously, uncorrected formes survive in a minority of copies and the discovery of each previously unknown copy tends to increase our record of them. Craven neglects to consider the many variants in the 1600 quarto of *Sir John Oldcastle*, which have been twice described in editions of the play, incompletely in the Malone Society reprint of 1908 and more reliably in Kathleen Tillotson's edition for the fifth volume of the *Works of Michael Drayton* published in 1941.

In an important article, Herman Doh[2] proposes a technique for measuring the various habits of compositors in their spacing of justified lines filling the measure. Two compositors in Thomas Heywood and William Rowley's *Fortune by Land and Sea* (1655), clearly identified on other evidence, were seen to have adopted two quite distinct methods of increasing space to fill out a loose line, the one introducing the extra spacing types throughout the

[1] *Papers of the Bibliographical Society of America*, 68 (1974), 361–71.
[2] 'Compositorial Responsibility in *Fortune by Land and Sea*, 1655', *Library*, XXIX (1974), 379–404.

line, the other, more crudely, increasing spaces only in the second half of the line, to produce a line with unsightly gaps in its second half. The reduction of these differences in spacing to a numerical factor provided a test which would, of itself, have sufficed to identify the stints of the two men. Application of the technique to Q2 *Hamlet* and F *Merry Wives*, by way of verification, suggests that it may prove to have some use in verifying and extending Shakespearian compositor identifications. Further analysis of *Fortune by Land and Sea* revealed that, as might be expected in a quarto of such late date, 'the great majority of spelling variants have no measurable relation to the pattern of alternate composition', a valuable reminder of the elusiveness of spelling evidence in compositor studies and the desirability of other kinds of discriminating habit.

David Daiches[1] celebrates the 250th anniversary of the House of Longman, publishers of the third edition, 1818, of Bowdler's *Family Shakespeare*, with a genial survey of the vagaries of Shakespearian publication from his day to ours, which will entertain the great variety of readers who are content to seek more up-to-date and accurate instruction elsewhere. J. H. P. Pafford[2] clears W. R. Chetwood from the stigma of inventing fictitious early editions of Shakespeare's plays, a charge first levelled by Steevens in 1766, by indicating that the list of plays in question, in *The British Theatre* (Dublin, 1750), gives hypothetical dates of performance, not publication, for the plays first printed in the First Folio, and that it is quite unclear whether Chetwood had anything to do with it.

Computer studies of literature, including Shakespeare, which the old-fashioned may regard as 'th'impostume of much wealth and peace', show signs of proliferating. Their value, as always, is determined by the quality of the human mind in charge of the input end of the operation. *Computer Studies in the Humanities*

and Verbal Behavior has devoted an issue to eight papers generated by the World Shakespeare Congress held in Vancouver in 1971.[3] Fred R. McFadden, jr., lists sixty-eight 'research projects in Shakespearean stylistics and pedagogy which would be adaptable to some type of computer processing', ranging from 'ultramicroscopic' study of Shakespeare's handwriting and 'computerized patterns of sexual terms in Shakespeare to show densities of incidence' to all manner of linguistic and phonetic testing and even 'decision-simulation games using Shakespeare plots and the computer'. B. Brainerd recommends the accuracy of computers in investigations involving the counting of large quantities of data, e.g. authorship studies, and their invulnerability to 'fatique [sic], oversight, distraction, etc.'. A later piece by the same author[4] discloses that the existence of a relation between the number of words a character in Shakespeare speaks and both 'his importance to the author' and 'his rank' is borne out by statistical analysis of the tragedies and histories, while 'the comedy coefficients are quite different from those of the other genres' – a conclusion whose lame impotence affords as sadly clear an example of sheer waste of computer time and of the principle that if you ask a silly question you may expect a silly answer as the most reactionary pre-electric sceptic could wish for. Marvin Spevack reviews computer-concording in the Vancouver collection. Elsewhere, he is joined by H. J. Neuhaus and T. Finkelstaedt[5] in outlining plans for the computer-compilation

[1] 'Presenting Shakespeare', in *Essays in the History of Publishing*, ed. A. Briggs (Longman, London, 1974), 61–112.

[2] 'W. R. Chetwood and the Fictitious Shakespeare Quartos', *Notes & Queries*, CCXX (1975), 176–7.

[3] Vol. IV, no. 1 (Mouton, The Hague, 1973).

[4] 'On the Number of Words a Character Speaks in the Plays of Shakespeare', *ibid.*, no. 2 (1973), 57–63.

[5] 'SHAD: a Shakespeare Dictionary' in *Computers in the Humanities*, ed. J. L. Mitchell (Edinburgh University Press, 1974), 111–23.

of a 'complete, systematic, and analytic Shakespeare dictionary'. As with Spevack's Shakespeare concordances, to which, together with the *Shorter Oxford English Dictionary*, the new scheme is geared, the main doubts arise at a very early stage. Presumably the basic text of Shakespeare will again be G. B. Evans's eccentrically edited *Riverside Shakespeare*, which at once rules out the possibility of completeness. The important questions of spelling, variants from collateral substantive texts and the status of editorial emendations are not even raised, let alone satisfactorily answered. The lexicographers' comments on the Oxford Dictionary likewise reveal a disquietingly uncritical acceptance of, for instance, the record of dates of earliest occurrence of words and meanings, long recognized as one of the least reliable features of the Dictionary. A new Shakespeare dictionary may be a desideratum, but a much more critical attitude to the bases of it will be needed than is displayed here before it can have any hope of improving substantially on existing reference works, let alone achieving any degree of completeness and system.

The remaining computer papers are on the compiling of 'A Fully Automated Shakespeare Bibliography', by D. M. Burton, and on computer-collation, by R. L. Widmann, who has also published the results, which confirm expectations at every point, of her collation of twenty-five editions of *A Midsummer Night's Dream*.[1] The issue closes with T. H. Howard-Hill's prophetic vision of 'A Common Shakespeare Text File for Computer-Aided Research', to be established on the basis of the magnetic tapes of sixty early editions of Shakespeare (or, more precisely, of facsimiles of them) which he prepared as the tools for compiling his Oxford Concordances.

The cold wind of recession has by now doubtless tattered the sails of some of the vessels so proudly launched by this manifesto, but the prospect of answers to many Shakespearian

questions of real interest and difficulty which depend on the analysis of large quantities of minute detail is undoubtedly increasing at a rapid pace as the substantial possibilities of computer-aided research begin to separate themselves from the dreams of Africa and golden joys.

W. R. Elton[2] returns to the tantalizing anonymity of the epistle added to the cancel title-leaf of *Troilus and Cressida* (1609), which he designates 'the only detailed commentary on a Shakespearean play published in the author's lifetime'. The tone of special pleading thus revealed at the outset does even more than the lack of substance in the argument to demolish his many-storeyed and circumstantial hypothesis, in which Peter Alexander's suggestion that *Troilus* was written for an Inns of Court occasion is assumed as fact and a web of inference, much of it fascinating in itself, gradually enmeshes John Marston of the Middle Temple, his wife's 'good friend' Henry Walley, publisher of the 1609 quarto, and Ben Jonson. The attractive notion of Marston as the procurer of Walley's copy-manuscript and author of the epistle must, for the time being, remain no more than that. Some particular points in a discussion of the two early texts are more substantial, especially the defence of the authenticity of the longer passages found only in the F text.

James M. Welsh ('A Misrepresented Reading in Folio *Tempest* 285 (I. ii. 175)', *Shakespeare Quarterly*, XXVI (1975), 213–14) lays the ghost of a non-existent variant, 'Heuen' for 'Heuens', at F *Tempest* 285, by reporting that, although the 's' is missing from the Lee facsimile (1902), it is present in the Chatsworth

---

[1] 'Compositors and Editors of Shakespeare Editions', *Papers of the Bibliographical Society of America*, 67 (1973), 389–400.

[2] 'Textual Transmission and Genre of Shakespeare's *Troilus*', in *Literatur als Kritik des Lebens*, edd. R. Haas, H.-J. Müllenbrock and C. Uhlig (Quelle und Meyer, Heidelberg, 1975), 63–82.

copy (now in the Huntington Library) from which the facsimile was made. John P. Cutts ('The Fool's Prophecy – Another Version', *English Language Notes*, IX (1971–2), 262–5) draws attention to a hitherto neglected version of the Fool's prophecy in F *Lear*, III, ii, in Bodleian MSS Ashmole 36/37, f. 60, item 74. It rearranges four couplets which bear close verbal resemblance to the F lines to make a single eight-line stanza. As the manuscript dates from the mid-seventeenth century, it seems as likely to derive from *Lear* as to represent a version intermediate between medieval analogues and Shakespeare. A. S. Cairncross ('*Antony and Cleopatra*, III. x. 10', *Notes & Queries*, CCXX (1975), 173) proposes 'Yonder ribaud Nagge of Egypt' as a convincing solution to a celebrated crux, supposing F's 'Yon ribaudred' to be the compositor's unhappy attempt to remedy of pie of 'der' from 'Yonder'. Eliot Slater follows an earlier (and inconclusive) analysis of the vocabulary of *A Lover's Complaint* in relation to Shakespeare's poems ('A Statistical Note on "A Lover's Complaint"', *Notes & Queries*, CCXVIII (1973), 138–40) with a fuller investigation ('Shakespeare: Word Links between Poems and Plays', *ibid.*, CCXX (1975), 157–63) of the relative frequency of occurrence of rarely-used

words in Shakespeare's works. His results, based mainly on words used no more than five times in a given text, suggest both the authenticity of *A Lover's Complaint* (and, incidentally, *Titus Andronicus*) and an association between its vocabulary and a group of plays comprising *Hamlet*, *Troilus*, *Cymbeline*, and, perhaps, *Lear*. In a separate note ('Word Links with "The Merry Wives of Windsor"', *ibid.*, 169–71) he applies a similar test of 'communities of vocabulary' to the dating of *Merry Wives*, which his results associate with a group of plays including 1 and 2 *Henry IV*, *Much Ado* and *Henry V*, rather than with the plays of 1600–2. Michael L. Hays ('Watermarks in the Manuscript of *Sir Thomas More*', *Shakespeare Quarterly*, XXVI (1975), 66–9) argues, on the basis of evidence both inaccurate and incomplete, that all the additions to the manuscript of *Sir Thomas More* were written on paper of the same stock, and therefore presumably on a single occasion. In fact, the measurement of the chain-lines in all the leaves and smaller slips used for the additions, as well as the four discernible watermarks, support his conclusion even more convincingly than the evidence he presents might suggest.

© RICHARD PROUDFOOT 1976

INDEX

INDEX

INDEX

INDEX

INDEX